# AUTISM OUT LOUD

# AUTISM OUT LOUD

## LIFE WITH A CHILD ON THE SPECTRUM, FROM DIAGNOSIS TO YOUNG ADULTHOOD

KATE SWENSON

CARRIE CARIELLO

ADRIAN WOOD

PARK
ROW
BOOKS

PARK ROW BOOKS™

Recycling programs for this product may not exist in your area.

ISBN-13: 978-0-7783-6837-3

Autism Out Loud: Life with a Child on the Spectrum, from Diagnosis to Young Adulthood

First published in 2025. This edition published in 2026 with additional chapter.



Park Row Books
22 Adelaide St. West, 41st Floor
Toronto, Ontario M5H 4E3, Canada
ParkRowBooks.com

HarperCollins Publishers
Macken House, 39/40 Mayor Street Upper,
Dublin 1, D01 C9W8, Ireland
www.HarperCollins.com

**Printed in U.S.A.**

26 27 28 29 30 LBC 5 4 3 2 1

*To Cooper, Amos and Jack.*

*You add color to the words,*
*sunshine to the rain,*
*orange to the morning sky.*

*You are every worry, every hope,*
*every triumph inside our hearts.*

*Our sons.*

*Our suns.*

# AUTISM OUT LOUD

# CONTENTS

# INTRODUCTION

What do a Midwestern girl, a Southern debutante, and a housewife from New Hampshire have in common? We each have a son with autism.

Jack, age nineteen.

Cooper, age thirteen.

Amos, age ten.

Throughout these pages are three wildly different stories of the autism bell curve, told by three different mothers living across the country from one another.

It all started with a Facebook Live in 2020. Thanks to the pandemic, the world had just fallen apart. Kate suggested we talk online about a current event related to autism and adoption. Adrian kept bringing up something called a cookie cake during the Live. Apparently, they are very popular in North Carolina.

We don't remember much of the details, but we do remember how hard we laughed during our time together. We do remember, through our screens, feeling a connection that we rarely experience in everyday life. From late-night texts to morning phone calls, we began to share the vulnerable, often messy side of building a family. How, at one time or another, we have each experienced the piercing loneliness that accompanies life alongside a child diagnosed with autism.

Ranging from nonverbal to high functioning, our children each have three very different autism diagnoses. Yet as mothers, we struggle with a universal challenge—how do we prepare the world for our child and our child for the world? Together, we grapple to make sense of the chaos and joy the spectrum puzzle piece has brought to their lives.

We have thirteen children between us. With autism often at the epicenter, we balance the ordinary life of hockey practice, potty training, high school prom, and trips to the orthodontist. This is often done with a heavy heart, as our younger children experience what we call *leapfrogging*—surpassing their autistic sibling in milestones and development, or achieving things that will always be just out of his reach.

We often say there is no manual for raising a child with autism. Here, we attempted to write our own.

How did we sleep train our kids? What is puberty like? How do you research a post–high school program for a neurodiverse student? Does the grief ever end? These are just a few of the questions we are asked. In this book, we answer them and more.

A combination of memoir and how-to guide, *Autism Out Loud* offers a glimpse into our life of medication, sibling dynamics, and marriage. Honest and unapologetic, we explore small triumphs and missed milestones. We share what worked for us, and what didn't.

During a virtual brainstorming session, we searched for the perfect title. Round and round we went, shaking our heads and making notes.

*Autism Out Loud.*

Once we landed here, a collective hush fell over the Zoom meeting. After all, if you ask anyone what they think of when they hear *autism*, these are the words upon which they eventually settle.

*Out loud.*

Whether it's a complete lack of inhibition when it comes to wearing clothes in church, or dashing onto the baseball field during a Little League game, or the pointed questions directed at pregnant women, our boys live life out loud.

By association, so do we. This is the beautiful by-product of a diagnosed child. Life alongside autism has taught us to embrace the raw, gritty pieces of our journey. To forgo life in nuanced shades of gray and look for the colorful moments instead. It is between the brilliant hues of pink and orange where pure joy unfurls like a blossom in the sun.

Whether you are in the throes of sleeplessness and meltdowns or living adjacent to autism as a grandparent, neighbor, teacher, or friend, there is something in our words for everyone.

This book is the story of raising unexpected children in a reluctant world. The story of finding joy in little moments and of piecing together new dreams out of the broken pieces.

It is about the power of community, and the important reminder that we are not alone.

Yet it is anything but sad. Each of our children will live a life full of joy and delight. Somewhere along the way, we have learned to surrender to a life we didn't ask for, and discovered we love it all the same. You will too.

# 1
# Who We Are

## KATE

Hello, I am Kate, the Midwestern part of this trifecta. Most people know me as Cooper's mom or Kate from *Cooper's Voice.* I am a wife, mother, and advocate who shares not only the challenges with life alongside autism but the joys as well, unapologetically in hopes that it helps someone.

Most people assume I am an extrovert. And that I am confident. They assume wrong. I am quite shy. But I have had to transform and become someone new. Because I have a life that demands bravery and a boy who deserves it.

When my son was diagnosed with autism at age three, my first thought was to take him and our little family and run away. I was terrified.

I have since learned that it is an act of bravery to share one's life and to feel one's feelings. Especially out loud. Even when it's hard to do so.

This chapter was the first thing that Carrie and Adrian and I wrote together. We had been doing weekly live videos together for quite some time, but this was the first written thing. None of us seemed to know where to start.

During one of our weekly planning calls, Carrie was in her office in New Hampshire battling a cold, Adrian was in North Carolina preparing for a trip to a water park, and I was on a five-and-a-half-hour drive to northern Minnesota for a presentation. How far north, you ask…? Ten minutes short of Canada north. The drive was ridiculously long, and I was thankful for the conversation that hopped from book to real life seamlessly.

As the conversation moved from marketing to process to outline, the other two opted to write the book in order. I made the case for starting with the sibling chapter. I was outvoted. They wanted to write chapter one first. Who We Are: Storytellers, Advocates, Friends.

It makes sense, I guess. Except, for me, it's the one chapter I didn't know how to write. In all honesty, I don't know who I am right now. I feel a little bit lost in space and time. As if I'm floating from hockey practice to bedtime to IEP meeting, which is a collaborative meeting with Cooper's school team to discuss his individualized education plan, to book meeting, juggling all the things, while doing nothing particularly well.

Motherhood is a lot more confusing than I anticipated. I'm not saying that in a ha ha, laugh out loud sort of way. I'm saying that because it is truly way harder than I anticipated. So is marriage and turning forty-one. And navigating the unique grief associated with autism that has found me once again.

Autism is the suitcase I carry every moment of every day. It's adjusting to the weight only to have it change. And it's coming to terms that, someday, I will be forced to set it down. And wondering who will pick it up for me and carry it the rest of the way.

Thankfully, the kids are okay. (Isn't that from a movie?) Better than okay, even. They are thirteen, eleven, five, and three.

Sawyer is smart, athletic, popular, and kind. Of all my children, he has the biggest heart. And even though he is my second-born child, in so many ways he is like my first. I've watched him leapfrog Cooper in nearly every way and grow into the bigger "little" brother role.

Harbor is my precocious child and I worry about breaking his spirit. The measure of success with Harbor is that I kept him alive. He is by far my most joyful child and always up for anything. And as the somewhat fuzzy future starts to come into focus, I see him leaving at eighteen and never looking back. It terrifies me. But he cannot be contained. He is larger than life.

And then there's Wynnie, our youngest and last. I never thought I'd have a daughter. After having three sons and thinking our family was complete, a daughter never crossed my mind. Nor did a fourth child. And if Jamie was sitting here next to me, he'd have me add a sentence that read "four kids is entirely too many!" But he can never seem to decide which one he'd get rid of when I question him on it.

Wynnie, or as we lovingly call her, Fred, softened our edges. When I was pregnant with her and trying to come up with a name, I fell in love with Wynnie. But Winifred felt too matronly, so we chose Wynter. Now we call her Fred. It fits her perfectly. Life is funny like that. She is the perfect combination of strength and tenderness. My friend Caroline, a mother of four boys, said to me once, "You know the difference between girls and boys? The real one? It's the dryer lint. With boys it's full of leaves, rocks, and twigs. With girls, it's glitter and bows and pink barrettes." And that's my Wynnie. She fills our world with shiny things.

Cooper, my buddy, continues to be my greatest teacher. He still carries the same diagnosis that he was given at age three—severe, nonverbal autism—but he has settled into his diagnosis. He has dreams of taking the Amtrak to California to see the whales and squealed with joy when he got a cell phone for his thirteenth birthday. He is growing up, a reality that is rarely talked about. Cooper is growing up. And with it, a paralyzing fear of the future.

My husband, Jamie, and I have been married for sixteen years, minus one year. Yes, we were divorced from each other, and remarried again. I was pregnant with Harbor and the ceremony took place in our living room. It's one of my favorite memories. Today, when we do get into an argument, Jamie will annoyingly say, "You can't divorce me twice." Marriage is hard, much harder than I thought it would be. And yet I am so thankful that I have this man who chose me not once, but twice, to be his partner.

But me. Who am I? I am a mom who lives in two worlds, the world of special needs and the neurotypical world; the two rarely cross over. I am nothing like the influencers I see online when I scroll through Instagram. My family isn't perfect. My children refuse to pose in outfits. And no one wants to do a video with me. I struggle as my children get older with what to share and what not to share.

When I give my most sought-after presentation, Finding Joy in the Secret World of Autism, I have a slide that lists my titles.

*Hi, I am Kate Swenson. I live in Minnesota with my family. I am a wife, mother, published author, blogger, influencer, business owner, caregiver, and advocate. Some of these titles I expected to have. Some I did not.*

Very rarely is a life a straight line. I know mine isn't. Mine is imperfect and yet I beam with pride when I share the story of us. I love sharing the unconventional ways we became who we are today. I am proud of my transformation as a mother and how I learned to stop running away from grief, vulnerability, and parts that hurt and instead share them with the world.

When I started my blog, *Finding Cooper's Voice*, secretly from my couch in Duluth, Minnesota, when Cooper was just two years old, I thought I was so witty picking that name. I even went as far as imagining the celebratory post I would make when we indeed did find Cooper's voice. *Autism* wasn't a word in my vocabulary yet, even though my son was drastically different from other little boys his age. I vividly remember smiling so confidently as I pressed Publish on my first post. Even saying to Jamie, "I started a blog. I'm a blogger." And him laughing when I refused to tell him the name. My plan was to keep my blog a secret, mostly so I could write about him.

*Finding Cooper's Voice* is my life. I get the gift of sharing our story and helping others in a variety of ways. My mission is simple: I don't want any other mother to ever feel as alone as I did in the beginning.

I never wanted to be an advocate. Really, I am a "reluctant" advocate. When Cooper was diagnosed, I never planned to pound the pavement for autism rights. I just wanted to help my son. Our ship was sinking, and plugging the many holes was my priority. But I learned very early on that when you advocate for one individual, you are making change for many.

I often tell a story from our hardest years. For Cooper and our family, that was ages four to eight. He was a runner with no understanding of safety or awareness of danger.

Our front and back doors had three locks apiece, our windows and doors had alarms, and we lived as if there was no front yard. If given the opportunity, Cooper would run toward cars without hesitation. He seemed to even be drawn to traffic. When we arrived home, the garage door had to be shut before releasing him from his car seat. It was that dire and it was terrifying.

I spent a lot of time and energy advocating for a six-foot wooden fence for our backyard. I had been informed that there were supports in place to help families like mine with home modifications to keep children safe through Medicaid-funded programs. They denied my request and offered a four-foot chain-link fence. I explained to them that Cooper could and would and had scaled many four-foot fences. The process went on forever and they buried me in paperwork, phone calls, and more. It felt as if they wanted me to give up and that possibly they were making it purposefully hard. But I didn't give up and eventually won my request for the fence.

Afterward, I found the courage to ask the director why she fought me so hard to get something that could and would save my son's life. Her response broke me: "If we gave a six-foot wooden fence to you, we'd have to give it to every family who asked." She explained that I set the precedent.

I responded frustratedly, "Think of the children's lives you'll save." Still to this day, many years later, families reach out to me and thank me for my advocacy because they now have a fence to keep their child safe. Remember, moms and dads: no one will ever fight harder for your child than you, and when you advocate for one, you are changing lives for many.

Having a child with a disability has changed me in the most profound ways. Without autism, there is no Kate as we know her. It took me years to admit that my son's diagnosis did consume me, a stark contrast of before and after diagnosis. I will never be the person I was before autism and I can say with certainty that this version of me is better. Fighting that was useless. So was looking at it as a negative thing, because it also brought countless gifts into my life.

I read something on a self-help website once about navigating grief. The author said that in periods of grief, it can feel like we have been given a box of darkness to unpack and cope with, often with no guidance. Although my grief at the time was different from what she described, I was drawn to the analogy.

I've never written about it in relation to Cooper. I worry that someone might think I am referring to him as a box full of darkness. Nothing could be further from the truth. His struggles, especially the ones most often not talked about, are the darkness. The cruelty of the world is the darkness. The lack of understanding is the darkness. His vulnerability is the darkness. The fear of dying and leaving him behind is the darkness.

He is the light. The gift.

It took me time, many years, to understand the difference between darkness and light. And how each has a lesson to teach me. Also, how we cannot have one without the other.

But during those difficult years I learned more about grief, and myself, than I had imagined possible. And that box of darkness turned out to contain marvelous revelations.

I get the gift of sharing our story. Of advocating. And friendship.

I get gifts of knowing kids like Cooper. The siblings like Sawyer. The moms and dads like me and Jamie.

Adrian. Carrie. Amos. Jack.

Buried in that same presentation that I have given countless times is a slide that reads: *"I started to believe that I wasn't meant to be happy."*

It took me nearly thirteen years to allow myself to be

vulnerable enough to share that. The first time I remember feeling it was right after we moved into a new neighborhood. The home that we thought was going to be our forever home. The morning after we signed the papers, the house officially ours, the doorbell rang, and two little boys whisked Sawyer out to play. I joke that I didn't see him again for a year. Shortly after that, Jamie brought the garbage out, and did not return. He had discovered the other dads living in the neighborhood.

I was pregnant with Harbor, my belly noticeable. I sat in the living room, a whole world happening outside of our home. Cooper, entirely nonverbal then, moved throughout our new house following an invisible path, his anxiety at an all-time high. I sat alone, the silence screaming at me. Maybe it was pregnancy hormones or maybe a mother on an uncomfortable journey to acceptance, but I saw my future. And it was just me and Cooper. Alone. Everyone else had left. And in my darkest moments, I convinced myself that everyone would eventually leave, and it would just be Cooper and me. And in a selfless way, I accepted it. I was meant to carry this alone.

The familiar ding of a text. My group chat with my friends, the moms who get it.

"Kate, how is Cooper doing? What did he put in the bathtub today?"

And suddenly, I am not alone anymore.

## ADRIAN

My childhood was an idyllic existence, if there is such a thing. A traditional all-American family with a stay-at-home mom and a doctor dad. I spent my days out of doors, where I ransacked the neighborhood's well-manicured yards on a gas-powered go-kart that Santa brought the year I turned seven.

Eastern North Carolina was a wonderful place to run wild, and boy, I did. Though born in the South, my parents were Yankees—transplants from Ohio. They didn't follow the guidelines required for the raising of a proper Southern daughter. Hence, the wild spirit. When I close my eyes, I see myself as a little girl. Tangled up in surf and sea, tan and scrawny, long limbed and gap-toothed. My mop of blond hair was cut short because my mother says I was averse to baths.

My story is not unique, and then again, maybe it is. Though I was welcome amongst my peers, there is no denying that I was unlike the others, and even then, I knew it—a tumbleweed amongst weeping willows. I knew back then that my path was different, but I couldn't have told you how or why. I had no way of knowing the curves that lay ahead, much less that I would have a child with autism. Though his physical traits resemble my own at that age—the shock of blond hair and loose limbs—his life has not been framed by the same freedom and independence.

The little girl with the big personality never lost her sharp edges, though she melted a bit when her big brother fell off this earth. She was fourteen years old when she was introduced to the first taste of grief associated with a diagnosis. It was cancer, and within a year, her brother was but a dream. My transition to the role of only child took a bit of getting used to and it wasn't until my later teens that I became the dutiful daughter. I graduated from Meredith College in Child Development and earned a master's in education from UNC–Chapel Hill and a PhD from NC State in Educational Research.

In the midst of that, I married a boy who I had known throughout college. Thomas Wood was the boy I fell in love with after years of friendship. He was cool and collected while I was loud and jovial. Somehow, we found our way to one another and we've been together over half my life. We've been married for over twenty years and have lived in Edenton, North Carolina, for most of those and it's quite home. His part and role in my life has been the largest—not just as husband and encourager, but father to our four children.

We have three teenagers and a third grader at the time of this writing.

Thomas is our oldest at eighteen and graduating from high school this year. He is an amazing young man with a sensitive spirit and empathetic heart.

Russell is next, and at sixteen he has always had a special place in my heart, as he is named for my older brother (Adam Russell). He is introspective and curious and loves all things learning. He has always been a protector of Amos.

Blair is fourteen and our lone girl. She came out of the womb laughing and trying to keep up with her big brothers. No one longed to be a big sister more than Blair, and when Amos arrived rather than the "sister baby" she had wished for, she promptly forgot she had wanted anyone else.

And finally, Amos.

Amos is ten years old and arrived several years after we thought our family was complete. With three small children, life was good and busy, and when I found out I was expecting at nearly nine weeks, we were shocked. When my husband and I shared the news that evening with the children, they were giddy with excitement. There has never been a moment that Amos wasn't wanted or loved.

I imagined that would be the final chapter of my story—the building of my own tribe. I had a husband and a parcel of children and planned to sail our tidy ship into the sunset. This paper version of life was charming and planned, even well executed. When Amos plopped into our family, I was introduced to the real version—messy, frightful, and amazing all wrapped up and no neat bow in sight. It was not the family I had envisioned building for myself.

A hardworking dad and a less-than-perfect mother wrangling three teenagers and a ten-year-old with autism. I hope our children feel our family is a shelter from the storm called life like I do. I hope they learn that perfection is overrated and real rules the day. I certainly have. My first three children were following the path I had imagined—one that mirrored my own growing up—when Amos came along. I knew he was different, too, and much like I had felt about myself, I couldn't articulate why or how. But I knew, and even though I sought answers and validation of my fears, I was dissuaded from jumping to the conclusion that my baby was anything but ordinary.

Amos propelled my writing journey and another tribe was created. A virtual community where strangers have come together and learned to depend on each other for strength, camaraderie, tears, solutions, and laughter. It has been the most amazing of tribes and a place where I have received far more than I have given. In my small community, there are very few people who walk the walk of my family and I need those who "get it." I depend on information related to Amos's nuances—our medication journey, potty training, and especially the infamous struggle of autism, which is sleep or the lack thereof.

And today, I tell you about the microcosm that has made my life better and that is the friendship between three women living similar lives. I didn't know online relationships existed outside of dating apps until I met Kate Swenson and Carrie Cariello. I have lived in North Carolina the whole of my life and run in the same social circles since childhood. I didn't know anyone else in my small town who shared my struggles and I was so very lonely. The tentacles of our online friendship have soothed my heart and given me hope.

At the end of the day, we all long for authenticity and a place to be accepted. Real is not the life we had envisioned for ourselves; it's never neat and tidy. Real is what is, our present reality, the life we ended up with and call our own, a messy, joyful, and crazed existence where we are wondering when we became the grown-ups.

Welcome home.

# CARRIE

My name is Carrie.

I was named after my mother's cousin. Her other cousin was named Alveena. In retrospect, Carrie suits me a little better.

My husband is Joe, formally Joseph. For reasons that have never been explained to me, he has no middle name. Perhaps it's an Italian thing. Or maybe by the time he rolled around—the youngest of six—they'd simply run out of ideas.

Joe and I have been married for twenty-five years. We have five kids. Our second, Jack, is diagnosed with autism.

Our firstborn, Joseph, is twenty. He is a junior in college. He has green eyes and a shock of wavy hair that is forever in his eyes. He is gentle and sweet, but he will eat your leftovers without asking.

Jack is nineteen. He just started another year in a residential space. It is a supported program with a lot of scaffolding to keep him moving forward. At six feet five inches, he is the tallest in our family—so far.

Charlie is eighteen, all dark eyes and racing heart. He looks the most like his father. A sports aficionado, I liken him to a puppy, or a kite—open the door and out he flies. He has never met a stranger.

Our daughter, Rose, is sixteen. She just got her driver's license. Watching her back out of the driveway the first time, hot tears pricked my eyelids, knowing I'd probably never need to pick her up from crew practice or a babysitting job again. I always enjoyed the time in the car with her, even if I was late a lot.

Henry, our youngest son, is fifteen. He is taller than me, but I still think of him as a little boy. He hates when I say this.

Jack was diagnosed with autism when he was eighteen months old. It was a chilly day in November. As we walked back to the car, our footsteps echoed throughout the parking garage. He was wearing overalls.

We lived in Buffalo, New York. I took the highway home from downtown. I got off on the exit and drove through our neighborhood. I felt drained, but also calm. I called Joe as soon as we got home. This was 2004, and cell phones were big, clunky devices that weighed down your purse. Talking from the car was impossible. He listened quietly as I explained what the doctor confirmed: Jack was on the autism spectrum. Back then it was classified as Pervasive Developmental Disorder—Not Otherwise Specified. Over time and a move out of state, the label would eventually morph into simply autism.

*My son Jack has autism.*

These five words would eventually shape my family, my marriage, and my life.

Back in 2004, however, I didn't know a single person who was diagnosed with autism. In fact, my only reference point was the movie *Rain Man*, with Tom Cruise and Dustin Hoffman. I watched it with my mother when I was in high school. We sat in our living room and marveled at the level to which Dustin Hoffman could portray a man so riddled with anxiety and rigidity. I was equal parts horrified and mesmerized. Yet for whatever reason, once the movie ended, I never gave it another thought.

When I told them the news of Jack's diagnosis, my friends nodded in sympathy. We all had kids around the same age. They asked all the right questions. They ruffled his hair and smiled when he reached for the vacuum cleaner in their respective closets, as opposed to the basket of toys all the other kids played with on the floor. Yet no one really understood my new reality. How could they? I barely understood it myself.

I was lonely. Working part-time, my days were also consumed with the needs of two toddlers, as my silhouette began to bloom once more with a third. Often Jack felt lost to me—as though I couldn't penetrate autism's inner sanctum to reach my little boy. He didn't seem to even know who I was. Beneath my rib cage, the timpani of fear began to beat.

In November of 2004, Facebook was not popular yet. Sure, it was sweeping the college campuses and connecting students to one another across the country, but it would be many years before the online community became a refuge for mothers and bloggers.

We moved to New Hampshire in the spring of 2007. With three little boys under the age of four, I was also wearing maternity clothes again. I remember I had a T-shirt with the word *baby* spelled out in rhinestones, with an arrow pointing in the direction of my bump, lest anyone get confused about my state.

A lifelong reader, over the next few years I discovered I also liked to write. I began submitting short essays to local print publications, mostly observational pieces with an emphasis on humor—why women prefer to wear big underwear, the rising popularity of spray tans. Joe was reading the local paper one afternoon and spotted a local publisher who was accepting manuscripts for nonfiction. "Hey, honey," he called over to where I was standing at the sink. "Maybe you should talk to this guy. Maybe you could write a book!"

A book. I turned the idea over in my mind as I rinsed the last of the dishes, but quickly disregarded it. Books were for other people to write, not me. I've since learned this phenomenon of self-doubt is called *Imposter Syndrome*—when we doubt our own skill and talent, and fear being considered a fraud.

Still, Joe left the paper open on the counter. I tucked the contact information into a drawer in my desk, in case I felt the courage to call. And I did, about three months later. That was the springboard into work as a writer.

The publisher was small—one person, in fact. He and I edited my first book in his kitchen. Sitting at the table while one dog snoozed at our feet and another one paced warily, we chose a photo for the cover and reread passages to check for cohesiveness. When we met to review the final manuscript, he suggested I start a blog as a way to build an audience. I was reluctant but agreed.

My first blog post ever was a letter to Jack on his eighth birthday. I tried to capture him for readers in that single point of time: a little boy with a fondness for cookies and an astounding memory for dates.

I found blogging was a great way to work through my experiences with autism and motherhood. Slowly, I began to share little snippets of our life online, including the more difficult aspects of autism. I compared the small moments of grief I felt throughout the day—when I saw another boy Jack's age playing with friends while he sat off to the side on the playground, for example—to the sting of a paper cut. The response to our story was nearly overwhelming. People, it seemed, were hungry for a glimpse inside the world with a diagnosed child. Slowly, my audience began to grow.

I had a circle of close friends in real life as well—women who were supportive and tried to understand as best they could what it was like to have a son like Jack. They listened when I needed them to, bought his favorite snacks whenever we came over, and generally provided a safe space for me to land and talk. Still, it seemed as though no one truly understood the world in which I was living.

By this point, Facebook had made its way onto the scene as a platform for social connections. I joined a few groups for parents of kids with special needs. The first one was called *Autism Magic Happy Fun Time*, a community for bloggers who shared the emotional roller coaster of life alongside autism. This is where I came across Kate's story.

I remember reading about how isolated their family was because of Cooper's severe autism—how few places they could safely go. With hardly any thought, I sent her a message, telling her she was always welcome to come to New Hampshire. It was 2014. Her son Cooper was four and Jack was ten.

Looking back, this was very out of character for me, but something compelled me to write it. A kinship, perhaps, or a perceived connection forged over the loneliness I continued to experience. I never expected to hear back from her. Yet a day later there was a message waiting. From that point on, we communicated fairly regularly. Through messages, emails, and eventually texts, we shared jokes, photos, and the worry that often kept us up at night. From across the country, we forged a friendship, albeit a virtual one. It would be nearly eight years before we'd meet in person.

I felt as though someone finally understood how messy, raw, painful, and dazzling this life could be. At the same time, I was fascinated by the difference between our two sons and their diagnoses—the way Cooper lined chairs up and hoarded paper, while Jack latched on to license plates and struggled with almost any kind of social interaction.

When the pandemic hit, Kate turned to creative ways to engage her audience, particularly with Facebook Live videos.

She invited me one day to join her, along with two other autism moms and writers, for a discussion about a current topic. This is where I met Adrian. Once again, I felt a nearly instant connection to her and her story.

Although we are very different mothers, and our sons have very different autism profiles, there is a common ground that binds us together.

Now here I sit at my desk, poised to write again. My story is not a new story. For the longest time, I thought it was about a boy. Now I am less sure. Like a wildflower reaching through the cracks in a sidewalk, it has blossomed into something tender and unexpected.

It is a story of marriage, of redemption, of loss, of hope. It is a story of pushing back against the parentheses autism imposes. The story of power in numbers—the importance of finding a community to call one's own.

With every word I write, I realize the world has much to learn. So does this boy Jack. Can each learn in time? My worry runs so deep, it's as though it's hardly there at all. I think of him, tucked away in his dorm-like space, working his very hardest to build a life around a diagnosis—or perhaps in spite of it—and my heart swells with pride. For life alongside autism is nothing if not a swirl of contradictions, some changing by the minute.

I believe in him. I believe in the world. I believe in second chances and smiles of goodwill. I believe because I have to believe. I have no other choice. I have no other choice because one day I will die. And as much as this idea stops me in my tracks, it is true. This is me, small and afraid.

For now, I live bravely.

I have no choice but to look to the sky and see sun instead of storms. I hear notes of music and listen for birds gone free. I smell incoming winter. The leaves are dying, floating, drifting, landing. Yet come springtime the branches will be green with newness. Newness. This is the light to which I hold tightly. These are the things that keep the very birds in the sky.

I hope you may take something from the sentences I've cobbled together here, in this book. I deliver them to you from the very bottom of my heart.

# 2
# Diagnosis Day

## KATE

People find me in a variety of ways. Facebook. Instagram. The viral video of me crying in my car. My first book, *Forever Boy.* And they find me at different times in their journey too. They suspect autism. They've just heard the word *autism* in relation to their child. They want to support a family member with autism. The list goes on.

I often say, "Your child has just been diagnosed with autism. Maybe it came as a shock. Maybe not. Maybe, like me, you already had an idea that something was going on, but you still felt the sting when the words were said out loud in relation to your own child."

The autism club. It's a strange feeling being initiated into a club you never wanted to be in. I will admit I wanted no part of it. But I know now that with it comes solace. Because once I was ready, I found comfort in this club. I found my people. But I am getting ahead of myself.

When we left Cooper's diagnostic appointment, in a way it felt like autism was given to him. It was placed on his shoulders by a young psychiatrist. And part of me wanted to politely decline. "No, thank you. You keep that. We are good." But it doesn't work like that. The diagnosis wasn't given to him. It was always there. Cooper was and is autistic, no matter what. No matter what we called it or where we lived. Denying would have been denying his true self.

I want parents to know that we get a choice in how we look at this. That, although not easy, and probably not right away, we do get to pick our reaction to this life-changing diagnosis. As simple as it sounds, in the beginning, it never occurred to me that I had a choice in how I looked at my son's disability. It was presented to us as something to overcome, to outrun, to diminish, even. I sure hope it's different now. Instead of being presented as a death sentence, I hope it's a ticket to a new life, one filled with happiness and joy and support.

I was missing my son's life, waiting for it to get better. I was living in this perpetual place of grief, where I told myself, "I'll be happy when he talks, happy when he goes to school, happy when he starts sleeping." There was always a when. But I couldn't live in that angry place forever. I couldn't be that person. I decided to choose joy. I am the only person who gets to decide how I feel. I get to choose. And so do you.

It wasn't easy for me, stepping off the path of the life I imagined into the unknown. And suddenly being expected to be the expert. The advocate. To be invincible and brave. I would do it a million times over again for Cooper. But it was terrifying. I joke that my autism manual got lost in the mail. The one that would tell me what to do.

I am an entirely different person than I was in the beginning when that piece of paper was slid across the table to me that read "autism spectrum disorder."

People often ask me when I knew my son was autistic. The questions come from well-meaning parents, looking at us, hoping that we aren't their future. I used to be the same way. Not anymore.

The answer is Cooper was different from the second he was placed in my arms. Of course, I didn't know the word *autism*. That would come much later. But looking back, and going on to have three more kids, I can say with absolute certainty, Cooper was different from the second he was born.

While most newborns snuggle in, grunting, starved, and exhausted from their journey, Cooper was wide-awake. Yes, his delivery was traumatic, which I share at every IEP table when they ask about his birth. But he perked up quickly. And instead of exhaustion, he wanted to sit up, look around, and take it all in. I will never forget his unbelievable head strength or how he was the softest thing I had ever felt.

The world has never made sense to Cooper. Not then, not now. From the very beginning he needed stimulation. I would later learn he was a sensory seeker, but back then I just knew he loved the bright light of the television and the snow falling outside the window. We would spend hours swaying in front of both. Eating and sleeping did not come easily for him. And if you were to ask me today, I would tell you that looking back, my sweet baby had anxiety as a newborn. But of course, I didn't know that then. I just knew that my baby was different from all the rest, and no one believed me.

We often hear the phrase "trust your gut" when we enter the world of motherhood. But what if our gut is just as confused? I think I was overly confident bringing Cooper home, with countless hours of nannying and babysitting under my belt. Immediately the learning curve felt more like a rapid jump instead of a nice sloping curve. I'm here to tell you that no matter how many babysitting hours you've racked up, books you've read, or parenting classes you've completed, becoming a mother in real life is a whole new ball game.

I asked for help right away. As I would continue to do for years to come. I was met with "relax," "calm down." "You are just a first-time mom." And "boys are just lazy, late bloomers."

I remember crying hot tears in a clinic room as our pediatrician examined Cooper. She looked in his ears, checked him for a tongue-tie, even checked his fingers and toes for hairs wrapped around them possibly cutting off circulation. Upon completion of her exam, she placed her hand gently on my shoulder. "Some babies are just challenging, Kate, and you got one." As time went on and he wasn't developing as he should have been, I was told to read to him more and to stop anticipating what he needed.

Eventually, the most dangerous thing ever said to me was "Let's wait and see until he's three before worrying." This is still happening today, and in many regions you can replace age three with age five. Every single day I tell parents to trust their gut. Sometimes you must make (respectful) noise.

The earlier a child receives an autism diagnosis and intervention, the more significant the positive impact on their communication skills, behavior, and overall development. Remember, your child is just one of a doctor's, teacher's, or social worker's caseload. You must keep pushing, because no one will fight for your child like you will. You are their best advocate.

I didn't hear the words *autism spectrum disorder* until Cooper was eleven months old. I mean, I am sure I had heard them somewhere but in relation to other children. Not my son. I was sitting in a lunch-and-learn at work, eating a sandwich and minding my own business. I was a project manager for a large nonprofit whose mission was to help children and families in a multitude of ways, and often we were educated about the work the organization provided in the community. I enjoyed learning but also taking a break from my work, so I often attended the lunchtime presentations. My head didn't snap up until the nurse said "not talking as much as other children." She went on to list other signs, such as not responding to their name, avoiding eye contact, not returning a smile, getting upset over a certain taste, smell, or sound, and repetitive movements, such as flapping their hands, flicking their fingers, or rocking their body.

Never in my life up until that point had I had a fight-or-flight moment like the one I was experiencing. I had to get out of that room. I tried to subtly sneak out, but my chair flung back as I stood, slamming into the wall. I froze. All eyes were suddenly on me. And just like an old-time cartoon character, tears sprang out of my eyes. I turned and ran. When I got to my office, I immediately locked the door. And I did what most parents do in a time of fear with their children. I googled.

The words felt foreign and scary as I typed them out. *Autism spectrum disorder.* Back then there weren't really blogs to follow. Facebook wasn't much of a thing yet either. The search results returned clinical websites. Black-and-white clinical information void of the color that Cooper brought into our lives.

I spent the afternoon making lists. Yes, he smiles. No, he doesn't speak. Yes, he shows love. No, he doesn't play. I eventually found the M-CHAT, an online screening tool to assess risk for autism spectrum disorder. By the end of the day, I'd completed the tool over a dozen times, each time getting a different answer. Your worst battle is between what you know and what you feel. My brain knew; my heart wasn't ready.

From that day forward I would sneak over to the library on my lunch break and read about autism, developmental delays, challenging toddlers, and other possible disorders. I loved the anonymity of the library. Of sitting in a corner all by myself and taking in information without judgment. No one knew I went there. It was my time. And I didn't feel the need to defend my choices to anyone there.

Then one day, I found myself sitting on a big comfy couch in the children's section of the library. I was reading a book on language disorders when a gaggle of children gathered around me. They jumped and climbed as they waited for their reader. Their excitement was contagious.

I asked the children how old they were, and little voices shouted "two" and "three." And that was the exact moment I knew my son had autism. All the books, all the research, all the screening tools were one thing. But seeing what autism wasn't told me everything I needed to know.

Six months later, just a few months shy of his fourth birthday, Cooper was diagnosed with severe level 3 autism with a language impairment. I felt instant relief when the word *autism* was said out loud. Not that it was autism but more because we finally had an answer. And in that instant, nothing and everything changed all at once. We drove home with a folder of information, none of which told us what to do next.

One in fifty-nine. That was the autism rate back in 2013.

One in fifty-nine children fell somewhere on the autism spectrum.

When we walked into the appointment, we were one of the other fifty-eight. When we walked out, we were the one. My head was spinning at the hurry-up-and-wait mentality of it all. But also, the isolation of it.

When we left Cooper's diagnosis appointment, I didn't

know one other child with autism or one other family who had a child with a disability. One would think, logically (although there is not a lot of logical thinking happening when one's world is turned upside down and inside out), that being placed into a group like this one would make me feel less alone. So, why did I feel so alone? Why did it feel like we had the only child with this diagnosis? Where were the moms like me? The kids like mine? I was motivated and paralyzed at the same time. And I'll tell you, vulnerably, it gets worse before it gets better.

I hate to throw a bunch of stuff at parents. Because I know either they won't remember it or it will overwhelm them. Or they will resent me. When someone is drowning, they need a life raft, not to be told how to feel. But there are important things that I wish someone would have told me after hearing the word *autism*. I wish these things would have been in the folder that was slid across the table.

Kate, Cooper is exactly who he is supposed to be. A diagnosis of autism wasn't given to him by a doctor, nor did he change the second the diagnosis was said out loud. He is the same amazing kid as he was before the label was given. Remember that.

Let him show you the way. He will lead you off the path of "typical" and into his magical world. Meet him where he is. Sit. Listen. Learn. Just be there with him as he studies the sky and dances to music you cannot hear. Be his shield too. The world doesn't understand autism yet. And while you may not yet either, you are now at the forefront of his journey.

You need to be brave for this child. You will encounter unkindness and fear toward his differences. The first time it happens it will take your breath away. And know there is no way to ready yourself for it. But once it happens you will truly understand what advocacy means. And it will give you a strength like you've never encountered before. It is a gift to protect these tiny humans.

Believe in him. Believe in him so much that people think you are out of your mind. And then believe in him more. You will be told all the things he will never do. The story of his future will be written for him in countless reports. Rip it up. Rip it up and write a new story. Yes, the chapters may be different from every other child you know. His story will be unlike the others. And that's okay. It will be just as beautiful and just as profound.

It all comes down to happiness. I know there are so many things you want and need for your child. But when you strip all of that away, the tying of shoes, scoring a goal, a smile for a driver's license photo, it all comes down to happiness. Is he happy? For us, right now, the answer is yes. That's all that really matters to me.

Lastly, look for the helpers. They are out there, walking the same path as you. Adrian, Carrie, and countless others. Lean on those who get it. You are not alone. Not ever.

But most importantly, I wish someone would have welcomed me to the club.

"Kate, you made it. We are so happy you are here."

## ADRIAN

Finding a diagnosis had been awfully important until the moment I got the wrong one.

"On a scale of 1 to 10, how important is it that you find a diagnosis for Amos?" the doctor asked. Her coat was crisp white and her embroidered name was followed by several initials. Seven years ago, autism became a part of my story.

An evaluation for autism spectrum disorder (ASD) doesn't just get penciled in on one's calendar. Months—and years, in many cases—go by and parents struggle to figure out what and why and where and how. Getting a diagnosis is not easy and it's even harder to figure out how to narrow down your options of where to begin. In order to understand how we landed there, we need to go back to the beginning.

When Amos was born, the hospital pediatrician noted a few anomalies—a sacral dimple, an eye that seemed unable to focus, and hypospadias. After an otherwise normal newborn screening, no one seemed overly concerned and we took him home to his three siblings. When he was ten days old, I had my first twinge that there was something different about this baby—my fourth baby—and it all started with his lack of a smile. When you share with your doctor that you're concerned over such a nuance, you're placated and reassured and sent on your merry way. After all, what's typical for a tiny person is pretty loose, and as long as your little person is gaining weight, everyone seems happy. But I was not happy. A mother knows. If you hear those voices telling you to ask more questions, listen to them.

Amos's development continued to lag. The empty spaces in his baby book seemed to accumulate and glare at me, daring me to write falsehoods in the tidy spaces meant for accomplishments. When Amos was eight months old, I noticed that while the other babies independently sat splashing in tidal pools, my son was unable to sit upright in the damp sand without toppling over. Following that summer—when he was around ten months old—I requested a referral for an assessment by an early intervention team. For the first time, someone saw what I saw—a beautiful happy baby who by now smiled and cooed, but was significantly delayed. That early intervention evaluation resulted in language and motor skills being identified as issues that required services. Soon after, we began an intensive occupational therapy, physical therapy, and speech therapy regimen. I tackled therapy sessions as a full-time job. Between home visits and private sessions at our nearby hospital, we averaged eight to ten per week the year following his first birthday.

Still, I struggled with the unknown, and after one of those morning therapy sessions, I strapped one-year-old Amos into his bucket car seat and we made the hour-long drive to a big bookstore. I was sure that if I just looked in the right section or dug a bit, I would find a book that delved into life with a child who had developmental delays. I needed a book that acknowledged what it felt like and what one should do when there was no "real" diagnosis. Though I scoured the shelves, I could not find it. I naively believed that having a diagnosis for my towheaded boy would equate to a solution.

Over time, we gained some ground and I had successes to note other than his first smile arriving at twelve weeks. He sat up at eleven months, crawled at fourteen months, and finally walked at twenty-two months. Still, we had no idea of the "what" that was responsible for Amos's differences. Securing a tangible diagnosis was a priority in those early years, and so I continued to request referrals for specialists. The array of doctors included an ENT who inserted a half dozen set of tubes for frequent ear infections, an orthopedist who prescribed orthotics for low muscle tone, a craniofacial surgeon who corrected a posterior tongue-tie, a urological surgeon who corrected the hypospadias, a pediatric ophthalmologist who patched one eye and prescribed glasses, a neurologist who scheduled an MRI, which showed a couple of anomalies, including delayed myelination and protruding spheres, and finally, a geneticist who performed microarray testing, followed by whole exome sequencing (WES), neither of which initially revealed any hidden secrets. Each doctor's appointment meant another checked-off exam/assessment/test, and still, my search for the elusive diagnosis was unfruitful. My musings overflowed on paper.

"With each day that passes and reveals nothing, I struggle for a balance between wishing and accepting, concern and overwhelming consumption, hope and an acknowledgment of our reality."

The words of specialists also filled papers, and papers filled notebooks. They were laden with reports and observations that felt cold and clinical. An oral motor specialist documented her observations:

"He is not moving the oral musculature. He has little to no upper lip mobility, and no lip rounding, NO cheek movement, he is always in a high jaw position (with a lot of extraneous jaw sliding as he attempts to motor plan for sounds), his tongue is not moving and there is no dissociation of jaw/lip/tongue movement."

As Amos neared three years old, I grew more desperate. The questions of his delay followed us everywhere—at the playground, grocery store, church, and even the drugstore. We were waiting for the language that by now no one promised was coming. I applied to see a team of doctors in New York City specializing in the diagnosis of rare diseases. When Amos was three and a half, our entire family traveled to the Big Apple and spent the better part of a week in testing sessions and exploring the city in between. The day before World Autism Day, we headed to the hospital for a final appointment. A neurologist came to fetch us from the waiting room and pronounced the verdict just minutes later.

*Autism*, I heard her say.

Autism had landed in our hemisphere and delivered a sucker punch. I listened as she explained that Amos's brain is wired differently than the rest of ours. It was the first time I felt someone knew what they were telling me and that it was likely to be quite accurate. And still, I wept as sadness fell like rain on my fearful shoulders—the what-ifs, the what-nows, the why-mes.

We had been looking for so long for the WHAT behind Amos's differences, but my brain had never contemplated autism. How had I missed all the signs? Love must be blind, I thought. I had no idea a diagnosis would feel so troublesome—no relief, no weight lifted, just heavy debilitating grief. Real life is messy and it doesn't take a pause for any of us, no matter what we're going through. No amount of wishing could turn back the clock to the life that was no longer. Had I known how easy life had been?

I was desperate to find something good about this moment when the face of my beautiful brother flashed through my mind. It's not cancer, I thought. At least it's not cancer. My Amos was healthy and whole and this diagnosis wouldn't leave me weeping on a grassy knoll overlooking a pond in rural eastern North Carolina.

Amos has autism, I practiced saying. This beautiful human had as much purpose as anyone I had ever encountered and it was up to me to cheer him along. And maybe, to follow his lead.

## CARRIE

"Mrs. Cariello?" the woman asks, squinting at a folder. "Right this way, please."

Lined with blue chairs, the waiting room is nearly empty. A cancellation landed us here a full six weeks before our appointment to see the highly sought-after developmental pediatrician. I'd gotten the call while I was at work. Excusing myself from a meeting, I raced out the door to pick Jack up from day care. I'd left Joe a voicemail on the way.

I stand from my seat and gather my purse and the diaper bag. I call out to Jack. He's standing at a kid-sized table, staring at a wooden puzzle in front of him.

"Jack? Buddy? Come with me. Come with Mommy."

With his eyes down, he turns slowly in my direction, but he doesn't answer me. I breathe a sigh of relief at his cooperation. At eighteen months, his emotional pendulum swings wildly throughout the day. Side by side, we cross the room. The nurse leads us down the hallway and into a small exam room.

November 16, 2005. George Bush is president. Hurricane Katrina has just destroyed much of the Gulf Coast. "Hollaback Girl" by Gwen Stefani plays on every radio station.

"He'll be in in a few minutes," she says and shuts the door behind her. Jack moves to the corner and studies the floor. I sit down and look out the window. I notice how overcast the day has become since the morning. The sky looks as though it has something to say, if only I could read the clouds. As we wait my mind becomes a slideshow.

The delivery room where Jack was born on Mother's Day, merely thirteen months after my oldest son. Joe sleeping on the vinyl recliner as I recovered before racing home to feed Joey and put him to bed. Jack's vacant stare, even as an infant. Here but not here.

Night after night, sitting up in the living room, rocking and soothing him as he whined and squirmed in our arms. Joe and I passed him back and forth between us, our eyes grainy with fatigue, my litany of worries unspooling between us like brightly colored thread. Always, I landed on the same refrain.

*Something is wrong with him. You know something is wrong.*

I'd watch Joe's profile in the darkened room as the words echoed around us like a silent scream. He never turned his head when I said them.

Tantrums. Epic, earsplitting tantrums that alternated with the eerie silence of a toddler who doesn't speak.

An entire jar of spaghetti sauce smashed on the floor of the grocery store, shards of glass mixed with red.

Sitting around the dinner table, Joe playing a game where he'd go around and point to all of us, trying to engage him. "Jack, see?" he'd say, pointing at me. "This is Mommy! *Mommy.* Can you look at Mommy?" I can't lie. It chilled me, realizing my son didn't even know who we were.

The time we took both boys to dinner at one of our favorite Italian restaurants in Buffalo, New York. Long since closed, it was called Rizzo's, and it was known for wings and pizza. I'd dressed them in matching pajamas—navy blue with white snowflakes—and as we sat and waited for our meal, people kept stopping by the table to ask if they were twins. Jack was around six months old, and sitting in the wooden high chair he seemed present, as though he was taking it all in, even if not quite interacting with the world around him.

I can bring myself back to that restaurant in an instant. I can smell the Buffalo sauce and the pizza. I can picture the kindly people with their gentle smiles and feel Joe's hand in mine across the table.

Why is this memory so clear for me? It is the last time I remember *not* worrying about Jack. We were simply a young family out together. The drumbeat of fear beneath my rib cage had not quite begun yet.

"Mrs. Cariello, hello," the doctor says softly, breaking me from my reverie. He closes the door and sits down in the chair opposite me. "I've been reading through all the paperwork you sent. Can you tell me a little bit about what's going on with your son?"

I look over at Jack. He is tracing his finger on the vinyl tile, down one side and up the other. He is absorbed in this self-appointed task—as though there are a requisite number of times he has to create this shape with his hands. I notice his fingernails need clipping. The room is hot. A wave of nausea comes over me.

"Well," I begin in a rush. "My husband and I are just noticing that he's not… He doesn't really speak. He doesn't have any words, not even *Mama*."

"Okay, I see that here." He picks a form out of the folder he's holding. "What else?"

"He never sleeps. I mean *never.* I have a son a year older than him at home, and they're just so different." I can feel myself on the verge of babbling, yet my words tumble out like a waterfall. It feels so good to talk openly for once—to admit honestly everything I've noticed since Jack was born.

"Uh-huh," he murmurs.

"He's not interested in any kind of games, like patty-cake or Itsy-Bitsy Spider."

The doctor is taking notes in the folder.

"He has trouble managing food," I continue. "It's as though he can't figure out how to move it from the front of his mouth to the back. He gets incredibly frustrated when we're eating."

The doctor nods. He looks over at Jack sitting on the floor and then back at me. I take it as a cue to continue.

"I guess it's a million little things, you know? I can't shake the feeling that something is just *off.* He never looks at me. He stares off into space a lot. But the slightest thing can set off a huge outburst."

I pause for a moment. I take a deep breath.

"I just want to help him."

*I just want to help him.*

All at once, Jack comes to life in the corner of the room, as though someone changed his batteries or flipped a switch inside of him. No longer content with the tile, he starts to roam the small space, picking up objects within reach and flinging them to the floor. He reaches the doctor and grabs the pen from his hands. He lets out an ear-piercing shriek. I feel a familiar pit in my stomach.

"Hey there, Jack! I'm your doctor." Jack turns away quickly. He looks up at the ceiling, then back down at the floor. His diaper rustles beneath his overalls.

"Jack! Hey, buddy, let's calm down. Come here. Come to Mommy. Sit with me."

He begins to whirl around the room as though he's listening to music only he can hear, yet it is anything but a graceful dance. Suddenly, he crashes into a filing cabinet. His knee collides with the metal corner. He begins to thrash and scream. I rush to him and attempt to gather him in my arms and soothe him. He flails away from me, his whole body physically rejecting my touch.

Just as quickly as the episode started, it ends. In the center of the room, he slumps to the floor, seemingly exhausted by the outburst. For a moment, the only sound is his breathing. I kneel next to him.

"Does he ever come to you for comfort?" The doctor searches my face.

With this question, the world around me snaps into focus. In an instant, I think back to all the times I tried to soothe him—at night on the couch, attempts at morning snuggles, hugs before I drop him off at day care. Each time, his limbs turn wooden in my arms.

I look back at the doctor. Tears spring unbidden in my eyes.

No.

I shake my head. I can't bring myself to admit the words that, no, my son never comes to me for comfort. I'm too ashamed. Yet I know in my heart this is the definitive moment. Somehow, this carries more weight than the lack of speech, the difficulty swallowing food, the sleepless nights. For me, anyway.

What happens next is a bit of a blur. Jack moves back to the tile and begins tracing again. The doctor leans back in his chair. He crosses his legs. Gently, he tells me that, based on the forms and our time together, Jack has Pervasive Developmental Disorder—Not Otherwise Specified.

"Your son is on the autism spectrum."

He goes on to explain what this means, but I have trouble focusing on what he says.

"He will likely always have trouble relating to people."

"One out of one hundred and fifty-eight children are diagnosed every year."

"We don't know very much about the spectrum disorder quite yet."

"His future is uncertain at this time."

Eventually, the appointment ends. I gather up our things and take Jack's hand in mine. I lead him out the door. We walk back to the car. The air in the parking garage is chilly.

My mind is still on the ride home—nearly blank. Yet at the very same time it races. Instead of a nostalgic slideshow of memories, I begin to peer tentatively into the future. As Jack stares out the window—his run-in with the filing cabinet forgotten—I try to imagine him at five, in third grade, then middle school. I think briefly of that afternoon with my mother so many years ago, watching Tom Cruise grapple with a brother he never knew he had.

*If only I had a crystal ball*, I think to myself.

As I grip the steering wheel, my life suddenly feels full of loose ends, when all I long for are knots—something I can grab hold of, something firm between my palms.

It's been more than eighteen years since that day in the doctor's office. This afternoon, I sit at my desk and stare out the window, thinking about my young son. Outside, the trees are covered in snow, though the sky bears the same metallic hue as my memory.

Today, the numbers are much higher. One in every thirty-four children is diagnosed each year. There is much speculation as to this increase, but when asked about it, I have no answer.

That little boy in overalls is a young man now. He towers over everyone in our family. He is everything I never expected he would be—tenacious and honest and determined and pure. Yet there are still days when I long for a crystal ball to see how it all ends.

And how I wish I could go back to that younger version of myself, although I'm not sure exactly what I could tell her that wouldn't frighten her more than she already was.

I think back to the doctor's words and the parking garage. I smile remembering his hand on my shoulder as I walked out the door. I smile further remembering what he said before I walked out the door.

"Give him a big family. It will be good for him."

The next morning, I discovered I was pregnant.

Some days are meant to be remembered forever.

It's going to be okay. That's what I would tell her. It's not going to be perfect or easy. But it's going to be okay.

# 3
# This New Normal

## KATE

*Severe nonverbal autism.*

Those were the three words I keyed into the YouTube search bar the day our new normal officially began. I had never let myself say those three words together out loud, let alone seek them out.

*Autism*, yes. *Nonverbal*, yes. But not together, and never combined with *severe*. Maybe subconsciously I worried that if I searched for them, they would come to fruition. In the end it didn't matter. The diagnosis found us.

For me, while it wasn't a surprise, the finality of it came with many realizations I had refused to fully acknowledge. My son may never talk. My son may never learn to read. He may never outgrow this. He may never live independently. Those realizations changed me, hardening me to the world while softening my heart to this boy.

The search results were nothing short of terrifying. Dark, grainy videos depicting young men and women in vulnerable situations. I imagined a parent standing above them holding a camcorder on their shoulder, filming when they should have been helping. The screams were so loud from my computer I found myself turning down the volume to keep my search a secret from the rest of my family. Guilt for looking. That is what I felt. And shame for being terrified of our supposed future.

I've often wondered if the beginning of our autism journey would have been different if I had seen videos of Cooper today, thriving in his own way. Putting his shoes on, attending his first day of summer camp, or typing "pool party friends" into our digital calendar. Individuals like my son, they are not just their hard parts diced up and shared in a report or in a video. They are whole, the sum of their parts, good and hard. A child, a sibling, a grandchild, a student, a friend. They are not just their diagnosis. That's why I share. To give parents of newly diagnosed kids a soft place to land in their new world.

*Enough*, I thought. I slammed my computer screen down so vigorously I worried I had broken it. I vowed in that instant that my son's story would be different. I felt motivated, determined that if I did everything in my power to help him, he wouldn't end up like the individuals in those videos. If I'm being truthful, I thought he'd outgrow autism. Or that we'd find a magic pill to help him. That the word *autism* wouldn't be a part of my vocabulary when he was older. Maybe we'd even laugh about how worried we used to be way back when.

*By kindergarten, he will be fine*—that's what I told myself.

I longed for a crystal ball to give me a glimpse into our

future. I sought out the so-called professionals, in person and online, desperately asking my questions.

"What about when he's five? Or ten? Will he have autism then?"

I pleaded with them to take pity on me and give me the answers I so desperately needed to hear. This could not be forever. There had to be a middle ground between severe and neurotypical, between YouTube video and reality.

"You don't know what the future holds," I screamed at a first-year clinical therapist. She seemed half my age, with half my experience of autism, when she told me he would most likely never talk. I felt vulnerable and exposed as I nursed Sawyer, while watching Cooper through the observatory window.

With each prediction, I felt myself losing confidence in my ability to make this better. *Maybe he'll learn to speak and play a game. Maybe he'll be able to go into the community without having a meltdown. Maybe he'll be able to live independently, work a job, and support himself as an adult. Maybe this will be okay.*

I believe we are made to do hard things. I love a challenge, a project manager by trade. Give me a mess, I'll clean it up. Give me an idea, I'll make it a reality. Give me a problem, I'll fix it.

That attitude carried over to my home life too. I was never one to be stuck. I believed for every action, there was a reaction. Want to run a marathon, train. Want to lose weight, cut calories. Want a better job, work harder.

Autism was the first thing in my life that I couldn't fix. Autism humbled me. It stripped away my confidence, leaving me to question who I was inherently. Suddenly, I was the one who was unsure. The one asking questions. The one questioning if I had the ability to carry this weight to the finish line. Autism turned the tables on me. Except I wasn't allowed to be meek or unsure of myself. I was expected to be the expert in this diagnosis, in this boy.

It's easy to read about autism. It's a whole different story to live it.

In those early days I settled into a place of acute grief, experiencing a combination of denial, anger, bargaining, and depression. This can't be real. Why him? Why our family? I hated all my friends who had neurotypical kids. This felt unfair and cruel, and I wasn't interested in being part of this pivot from the life I had planned. I pleaded and bargained with God, offering an arm or a leg in exchange for my son's well-being.

As a society we must address grief in special needs parenting. It shouldn't be a taboo subject. There is a loss. No, not a loss of a child. There is a loss of the life we imagined. I thought my son would talk. I thought he'd be able to tell me he loved me, drive a car, and make me a grandma. With those losses come grief. Parents don't often say it. But parenting a special needs child can be lonely. Physically lonely, but emotionally too. Loving myself while I lost myself to autism was something I did not do well in the beginning.

The weeks and even months following Cooper's official diagnosis felt odd. You know that old saying "hurry up and wait"? I was all ready for the sprint of autism. I had my shoes on. I had trained for the race. I was at the start of our new life. But there was nowhere to go. We were already receiving all of the help our area had to offer Cooper. He had been evaluated by the school district and qualified for a special education preschool in the fall. But it didn't feel like enough.

Slowly at first everything began to change. We moved our family of four from our forever home in northern Minnesota to the Twin Cities, a metro area that provided more services for Cooper. Our days became appointments and therapy and straddling two worlds: the real world and the autism world.

We became reactive instead of proactive, constantly plugging holes in our sinking ship. I began pushing everyone away. It felt easier to live this life alone.

I lived in darkness, figuratively and literally, for many years.

We couldn't have lamps because he would break the light bulbs with his hands. That sentence right there, that's the one that people always gasp at when I describe our son's most challenging years with autism. They chuckle when I follow it up with stories of cooking dinner by headlamp. I paint a picture of Jamie, Sawyer, and me gathered around a candle in the living room making s'mores. A fuzzy blanket haphazardly thrown over four chairs creating a fort over our heads. In those days, we couldn't leave the house as a family of four—not safely, anyway. So, we did our best.

I've heard some autism parents say they had to let go of the fantasy of the life they wanted to free themselves and accept reality.

Ages four to eight, those were the years that defined our family. Every decision we made was looked at through the lens of autism. From where we lived (not by a busy street or a pond), to where we worked (a place with a flexible schedule), to how we spent our time. Our world got very small in those years post diagnosis.

Isolation is the silent killer of families with special needs and most of the world has no idea. I suppose our neighbors thought we were homebodies. Or maybe even antisocial. That's not true though. We just did what we had to do to keep our son safe.

Exterior doors had to be triple locked. Alarms were placed on the doors and the windows. All to keep him out of the street and ponds and safely in our home. We couldn't go in the front yard because Cooper would obsessively run toward traffic. We couldn't have mirrors because he would break the glass. We couldn't have picture frames on the walls because he would take them down and stomp on them to get the photos out.

My days started at 3:00 a.m. with him racing out of bed, with unbelievable energy. I would stand next to the VHS player, frantically pressing the fast-forward and rewind buttons, on a thirty-second clip of *Thomas & Friends*, to keep him happy and from waking his brother with screams.

The nights were so long I used to worry the sun wasn't going to rise. *Is the world ending?* I would think, waiting for the light to find us.

Chairs were lined up throughout the living room. Four red kitchen chairs, four folding chairs, and a few more miscellaneous ones. When I see photos of them now, I smile and wonder why we had so many chairs.

Cooper and I have never blended in. I would be lying if I said that wasn't hard sometimes. But I do remember the first time I didn't care.

We were walking along a path, through our city, to our local park. It was mostly silent except me narrating every so often. Truck. Tree. Cloud. Stop.

In a weird, out-of-body experience, I saw us clearly. A middle-aged mother walking a person not much smaller than her but yet not quite a man. He was wearing a red shirt. She was holding on to him tightly. She hugged him and kissed him often. She tickled and whispered and held his hand. Every few steps she would pull him close.

I flip-flop between two thoughts. We made it. Look at us out walking in the community. And, how did we get here? Right here. Not knowing how to safely walk or how to talk. A flash of dark, grainy YouTube videos fills my mind. We were them. We'd become what I was most afraid of.

Cooper quickly brings me back to reality. He touches my face, turning my head to show me something. Across the way, at the entrance to the park, there had to be a hundred white chairs neatly lined up. He points excitedly, then gasps and throws his head back and laughs with unbelievable joy.

I feel people staring. I don't care. He begins running toward the chairs. At first, I wasn't sure what he would do. He hadn't lined our own chairs up in ages. But like most parts of his autism, this too was cyclical. Most things return.

When he reached the front row, he stopped abruptly, looking back at me, waiting for me to catch up. Then, in the most beautiful way, he began moving his arms in unison to music that only he could hear. He was a conductor directing an orchestra.

It was my turn to gasp and to be educated. I finally saw the world through his eyes. All those years with chairs throughout our living room, seemingly dividing our world in two. The frustration I felt having a foot in two different worlds, trying to be the bridge between.

It's amazing, really. The way he moves between two worlds. The way he lives so fearlessly. The way he not only waits for me to catch up but, when I'm ready, leads me into these next phases of his life and gently reminds me that it's okay. It's okay to be different.

Accepting the gift of sight that he shares with me, I went and stood next to him bravely, shoulder to shoulder, and pretended to hear the music too.

## ADRIAN

Twenty-four hours after being handed an autism diagnosis, I found myself pushing Amos in a grocery cart and picking out a sheet cake at our local grocery store. It was smothered in blue icing and I smeared the words *Happy Birthday* until they resembled messy clouds. That evening, our family gathered around that cake and I willed the tears not to fall. Life had changed more than I knew possible, and despite my grief, I was determined to make friends with our new normal.

Just three years before, I had been lying on a table in my ob-gyn's office waiting for an ultrasound. My husband and I were raising three fairly typical children who were ages three, four, and six. We believed our family was complete and life was busy and good. That morning—while I was in yoga class—the thought occurred to me that I hadn't had a real period in over two months. I rolled up my mat and casually asked my instructor (who is also my cousin) if she had any pregnancy tests lying around. She looked at me quizzically and I assured her it was very unlikely since I had been on birth control since the birth of our daughter. She found a test buried in a bathroom drawer, which I unwrapped, and after following the instructions, I sat in her kitchen to wait the required allotment of time. After a few minutes, curiosity got the best of me, and when I peeked, the color drained from my face. My ob-gyn's office was beside my cousin's house, so I walked through the back door of the office and announced we had an emergency (you know you live in a small town when that's a viable option). The office manager took pity on me and told me to come back in thirty minutes. Before I knew it, I was shifting on green pleather covered with crinkly paper. Minutes after the cool gel was slathered on my stomach, the ultrasound wand revealed a white scene amongst the black of my womb.

"What is that?" I asked.

"It's your baby!" he said. He estimated I was about nine weeks along.

That was the end of normal as I knew it. My previous pregnancies were all planned and this very much was not. After a bit of crying, I called my husband, who was shocked but happy. We adjusted fairly quickly to this unexpected child and began thinking about our future with him. I imagined a rough-and-tumble fourth child, one who would be happy tagging along with his three older siblings, eager to keep up and participate in all the things—and we sure had things.

Our family was in constant motion and we stayed on the move. We filled every school break with a road trip, a plane trip, or even a camping trip. It was nothing for me to hop on a plane with my three littles and go to Florida to see their grandparents for a long weekend. My husband often stayed home to work and I became a pro at juggling three children. While I knew a baby would complicate our well-established life, I was confident we would adjust and quickly land on our feet. Instead, this baby would rock our world, and I said goodbye to that old semblance of normal.

From the very beginning, Amos required a tremendous amount of my time and attention. Though we didn't know he had special needs as a baby, he did have several medical issues that required frequent appointments and multiple surgeries. Juggling four children had proved to be beyond the scope of the difficult I had expected. Once he outgrew his stroller, traveling was tough and going to sporting events was no longer possible. We hired babysitters or my husband and I took turns participating or being spectators at the activities of our big three. When we attempted to take Amos to cheer on a sibling, he had to be watched like a toddler even though he was in kindergarten. While the other younger siblings played games amongst themselves, he would flee at a moment's notice. One time I was too engrossed in a conversation with a friend, and before I knew it, he had darted on the field and was rolling in the net by the time I caught him.

Our new normal was also humbling. There is nothing that makes me feel quite as vulnerable as chasing a little boy across a soccer field in the middle of the game. My old normal involved sitting on the bleachers, munching popcorn, saying hello to friends, whereas this new normal was consumed with juggling special needs and often being on display. Though we tried to carry on our old existence, it proved trying. I remember going out to dinner and my daughter had brought a jar of change to purchase some candy after the meal. When Amos's iPad unexpectedly died, he not only threw it, but shoved her jar of change off the table. Shards of glass and coins exploded on the old wooden floor and her face dropped. She held it together, though, and, with her older brothers and dad, picked up the pieces of the jar and gathered the spilled change. Though life was not following those once-choreographed plans, our family was learning to pick up the pieces.

Feel all the feels, I would tell them and myself. When Amos broke something, I wiped away the tears. When one of them voiced their annoyance, I really listened and sympathized rather than just trying to smooth over the hard parts. We learned to navigate this new life together, and over time, my big three developed resilience and participated in the care of Amos.

One trying afternoon, my oldest son arrived home from school and noticed I was at the end of my rope after a long day with a discontented Amos. He offered to take Amos outside to swing and I was so appreciative and marveled at this newly sown empathy. My daughter was quick to offer hugs and smiles after a meltdown and demonstrated how easily forgiveness should come. My middle son would always position himself between Amos and a perceived danger whether on a sidewalk or in the ocean. On almost a daily basis, they would shout or call me in excitement over the smallest feats. Nothing was too little for celebration—Amos sipping from a cup, when he learned to wave goodbye, nodding yes, even stepping down from a curb rather than crawling. Their delight sparked the new way our family defined success.

That doesn't mean I didn't struggle or grapple with the new normal. Unfamiliar or unpredictable community settings struck me with bouts of heartache. I remember going to a ribbon cutting in our small town for an amazing new playground that was accessible for kids with special needs. It was a fantastic place, beautiful and functional, fun and far beyond anything our small community had ever known. My heart smiled as newly diagnosed Amos flew up ramps and down interesting sensory slides. He needed that playground and my struggle was in the grappling of that acknowledgment. I had not envisioned a world that would need to be tailored to our family and longed for normalcy, not special needs. I loved him so much but couldn't make my mind obey my heart. I longed to quell the tears lodged there, but that playground was a reminder of the unknown abyss which loomed large on the horizon. I shrugged off those pesky feelings and chose joy in that moment. I joined Amos on the shiny new equipment and we flew down the slide together, played chase on ramps, and I pushed him on the zip line. Later, when quiet fell and children were tucked into bed, I finally shed those tears and allowed the grief to wash over me for this newfound normal. Acknowledging the hard meant it didn't own me and I needed a life steered by joy no matter our normal.

A year after the diagnosis, I felt ready to tackle the world. In a moment of naive confidence, I signed Amos up for his first taste of rec sports. I would soon be humbled by the rite of passage that marked three- to five-year-olds in our small town. Practices and games were a rite of passage for small-town youngsters in early spring and I was reminded of my former life with Amos's older siblings. I had enjoyed clambering up noisy bleachers, watching the kids on the field while exchanging gossip and news with other parents in the stands.

A minute or so into Amos's first game, I realized my days on the bleachers and gabbing on the sidelines had effectively ended. On that cold Saturday morning in March, I was the only grown-up on the pint-sized field chasing a small boy with spaghetti legs and hand-me-down cleats who gleefully twisted himself in the other team's soccer goal net. As I gathered four-year-old Amos into my arms, I swallowed my pride and remembered that just a few years ago, he was the boy I had wished would walk. He had indeed come so far.

Soccer turned out okay in the end. Amos did kick the ball, though not in a team sort of way. When instructed by the coach, he connected that little old foot with the ball. I sat on a bench surrounded by little boys and did my best to show Amos the beauty of being part of a team. When he ran, I ran, and when he sat, I sat, and when he wandered astray, I gathered him in my arms and told him I was so proud. And really, I was proud—of both of us. The clever little boy and the mom on the field who had never been anywhere but on the bleachers. I was filled with gratitude for the coaches who called my son by name and those parents whose faces radiated joy from their perch on metal slats.

Today, Amos is ten years old and autism doesn't sting so much anymore. We have gotten better at juggling his needs amidst the rest of our family and navigating our new normal, whether sports, dinners out, or family vacations. We try to ensure that our other children have experiences, even if Amos cannot participate in the same way. Sometimes we leave him at home and sometimes we alter plans. This past spring, my husband planned to take our big three for a few days of skiing at Jackson Hole and I planned to stay home with Amos. It was my daughter who casually pointed out that Amos had not been on a family vacation since a trip to Mexico when he was still a stroller-happy toddler. I pushed back and cited the many trips we had taken together to see Florida grandparents and weeks at the beach.

"I mean a REAL vacation, somewhere new," she clarified.

After mulling over her observation for a bit, my husband and I decided she was right. I would plan to be Amos's person and Thomas and the big three could carry on with their planned activities. We canceled the Airbnb and moved us to a condo/hotel, as we knew a pool would be a welcome respite to fill time, especially if skiing was a no-go. I also made arrangements for two days of adaptive ski lessons and crossed my fingers that we would have success.

I had been raised to see success as the inevitable result from working hard. Our new normal recognized a strict definition was not realistic. With the birth of Amos, the landscape of our new normal was far more forgiving when it came to success. For example, I would no longer define success as a full day of navigating the bunny slope. I considered and voiced aloud to my skeptical family that real success would be getting Amos into ski boots. They laughed and visibly relaxed with this lowering of expectations as we prepared for the big week. The new normal meant we would be holding our collective breaths as we prepared for so many new firsts—first time taking two planes to reach a destination, first time putting on ski boots and being strapped to sticks on slippery snow, even the first time watching available TV shows rather than demanding YouTube. It was an amazing trip and success was ours because we embraced our new normal.

We had just arrived home when his sister made mention of his success. She smiled with the memory of a trip that didn't include a family skiing the days away together or going out for leisurely dinners.

"Mom, Amos was really good at Jackson Hole, wasn't he?"

"Yes, he really was," I said with a smile and thought back to what I once considered a normal life, which is all I ever wanted. I wouldn't trade this normal for any other.

# CARRIE

The first person I told about Jack's diagnosis was a stranger at the Bronx Zoo.

Sure, close family and friends knew something was up, but I hadn't found a way to officially tell everyone yet. I couldn't figure out the best way to do it. An email? Phone calls? Wait until we were all together for the holidays? Hallmark doesn't exactly have cards for this kind of thing.

*Dear friends and family,*

*I am happy to announce that, after nine zillion appointments with various specialists and doctors, we have learned that our son Jack is diagnosed with autism spectrum disorder.*

*We are still processing this news ourselves. We don't know quite what it means yet—for him or us.*

*Please be patient with us as we figure out what the rest of our life may look like. We may disappear from the social landscape for a bit. Don't take it personally. We'll be back.*

*In the meantime, feel free to send pizza.*

*Warmly,*
*The Cariello Family*

That would be great, wouldn't it?

Instead, there I was, on what seemed like the hottest day of the summer, chasing two-year-old Jack through animal exhibits. He ducked and wove around legs and strollers, picking pretzels out of the garbage and shrieking at the birds in their cages. And that was in the first ten minutes.

I was visiting my father. Joe stayed home with Charlie, with plans to build a play set in the backyard. I dutifully drove the three hours to New York with Joey and Jack in the back seat. I was seven months pregnant at the time.

When my father suggested the zoo, it seemed like a great idea. He and his wife could help manage the two toddlers with me and it would be a nice way to pass an afternoon. We'd stroll through the pathways, point out the giraffes, and maybe get some lunch. How wrong I was.

The minute we got there, Jack was completely overstimulated. Though I didn't possess the explanation for deregulation that I do now, it was obvious he couldn't cope with the crowd or the noise. The moment we walked through the gates, he started hitting his head and flapping his hands.

This might be a good place to mention we inadvertently went on "free" day. That's the day when the Bronx Zoo generously opens its doors with no cost of admission. Although a wonderful concept, it also means everyone and their neighbor turn out for a trip to the zoo. People blocked the pathways and lined up in front of the exhibits.

People stared. I noticed they were looking at me, judging. When Jack dropped to the ground after plucking a cheeseburger off someone's plate and attempting to eat it, I wanted to curl into a ball and disappear.

We soldiered on, as my father is not one to call a day earlier than planned—even if said day was free. Painstakingly, we trudged through the displays. I wished I'd thought to bring a stroller, even though by that age, Jack usually refused to sit in it.

Desperately, I wanted to tell our story that day. I wanted to explain how six months earlier, we found out he had autism. We were still adjusting to our new normal.

It wasn't until the very last ride of the day—a tram ride through the remainder of the park—that I broke my own silence. The line was very long, and it wrapped around itself. Jack was kicking the ground and bumping the people in front of us. More than once, they turned around and glared. After a few minutes, he broke free of my hand and bolted away. For perhaps the dozenth time that day, I chased after him.

Huffing and puffing, I corralled him and brought him back to the line, potato sack–style. I wove in and out of people to find my father standing with Joey. People stepped aside—some willingly, some begrudgingly. I couldn't read the expression on the man behind us. He had a baseball cap on backward.

All at once, something snapped inside me, and I said the words I'd been trying to form since we walked through the gates. I turned to the man in the hat and said, "My son has autism."

*My son has autism.*

My voice was strong. The words felt like I was trying on a sweater to see if it fit. I didn't apologize—although there would be times in the future that I would. On this day, I said them as much for me as the man in the baseball cap.

From that point forward, I said them often. At the grocery store, in the mall, during meetings with his new IEP team. Those four words became part of my new normal. All at once, they broke me open. They hurt me. They healed me.

Over the years, I've talked to parents who prefer to keep their child's diagnosis private. They worry about being defined by the label or pigeonholed somehow. While I respect this choice, there was no hiding Jack's autism. It was as much a part of him as his blue eyes or the freckles on his nose. I worried that if I didn't explain him, people would come up with their own labels: naughty, loud, or rude.

Early on, one of the defining characteristics of Jack's autism was his speech delay. Even once he gained speech around the age of four, he was slow to respond if he was asked a question. It would be years before I understood that autism speaks a listener's language and I could explain it in those terms.

In the meantime, it was my job to help people learn to wait

around him—not to bombard him with too many questions or sigh impatiently as he searched for words like so many needles in the proverbial haystack.

It was my job to speak for him, root for him, and fight for him. I was plopped right into the role of advocate—whether I wanted it or not.

Mostly, it was my job to share our story. The inclination is to turn into what they call *Mama Bear*—a state of fierce, and at times hostile, protectiveness. Yet that moniker never sat quite well with me. Instead, after a few failed attempts at defensiveness, I opted to offer a connection instead. To explain my son and his autism, yes, but to do it in a way in which people could relate.

As I explained autism, another idea bloomed in my subconscious, like a flower reaching toward the light.

*Who are we?*

This is what I asked myself over and over again. Who are we now, as a couple? Who am I? What does this mean for our other kids? Because autism is a family diagnosis. It isn't contained to one person. It affects us all. Perhaps this diagnosis was a chance to discover who we wanted to be.

I always say Jack drew us back home. He pared life down to the essentials and brought us to the basics: dinner at the table at night, church and breakfast with Grandma on Sundays. Fewer activities, because he couldn't tolerate racing from field to field on Saturday mornings.

About three years ago, I participated in a virtual event for parents of special needs kids. Through the screen, an earnest young mom asked if I had any recommendations for her five-year-old's upcoming IEP meeting. Was there a particular service or therapy that benefited Jack the most?

I didn't even think before I answered. Desperately, I wanted to give her the answer she longed to hear, that yes, extra time with the speech therapist and more goals added to the already long list would transform her little boy.

"What helped Jack get to this point?"

I wish I could say there was a formula to this autism journey—if you do A, B will follow. The truth is, there wasn't one particular therapy or service that helped get Jack to where he is today. I also once pinned all my hopes on the conference room and the sheaf of papers that I clutched in my hands. But it doesn't work that way.

Our first IEP meeting was in Buffalo, New York. Prior to that, I had never heard the words *Individualized Education Plan* in my entire life. I assumed everyone had the same plan for the same day at school. I never knew about things like accommodations.

It's important to remember you are trying to raise a whole child. A child who can forgive, and order in a restaurant, and cheer someone up after a bad day. One who can sit in church, or at his brother's baseball game, or through brunch at a fancy-ish restaurant. A whole child doesn't spring out of a conference table or leap off a page covered in black-and-white goals.

*Tell. Discover. Decide.*

Unwittingly, these three tenets became my mantra over the years. In other words, it's only in looking backward that I realized they were the principles which guided me through the unknown terrain of life with a diagnosed child.

I told our story. I told it even when people warned me not to share. I told it even though, at times, it fell upon unhearing ears.

We took the chance, as a family, to discover who we were—and who we could be. This didn't remove the sting of autism altogether—nothing does that—but it helps ease the heartache just a little bit. When viewed through the lens of possibility rather than limitation, this diagnosis took on a whole new meaning.

*My son has autism.*

The first time I said these four words, I was sweating beneath a summer sun.

The man behind me in line looked at me and smiled with his eyes.

"It's okay."

*It's okay.*

A good verse inside a Hallmark card if I ever heard one.

# 4
# Anxiety

## KATE

"What is autism?"

I knew this question was coming.

It was World Autism Day 2018, a day I didn't even know existed just hours prior, and we had invited all the kids in the neighborhood over for ice cream sundaes and cupcakes in our driveway to celebrate our son Cooper.

Cooper was eight years old. It may be hard to believe, but back then, there wasn't much for community in the autism world, online or in person. So, when a post showed up in my Facebook feed informing me that April 2nd was World Autism Day, I was a bit surprised. I had no idea there was a day.

Were we supposed to celebrate? Or be sad? Was this our "coming out" day?

As I scrolled through posts, I read statistics that weren't in our favor. It all felt heavy over my morning coffee. It was then that I made the decision to celebrate and share autism with our neighborhood.

Fifty cupcakes and five gallons of ice cream were ordered. Balloons came next. An invitation on the neighborhood Facebook page third. Finally, a text to my husband about our party plans. I live by a very simple philosophy: *Anything worth doing is worth overdoing.* I didn't know if anyone would come. Would they think I was silly to celebrate autism? We were relatively new to the neighborhood and Cooper hadn't made it easy for me to meet our neighbors. The isolation that accompanies autism was the hardest part for me. I was indeed "coming out."

Hours later, as the kids and their parents gathered in our driveway, I thought to myself, *I did it.*

We were given so many predictions about Cooper's future when he was diagnosed. Some people tried to tell me that his life was going to be sad and lonely. They told me all the things that he would never do or accomplish. I let those predictions steal the light from me for a lot of years. But as time went on, I learned to accept that our life was going to be different.

The party was a success. Cooper greeted every single one of our guests with a quick wave and a smile and even hugged some that he deemed his favorites. Cooper has always loved a big, tall, burly man. He loves a bald head and tattoos. Why? We have no idea. But when he sees them, stranger or not, they get a hug.

He used his speech device to tell people that his grandparents were coming in two days. He held up two fingers to inform a few of them that he was waiting on two DVDs from eBay.

He took a break and went to the mailbox with his dad and returned with a brand-new train magazine. And when he got overwhelmed by the noise, he signed "help" to me, and we made him a safe space right in the middle of the celebration. I've learned to give him all the space and time that he needs. And when he's ready, he will return.

I snapped a photo of Cooper wrapped up in blankets in the center of our driveway while the party happened around him. Near but far. I have always described Cooper with that phrase.

I was scooping ice cream into cups, feeling pretty good about my advocacy, when I heard a little voice say... "What is autism?"

There had been no mention of autism up until this point at the party, and for a second, I felt taken aback by her boldness. I let out what probably sounded like a laugh, only because I was nervous, and it was a hard question that I truly didn't have an answer to. Maybe I was even a little annoyed that she asked.

If I had to guess, she was six years old, around Sawyer's age. I didn't know who she was specifically, just that she lived down the street. Her mother stood behind her, smiling. I've learned over the years that children will ask questions that parents are afraid to ask. It's beautiful, really.

I stumbled a bit over my answer, but I did my best.

I told her that Cooper is just like her and me, only he does things a little differently. He was born with autism, which means he hears and sees and smells and feels and communicates differently a lot of the time. But he also loves cupcakes and trains and friends and swimming. And he really loves it when people say hi to him and sit next to him.

She asked a few more questions. Like why he sits on the

ground and flaps his arms and yells sometimes. I did my best to answer each and every one as honestly as I could but worried throughout that I was getting it wrong. One of my ongoing fears is that children will be afraid of my son.

I pray that parents tell their children about kids like Cooper. The ones who spend their days in other parts of the school and aren't recognized in the yearbook photos. I hope they encourage their kids to ask questions and say hi.

But what is autism? If I stumbled over my answer, how could anyone get it right? Countless times I've found myself studying Cooper, trying to separate autism from boy.

How do you explain a person, a family, an entire world, in a few sentences, over ice cream?

I knew the clinical answer. I even had it memorized. While at a seminar after Cooper was diagnosed, I wrote it out on a piece of notebook paper in red pen. I underlined words, bolded a few others, and scribbled some out too. Ever since then, I've carried it in my heart.

*The CDC says autism spectrum disorder (ASD) is a developmental disability that can cause significant social, communication, and behavioral challenges.*

That description meant nothing to me. It was too black-and-white, void of the sunshine and mystery my boy brought into my life.

When Cooper was diagnosed with autism at age three, no one told me anything positive about autism. Not one thing. No one told us about the absolute joy he would bring to our world. Instead, they told us all the things he would never do. From the very beginning, autism was presented as something to overcome, to change, to eliminate, even.

Only, the lesson to be learned is that autism can't be eliminated. There is no Cooper without it. His autism is woven throughout him. I picture colorful seams sewn throughout his arms and legs with rays of light peeking through. His autism can't be separated from him because it is who he is.

Asking what is autism is is like asking "Who is Cooper?" "Tell me about your boy" would be a better question and a much easier one to answer.

Our first World Autism Day taught me something invaluable about my son and ultimately my purpose.

In my early years, when I reluctantly stepped into my role as an advocate, I thought my job was to teach my son about the world. But as time went on, I started to see it differently.

Cooper is exactly who he is supposed to be, unapologetically.

My purpose is to teach the world about my son.

In 2018 we welcomed our third baby boy into our family. We named him Harbor after our favorite city, Two Harbors. We joke that we couldn't have handled two of him. At the same time, Cooper's challenges peaked. When I share today to parents of newly diagnosed children, I tell them our hardest years were ages four to eight. I don't tell them to scare them. I tell them to help them.

Because age eight is when everything changed in our world. Age eight was when I redefined the definition of Cooper's autism.

When Cooper was first diagnosed, I thought we hit the autism jackpot. While life was challenging because he couldn't communicate, we were okay. Yes, we had struggles with sleep and lack of safety awareness and communication, but we didn't have aggression or self-injuring, the darker parts that aren't shared often. But at age eight, everything changed.

Our home no longer felt safe. It was as if Cooper had created a list of unwritten rules that we had to live by, but we didn't know what they were. And even worse, they changed sometimes by the minute.

We did everything we could not to upset Cooper. Which,

as you can imagine, is incredibly challenging when you have a family, especially young children.

I navigated his world uncertainly trying to help him, researching, trying new things while keeping everything the same, analyzing everything, all while slowly losing my mind.

I was taking a much-needed walk with a girlfriend, who also happened to have an autistic son, who was much older than Cooper. I felt comfortable sharing with her how challenging life had become.

I tend to combat trauma with humor. It's who I am. I have to laugh; I have to make things funny.

I told her how we couldn't turn left in the car anymore. If we turned left, it would send him into hysterics. "We just keep turning right! We never get anywhere.

"We can't stop at stoplights, or get gas, or drive by a boat trailer, and last time we slowed down for construction, he jumped out of the car."

She nodded as I spoke, listening.

"My life is controlled by what devices are charging, the strength of the Wi-Fi, a lump in his sock, a beep of a truck backing up, and swimsuits. We can't even mention the words *pool* or *swim*.

"This has to be more than just autism," I said to her. I could hear the desperation in my voice.

I described it to her as something creeping in at random times, grabbing ahold of my boy and serving up an emotional and physical beating until he was barely recognizable to me.

"He changes. You can see it in his eyes. It's like he's a different person."

I would give anything to be able to fend off this awful intruder for him. To remove all the pain and confusion and just leave behind my boy.

I spoke of self-injury, aggression, and property destruction—the shameful parts that were breaking me.

Kids are supposed to skin their knees. They are supposed to fall off their bikes and take a tumble or two down the stairs. As parents, we are supposed to protect them from strangers and monsters under the bed. But not from themselves.

I didn't know about this part when I was pregnant. I didn't know I'd have to protect my baby from himself. This is an aspect no one talks about. The mental health parts. The realities of the day-to-day of keeping a human safe, who doesn't understand safety.

This is why I share. Why I tell our story whenever I can. To remind parents that they are not alone. We may not walk the same road, but we can lean on each other. And write our own chapters in our books, knowing that our stories can help each other.

And then my friend said five words that changed everything I thought about autism.

"Kate, that sounds like anxiety."

I think I laughed at her. Maybe even snorted a little bit.

Anxiety? What could a child have to be anxious about? The anxiety I knew happened before giving a speech or meeting someone new. Not turning left at a stoplight.

Cooper has autism. Just autism. Or was it more than "just" autism?

I did what I always do. I dove into research, scouring websites, articles, and blogs for any information about anxiety—desperate to figure out if this new *A* word was the thief of my son's joy.

I found out there were many different comorbidities that could accompany autism. Anxiety; depression; ADHD; epilepsy; OCD; sleep, feeding, and intellectual disorders; and so on.

I learned anxiety is one of the most common mental health disorders affecting children and adults on the autism spectrum and often the most overlooked. According to research studies, about 40 percent of youth with autism—and up to half of autistic adults—meet the clinical criteria of anxiety disorder, such as social anxiety, phobia, panic disorder, or generalized anxiety.

I began reading stories of anxiety along with obsessive-compulsive disorder in autistic children. I saw bits and pieces of our life in others. We weren't alone.

My son had crippling anxiety and OCD that no one had ever mentioned before. No doctor. No therapist. No teacher. But even more mind-blowing, all the challenging parts of Cooper that I had been lumping together for years and calling autism actually weren't.

As a visual thinker, I imagined a brightly colored hot-air balloon held down by ropes. His autism was the balloon. His color, his unique parts, his quirks. The ropes that held the balloon down, those were anxiety, ADHD, and OCD. The ropes kept him from flying. And they kept us from living.

Medicating Cooper, for any reason, never crossed my mind. While I had begged doctors for anything to help him stay asleep, which we never found, medicating for any other reason had never come up. In fact, every time I brought a concern to his doctors, I was told, "Oh, that's just autism."

*All kids with autism get ear infections.*

*All kids with autism have constipation.*

*All kids with autism have sleep disorders.*

And ultimately, *there isn't a lot we can do about autism...*

I am not a soapbox person, but if a doctor says, "Oh, that's just autism," I tell parents to stand up and leave, immediately. Many of the comorbidities that accompany autism are treatable and can be helped. It's imperative that we demand help for our kids.

Armed with facts and hope, Jamie and I brought Cooper to a doctor to help with his anxiety and OCD. For the first time, we felt seen and understood, and for the first time in Cooper's life, we didn't have to beg for help.

"I really think starting him on an antianxiety medication would be beneficial."

I was apprehensive. I didn't want to drug my child. I didn't want him to be a zombie. I had always been against medicating. There is a stigma around it. A shame, even. Parents didn't openly talk about this sort of thing. I'd seen many parents ask a question in desperation about medication in a Facebook group, only to be crucified just for asking.

And to be clear, I would never judge another parent for medicating their child. For me, though, it felt like giving up. Like a last-ditch effort to help. I was wrong and not just a little bit wrong—I was unbelievably wrong. I would soon learn that, like therapies, medications can be a wonderful tool to add to your toolbox.

Forty-eight hours after we started Cooper on antianxiety medication, we knew we had made the right decision. At nine years old Cooper sat peacefully for the first time. It was so monumental that when I called Jamie in from the garage to see, we stood together and cried. Then made our way to him and for thirty minutes we sat calmly next to our boy.

From that day forward we watched the light come back to our boy as anxiety lessened its grip on him.

He joined our family for a movie. We ate dinner together. He held his baby brother. He even said his first word, *mom*.

The transformation was stunning, and if I hadn't witnessed it, I may not have believed it.

Before medicating, I assumed medicine would take away his personality. Change him, even. I was wrong. Medicine combated his anxiety and OCD and gave him back his personality. Medicine should not be the last resort and I tell that to parents whenever I can. I see the worry, the guilt, the fear when parents ask me about medicating. I just share our story, honestly. Medication saved Cooper's life and gave him a chance to thrive.

Some people don't believe in anxiety. They think it's a made-up thing. I laugh because I've heard the same thing about autism. It's bad parenting. It's a child without discipline. Maybe at one time I even thought those things. That was before my son.

At thirteen, Cooper is still greatly affected by both anxiety and obsessive-compulsive disorder. Only it looks different now. We look at them as the fierce sidekicks to autism, a trifecta of sorts, ones that we can't seem to shake.

One day he will appear calm. It may even last weeks or months. We will breathe easier, take more chances, try new things. But like the flip of a switch, his sidekicks creep in and consume him.

Our days become obsessions of things and lists and places to go. A bullet train in Japan. Three sleeps until Grandma comes home. Two days until the Duluth Depot. Or random things. Things he lost two years ago. Things he doesn't have words for. Maybe an ad on a YouTube video showing the latest train magazine. Even a blemish on a piece of paper or mud on his shoe. Things coming in the mail. He is always waiting for something. Counting down. He carries a giant white board from room to room to bed to bus. On it, written in blue marker, the things he waits for.

One day he is fine. The next he is not. We live day to day with anxiety.

At times I feel like his emotional support person, repeating and writing and wondering if I am doing more harm than good.

We are connected. Mother and son. I translate what he cannot understand. I know how to calm him and talk him off the ledge, but what if someday I cannot? I feel the weight heavier some days.

For the hundredth time today, he looks to me with desperation, holding up three fingers, pointing to the sky. I know what he needs.

"Yes, Grandma will get on an airplane and come home, Cooper. Yes, you can stay three sleeps."

What is autism?

Autism is everything all at once.

## ADRIAN

In those early years, I blamed autism for almost everything—his lack of speech, the meltdowns that accompanied daily activities like putting on shoes or getting in and out of the car. My mind whirred with all the things I associated with autism.

I wondered how we got here.

I wondered what to do.

I wondered how we would survive.

Each day, we encountered things that threw Amos into a tizzy, and so we began to retreat. I was forced to hire a sitter to accomplish the most mundane and simplest of tasks. Running errands like going to the grocery store or bank or picking up a prescription proved to be too much for Amos. I had never noticed how many triggers lurked out in the world. Groups of people and automatic flushers in public bathrooms could cause us to leave a cart full of groceries or a long line. Family outings were particularly difficult because his siblings were also affected. I remember the night a buzzer at a church basketball game wrecked what had once been a predictably easy family outing.

It was a Saturday night in February at church basketball that nearly broke me. That night, our sitter canceled at the last minute and my husband was away duck hunting. I considered the three older siblings, who were dressed and ready to go, versus four-year-old Amos, who declared quite vehemently "No basketball!" when I shared our plans. His older siblings were looking forward to an outing on an otherwise dreary day. Though church basketball was something we had always done as a family, we had never taken Amos. He preferred the safety of his routine at home, and not only did the big kids have fun, I also relished the break. Being in public with Amos equated to running a full-court press. It was a nice respite to sit on the bleachers and chat with families, eat a $2 hot dog and call it dinner while enjoying some good-natured rivalry between eastern North Carolina parishes.

Against my best judgment, I decided to persevere. As soon as we walked into that big old gym, the buzzer rang out loudly and the tears began to fall. What Amos couldn't say in words, he demonstrated with body language. He sprawled on the floor of the echoing room while casting a side-eye, wary of the clock that he seemed to understand connected with the buzzer that sounded at random. When the buzzer went off, he panicked. I pondered what to do as he gripped my shirt and somehow we ended up in the bathroom. Amos and I cuddled with his blankie on a surprisingly comfortable bench before I attempted to move outside the open door, eager to catch my daughter's game. When I was unable to coax him out, a hot dog and a cookie helped to quiet him. I left him in the bathroom and stood outside the open door because my daughter mattered too. He was begrudgingly content on that bathroom bench and I was able to watch her performance. I alternated between cuddling him and cheering from the bathroom's doorway—a brief respite from the struggles that were becoming routine.

In the following year, Amos's erratic behavior became more unmanageable. The simplest of things spawned outrage and resulted in writhing and kicking and yelling. The rest of us would stand helpless, wondering how we would survive autism. He threw things, kicked bookcases, melted down over itchy tags, and flopped on the floor in rage. As time went on, I was less able to articulate the why behind his behavior. After opening up about our struggles, an acquaintance recommended that we get some help from a different type of specialist. Soon after, I made an appointment with a pediatric psychiatrist specializing in autism.

We spent all day at the Center for Autism and Brain Development, nearly a three-hour drive from home. This was a place that "got" us—friendly faces that didn't blink at the sight of my unkempt five-year-old, who arrived shoeless. After various formal assessments and questionnaires, I babbled on and on about our struggles with Amos, who played with blocks nearby. The doctor allowed me to continue, and when I paused to take a breath, he spoke gently.

"What you're talking about is anxiety, *not* autism."

That was the moment I learned that autism had a cousin named anxiety. Scarcely discussed, anxiety was the culprit behind Amos's explosive tantrums. His doctor conveyed that anxiety was the underlying reason for the pinged remotes which broke televisions and iPad screens or the kicks to furniture when it was time to leave the house. Before that appointment, I didn't know that children could be crippled by anxiety. After struggling for years, life would take a turn for the better.

We talked about the multiple strategies and interventions that would help Amos cope with daily activities like getting dressed, going to school, sitting at circle time, and even leaving the playground. I learned about the benefits of using picture and word schedules, task boxes, more classroom help, and even available training for teachers—all integral pieces to helping Amos.

The doctor also introduced the topic of medication. I vaguely knew it was an option, but had doubts about prescribing it to children. The first time a medical professional had broached the subject of medication with me had been several months prior. I had jokingly asked a pediatrician what we could do about our little boy who never sat still. She casually suggested a stimulant, and before I knew it, a prescription had been called in. I felt uncomfortable leaping off a cliff like that with so little knowledge about why and how medication may work. No one wants to give their child medicine and I never thought I would—until I did. According to the Anxiety and Depression Association of America (ADAA), nearly half of children with autism demonstrate "clinically elevated" measures of anxiety. Armed with the knowledge that it was anxiety and not autism who had stolen my son, I had to do something. Along with a host of other things like interventions, hundreds of hours of therapy, picture schedules, and detailed IEPs, we decided to try medication.

Soon after that appointment, four and a half milliliters changed our life.

In the first few months, the doctor had us try several medications. The third one was our first light switch. I remember the text from his teacher that very first day. She shared that he had sat in circle time for five minutes. Within a few months, I could list the positive behaviors that we were seeing in Amos. He was talking considerably more and communicating his needs like being hungry or thirsty or missing Mommy. I was able to get him dressed in the morning without a meltdown. After years of being awake, he began sleeping through the night on a regular basis. He continued to progress at school—completing worksheets and waving goodbye to friends. In six years, he had never *ever* waved goodbye.

Though medicine brought his anxiety to a manageable level, he was increasingly more active and impulsive. The way it was explained to me was that he was so often exhausted from the meltdowns that he had little energy left to give in the day. Fewer meltdowns meant a more energetic Amos and that meant different needs and solutions and, for us, a different medicine. I know medication is a tricky topic and may be something that a family has never considered or has deemed unnecessary. Before Amos, I, too, had wondered about people medicating their children. After all, my big three sailed through life and I mistakenly gave myself the credit for their successes.

Medication for anxiety and ADHD is no different from medication for diabetes or cholesterol.

Pride comes before a fall, I giggle to myself now. At our doctor's recommendation, medication has been utilized to help Amos be the best version of himself. In the beginning, I thought giving Amos medication would be one and done, much like taking ibuprofen for a headache. Instead, it's been a merry-go-round, and over the last five years, we've experienced side effects and changed types and doses too many times to count.

I remember sending an email to his doctor with the subject line of "SOS." I shared how Amos was doing really well in the mornings. He was dressed, willingly wore his glasses, and he agreeably got out of the car when we arrived at school. In sharp contrast, afternoons and evenings were filled with meltdowns. Had the behavior started when we started new ADHD meds earlier that week? The first day was good, but his behavior deteriorated by the next day and continued the entire week. I couldn't be sure if the root cause was the new medicine or something else. The doctor responded to my SOS: "Stay with me, I promise we're gonna figure this out together."

And we have. With each year, I note real progress. I see the benefits for Amos and I'm grateful that I sought help and listened to an expert in spite of my own beliefs. We are still on the medicine journey, but now Amos can sit through a haircut without going ballistic, whereas a couple of years ago, you may as well have tried to get a cat in the bathtub. Second grade was the second year in a row that he was mainstreamed—spending large chunks of time in a typical classroom—which hadn't happened since preschool. With the proper support, he enjoyed swimming lessons with his typically developing classmates. His teachers worked hard to follow his cues and know when to push him and when to offer a break. We have crawled out of the dark space that felt endless and witnessed a child transformed by joy. Far from perfect, but pretty damn good.

The next winter, we were back at church basketball. This game was at the church of a good friend, and when she asked if we were planning to go, I explained the dreaded buzzer. She called me back a few minutes later to say that she had reached out to the coach and he was happy to disconnect the buzzer. Amos was skeptical of my promise regarding the silent buzzer but was brave enough to go inside. Though unwilling to sit on the bleachers, he stood in the doorway and watched the big boys play basketball. His older brother saw him there and smiled. After the whipping of his middle school team, I expected bemoaning of the loss, but it never arose. Instead, he wanted to hear all about his little brother who had faced his fears and stood firm in the threat of that scary old buzzer. The real competition belonged to the smallest member of our family—a battle between Amos and the blasted buzzer.

On that evening, victory belonged to Amos.

# CARRIE

"I don't know what to do," I heard Joe say quietly. "It's like we're losing him all over again." Listening to my husband hold back tears on the phone with his sister broke my heart.

Jack was six. It felt as though we put him to bed one night, and the next morning he woke up a different child. I had never seen anything like it. He fell asleep a somewhat quirky little boy who was obsessed with license plates, asking people their birthday, and foaming hand soap from Bath & Body Works. Overnight, a flip had switched inside him, and panic gripped his young spirit.

All at once, he refused to go outside because he was afraid of the cold, even though it was a mild March in New Hampshire. Then he was afraid to go to the bathroom because one time he went in a public restroom and the toilet flushed while he was still sitting on it, so he could never ever use one again. He had accidents—lots and lots of accidents.

He was terrified of dogs. He worried about them constantly. If we saw one in the street he would scream. He started talking to himself. I don't mean a quiet little reminder to pack pretzels for a snack, or a softly hummed nursery rhyme. I mean he was having full-on expressive conversations with himself. He gestured. He grimaced. He jabbed his finger in the air while he muttered. It chilled me to the bone watching him converse with an imaginary person inside of his own mind.

Like a train leaving the station, his symptoms escalated within a matter of weeks. Soon, it was difficult to get him to leave the house. He asked us what time it was a dozen times an hour. He chanted odd sayings about painting babies blue and eating his friends.

I knew very little about anxiety up until this point. Like

the word *autism*, it seemed to belong to other people—other families—or only in the movies. Slowly, the idea that this was what we were looking at began to rise to the surface of my mind.

*Anxiety.* A harsh word with the letter *x* almost smack in the middle. Nothing good comes from an *x* in the middle.

In the end, medication was our only way out.

Joe and I sat in the exam room with our small son between us. For the first time in nearly a month, Jack seemed almost calm. He'd only asked to check my watch a handful of times. By the time the pediatrician bustled in, I thought perhaps we had overreacted—maybe this was just a false alarm.

"Does he, I don't know, look anxious to you?" I asked the doctor tentatively.

The doctor then told us that Jack was riddled with severe anxiety, that anxiety is often comorbid to autism.

*Comorbid.* I turned the word over and over in my mind as he and Joe continued the conversation. It is an ugly word. It calls to mind darkness and death, which I guess makes sense because even though Jack will never die from anxiety, it also doesn't let him fully live.

The doctor took out his trusty prescription pad—this was back before iPads and laptops made digital orders—and wrote on it.

At first, we resisted. We held up our hands emphatically and said *no.* We desperately wanted an alternative.

Then one night, we tried to take all the kids out for dinner. It was a restaurant we'd been to plenty of times before, yet when we pulled into the parking lot, Jack refused to get out of the car. He huddled in the back seat, muttering softly to himself about blue paint. It took nearly an hour for Joe to convince him to come inside and sit. On the ride home, Joe and I quietly agreed it was time. He couldn't live like this anymore, and neither could we.

Jack's been on medication ever since. At first, Clonidine to help with sleep and quiet his mind. Eventually, Zoloft for adolescent depression. When he left for his college program, we introduced Guanfacine to help with impulsive behaviors. As much as I hate it, monthly prescriptions are the only way to keep him afloat. Still, it isn't a perfect answer. The medicine simply smooths the edges so he can put one foot in front of the other. They don't erase the symptoms altogether.

There was a time when I judged parents who gave their kids medication, the same way I judged things like bribery for putting jackets on and cookies before dinner. Now that I have done all three, I can safely say you just don't know what you'll need to do in the moment.

Research tells us anxiety is an emotion, often characterized by inner turmoil, dread, and the expectation of a *future* event. It is not the same as fear, because fear is the response to a real, actual event.

It eats him from the inside out. This is what research and science don't tell you. They don't explain the way anxiety is a fire that burns around the clock, demanding all the air in the room until you can hardly breathe.

People ask me if I could, would I take Jack's autism away.

Yes. Maybe. I'm not sure, to be honest. But I would take anxiety away in a heartbeat.

The truth is, I don't even know what pure autism looks like anymore. Jack's vulnerabilities as related to the spectrum have always been regulation, rigidity, executive functioning, social skills, and working memory.

In other words, he has trouble keeping his body still. Throughout the day, he engages in what's called *self-stimulation*, or *stimming*. The hallmark movements for autism stimming are often flapping hands. Jack paces. He flicks his fingers. He rubs his face—the bridge of his nose, his temples, his forehead. He also clasps his hands together and bends over at the waist. It reminds me of someone trying to keep warm at a campfire.

Ever since he was a little boy, schedule and routine have kept him tethered to the *here* and *now.* Dinner at the same time, a compulsive need to figure out what we're doing for Halloween even though it's the middle of July, daily calendars with reminders for everything from when school starts to doctor's appointments. In life alongside autism, these are the anchors which slow life's oceanic waves.

His rigidity doesn't end there. He is very literal. He thinks in terms of black and white. One time I pulled into the mall around the holidays, and exclaimed the parking lot was a zoo. He was probably seven or eight at the time, and he spent the rest of the afternoon perseverating on elephants walking through the stores.

*Perseverating.* That's another great word we're familiar with: it means to fixate, or intently focus on a thought or an idea. Jack's perseverations have ranged from clock radios to the windchill factor to asking everyone he met when their birthday was.

There is also a phenomenon known as *sundowning.* Common in people with Alzheimer's disease, it refers to a state of restlessness, confusion, or general unease that occurs in the late afternoon and lasts into the evening. Though it would be many years before I had a name for it, when he was about five, I noticed Jack's mood would noticeably change around 4:00 every afternoon. He'd start pacing even more, asking the same questions over and over again.

Here we had this bundle of deficits, if you will—things he will need to work on for likely the rest of his life. Then anxiety came in, threw gasoline all over the place, and lit a match.

In terms of monitoring Jack's anxiety over the years, I have only one word. *Cuticles.* I know, right? What does the bottom of the fingernail have to do with anxiety? Well, oftentimes they were the first thing I'd look at when Jack came home from school each day, because his fingernails tell a story all their own. They are my barometer for gauging how anxious he feels at any given moment, because he chews them until they bleed. Even now, living hundreds of miles apart, it's the first thing I check when we FaceTime.

When Jack was in middle school, we added another diagnosis, completing what I call the third corner of this trifecta: autism, anxiety, and obsessive-compulsive disorder. It started out innocently enough—he just wanted to wash his hands more often than usual. Then, the way a spill on your shirt becomes a stain, it spread further and deeper into the proverbial fabric of his life.

He washed his hands ten, twenty, and eventually thirty times an hour. His fingers were chapped and red, the tips almost bleeding. If anyone got sick in the house, he flew into germ-containment overdrive—wearing a mask and gloves long before the days of COVID. (If you're wondering why a household would have masks and gloves before March of 2020, well, my husband is a dentist. We have that stuff lying around all the time.)

Perhaps one of the most difficult aspects of anxiety is that for years, Jack had no way to describe how it feels to him. The closest he ever came to capturing it was the night we all watched *The Wizard of Oz* together. Jack was about ten years old. Once the movie ended, he sat straight up from the nest of blankets he'd arranged for himself on the floor.

"The Lion," he announced, "has autism."

"Jack, buddy, why would you say that?" I asked.

"Because. He is afraid all the time."

My eyes welled with tears. Hearing my little boy describe

the fear he lives with every single day was simply heartbreaking.

Over the years, I've learned two terms that help quantify the phenomenon of anxiety.

*Fight or flight* is the physiological reaction we experience when we are faced with perceived threat—our nervous system tells us to either stay and fight it or turn and flee. Jack spends about 80 percent of his time in fight-or-flight mode.

A *tandem nervous system* describes the way Jack uses the people around him to regulate—if someone's nervous system is high, his nervous system automatically rises to meet it.

At nineteen, Jack still struggles greatly with both anxiety and obsessive-compulsive disorder. Still, he mutters to himself throughout the day. He keeps to a strict routine. He asks the same question dozens of times in a row. Sometimes I think of anxiety as a fog that hangs between us. As hard as I try, I can't quite reach him through the haze. Our conversations are more like two court reporters trading information about the weather or Disney movies.

I want to talk to my son.

These are the words I hurl at my husband during yet another debate about the cost of yet another program. My voice is jagged, raw. This is the sentence that circles my brain daily.

*I want to talk to my son.*

I want a real conversation, beyond what's next on the schedule and what we ate for dinner on Mother's Day of 2015. Jack has one foot firmly fixed in the past, and the other rooted in the future. He has no sense of *now*—of living in the moment. He misses so much of what is right in front of him.

At the same time, his constant questions and need for reassurance feel personal, as though we have no established bond of trust. As ashamed as I am to admit it, I often choose frustration over compassion. I remind myself anxiety is not his fault. It is not a choice.

*For now.*

When it comes to Jack, this is something I say a lot. For now, he is sleeping. For now, the pills are working. For now, there is enough air in the room to breathe.

For now.

I want to talk to my son.

# 5
# The Special Needs Sibling

## KATE

"At least you have your other kids," the comment read. "Be grateful for them." This was not the first time I'd received this type of scolding, nor would it be the last. The comments eventually evolve into conversation about how having a typically developing child should somehow erase the grief of having one who isn't; how my other children are "good" and how their milestones should surely cancel out the pain of Cooper's disability. These comments make me sweat and feel like I am walking through a minefield. I must tread lightly.

I know how lucky I am. Truly. But can one or three children developing typically make up for one who is not? The answer is no. But the reality is, they can ease the sting.

Raising three neurotypical children alongside a brother with a disability fills my heart with joy while simultaneously crushing it, reminding me that this autism life is often a double-edged sword. A constant contradiction of joy and grief, both coexisting and intertwined. Neither wrong.

Joy that one is babbling. Grief that one is not. Joy that three are developing typically. Worry, anger, heartbreak that one is not. These are not singular occurrences. They happen daily and will for the rest of my life. Watching my son pack a bag for his first sleepover. Sitting in the stands while he scores a goal in hockey. Standing next to him as he writes a valentine to his dream girl. Life keeps going for some and seemingly stands still for another.

The greatest lesson I have learned in my life is that two or three or even more emotions can be true at the same time. Grief, joy, love, and heartache can all be felt in the same instant. Competing. And none of these emotions are wrong.

Each of my other children has already leapfrogged, or surpassed, their older brother in nearly every area. Easily each of them has learned to speak, play with a friend, use a fork, put on their shoes, and so on.

It's a wonder to see, really. How effortlessly typical development can be. And how so many take it for granted. To this day I gasp when I see children sitting in a circle, walking in a line, singing on a stage. Why should one have to work so hard to do what most take for granted? I have learned to celebrate my children's growth and silently grieve what could have been, when the contradictory moments find me.

"Were you scared to have more children after Cooper?" That is the question that I am most commonly asked. Typically, moms message me, or email me, or even pull me aside in real life, and ask. I get it. I truly do.

I tread lightly when speaking about our decision to have more children after Cooper. I don't ever want to shame a family who has just one child, whether they chose to or not. I don't want to come off as bragging because I had four. Never. But I can say with absolute certainty that siblings have been the biggest blessing to Cooper in development, growth, and life in general.

The answer to the question, like most things in our world, is complicated. I had always dreamed of having lots of children. The therapist in me knows my longing for a big family came from growing up as an only child. My magic number was three. My husband's number was two. We landed at four.

When I found out I was pregnant with Sawyer, I cried. Of course I was happy. But I was also truly terrified. We didn't have a diagnosis for Cooper yet, but I knew something was coming. And life was hard.

Logistically, could we handle raising other children alongside Cooper? What if we had another child with autism? Would it be fair to Cooper? Would it be fair to a sibling? These are not easy conversations between a husband and wife and most end in either tears or a fight. But ultimately, the decision was made for us. Sawyer was a surprise. So was Wynnie. And Harbor in between. A friend teasing me, "Haven't you figured out yet how this is happening?"

I have never known motherhood without autism. But there is more to it than that. Cooper being our firstborn means his three siblings have also never known a life without autism.

Someone once said to me, "Siblings to children with disabilities are not special. And they shouldn't be treated as such."

I'll tell you this… In all my years of sharing on social media, very few statements have bothered me as much as that one.

It's so definitively wrong. Siblings to kids with disabilities are special. The best, really. People don't always talk about siblings, the ones who are asked to be strong, adapt to the unexpected, and grow up a little bit faster. The ones who learn to love a little differently, listen a little more carefully, and advocate not only for their siblings, but for themselves, a little more loudly.

Autism is a family diagnosis. Yes, it's only Cooper who carries the label, but it's all of us who feel its effect. Sawyer, Harbor, and Wynnie are all growing up with a brother who has a disability, something I never did. I have watched each of them realize their older brother is different. I've seen their frustration and at the same time their willingness to help, to lead, to protect. The word *autism* is a part of their vocabulary. They aren't afraid to say it.

People are always curious to know how each of my kids interacts with Cooper, specifically Sawyer. He is the one I share the most about in relation to his brother's autism. Most recently, a reel I created of them went viral. Even making its way to *The Today Show* social media.

The video shows Cooper practicing saying his brother's name while Sawyer cheers him on. When I spoke to the reporter, I told her how genuine Sawyer's excitement was when his name came out. When he was six and Cooper was eight, Sawyer begged Cooper to say his name. I was holding him in my arms when he realized that his older brother might never speak.

The video ends with Cooper using American Sign Language (ASL) to communicate that he "loves" Sawyer.

"Awww, I love you, too, buddy," Sawyer replies. He then rests his head on Cooper's shoulder.

When people ask how they got there, I always say it took time. Lots of time. But it also took something else. It took creating a safe space for them to figure each other out. All questions and feelings are allowed in our home without judgment. Now, that doesn't mean I always have the answers, because often I don't. But I encourage the questions.

Not too long ago, Harbor, all but four, ran upstairs and loudly said, "Mama, did you know my brother doesn't talk?" I tried my best not to laugh, but it was so adorable the way he asked it.

"For real, Mama, I was with him for a long time, and he didn't say a word. Not one. Did ya know?"

I did my best to explain autism. To explain Cooper. He listened, eyes wide. Before he ran off to play, he proudly said, "I'll tell him it's okay, Mom. I can just talk for him."

Another time, Harbor was relentlessly asking me questions about kindergarten and turning five. Much like Sawyer, he desperately wants to be older. On the daily, he asks me if he's taller and bigger and faster. But one morning, he asked me what will happen when he turns twelve. I didn't quite understand, so I asked some clarifying questions. His response shattered me.

"I don't want to turn twelve, Mama, because then I will have autism like Cooper. I don't want to stop talking."

Of course he was terrified, although the thought never occurred to me. This is complicated stuff.

Wynnie has had the least time with Cooper. Their relationship is still in the early stages. Yet I notice his fondness for her, his unending patience as she climbs on him and touches his treasures. He tattles on her. She tattles on him. Recently she has started mothering him. Helping him with his shoes, grabbing his hand in a parking lot. There are ten years between them and yet she has assumed the older sibling role already. When she graduates high school, Cooper will be in his late twenties. What will their relationship look like then? Another question I don't have the answer to.

It was a child therapist who first told me about parentification, a term I had never heard before. I had brought Sawyer in with some concerns and my hope was that he would open up and share what was bothering him. I had my own suspicions, of course.

I call Sawyer the boy in the middle. In every photo of our family, Sawyer is directly in the middle, arms stretched out wide, holding his siblings protectively. We don't pose him like that…he just instinctually does it. Of all my children, Sawyer is the one I worry about the most. That surprises people sometimes.

Sawyer is sandwiched in between autism and two very busy toddlers. He's easy a lot of the time. And easy is great. But all kids need something. I worried I was missing it.

In the summer of his tenth year, for a week straight, Sawyer broke down every night crying, which is what ultimately prompted me to make the appointment. The reason always being…Cooper. I didn't realize that Sawyer would carry so much, that he would worry so much about his brother.

We weren't new to the questions; he'd asked many over the years.

He asked me if he will be the older brother someday.

He asked me if God is still building his brother's voice.

He asked me if his autism will ever go away.

He asked me if he would ever be an uncle. And if Cooper will live with him someday.

Each question was like a paper cut to my skin. Aching for the boy who once asked me if he could have autism, too… so he could be just like Cooper. And then the root was exposed. Bullying. Because of autism.

He told me that a student at his school made fun of autism. Used the word as a slur. Teasing and flapping his arms. Mocking and making noises like Cooper does.

And saying, "Look at me… I'm Sawyer's brother. I have autism."

And then I watched my son turn angry. Angrier than I have ever seen before. The fierce protector in him came out. We talked for a long time, me and him. About how the hardest question is always why. We talked about right and wrong and about feelings, big and small. And what it means to be a brother to Cooper.

We spoke about the invisible weight that he carries. One that he didn't ask for.

I've watched him tie his older brother's shoes. And wipe his mouth. Buckle his seat belt. Hold his hand as he leads him through a parking lot. Never forced. He just does these acts of kindness. Because he loves him. The loyalty is fierce.

"He's my brother, Mom. My big brother."

I made the call the next day.

I told the therapist before his session about Sawyer's need to protect Cooper as they aged. I painted a picture of the two boys, sitting on a boat, side by side. Sawyer holding on to his brother's life jacket, even though he doesn't need to. Cooper is long past the days of jumping out of a moving boat. Yes, it happened in the early years. Now he likes to sit and watch the water churn up when we go fast. Sawyer doesn't need to hold him, and we tell him so. So, why does he?

According to parentification theory, when the siblings of people with disabilities assume adultlike duties, this role reversal is known as sibling-focused parentification. It has a significant impact on siblings' distress levels and the quality of family relationships.

This theory terrified me.

We have never placed pressure on Sawyer to care for his brother, even though I've been accused of doing so. I almost felt as if I should defend myself to this therapist. But he seemed to know what I was going to say.

"This just happens, Kate. It's nothing you or your husband did wrong. Sawyer has grown up in a home full of love and care for Cooper. He is just doing what has been modeled for him."

No one prepared me for the guilt I would feel in relation to my other children. And maybe nothing would have. Over the years my guilt has often turned to panicked thoughts…

"I've got to protect Sawyer. I've got to fix this. I've got to make this up to him."

I did what I always do. I wrote. Only this time, I wrote to Sawyer directly. I purged every ounce of worry and self-doubt that I have about raising an autistic child alongside a typical child.

I thanked him for being my son. For being with me on my hardest days. For filling the silence with sounds and questions and laughter.

I thanked him for growing up and giving me all of the typical parts of motherhood, many free from worry.

I thanked him for talking and playing and demanding that I be present in his world.

I apologized, too, for missing things. I explained about the choices I had to make and how most of them were not easy. And then I told him we had a choice in how we looked at this life we had been given. We could let autism harden us or we could change the world for him and others like him.

To this day when I read that letter publicly, people sob. I know it's because they see themselves in our story. They see their own sons and daughters. A while back I received a response to my letter. Only it wasn't from Sawyer. Not yet, anyway. It was from a woman, an adult sibling. It came when I most needed it.

*Dear Mom,*

*I read your letter today. You should know that the person I am today is because of you, and because of my brother.*

*Know that I never resented the focus on him. Not really. I watched, and learned, what it means to love someone. To nur-*

*ture them. To not only care for him, but to allow him to care for us. Not in the traditional sense, but in his way.*

*Love is not a spoken language. He makes me laugh, deep belly laughs, and smile till the creases in my face hurt. He is pure, and the euphoria we feel when he is happy and with each small step forward is unlike any other joy.*

*Being with him simplifies life to what really matters. Cynicism and self-absorption fade away. We experience life in full color.*

*Those are the times that make the grief, the stress, the anger at the world's injustice seem unimportant, if only for a while.*

*And those times you spoiled me? These helped me to learn to appreciate the sweet moments, and to take nothing for granted. That the chaos of life is tempered by levity.*

*You wondered how I would feel about my brother, now, as an adult. You never had to tell me what my role would be; I knew. There was no doubt. As I grow older, and you grow older, I worry too about outliving my brother, just as you do.*

*He factors into my every decision. But it is not a sacrifice.*

*My best qualities are inextricably linked to my brother. I have an empathy and interest in others I would not have without him. I understand the difference between treating someone equitably and treating someone equally.*

*You taught me this.*

*In a way you could say my brother keeps me out of trouble. I don't waste time on the wrong people.*

*I have a list of qualities I look for in a partner because I am looking out for someone who will love us both. This may also seem like a sacrifice, but it is not. I want a partner who sees innate value in others, and who can move beyond fear to meeting him where he is.*

*He is a gift. He is the reason I now teach children with autism.*

*When I was offered the job, I wondered if it was a good*

*idea. Would it be too hard to work all day, sharing in the pain and joys of other families, to come home to ours? But then I realized: would anyone else love these students the way I do?*

*Six years on, I have no regrets. And I want to change the world for my students. Which is why I am now getting my doctorate in autism education. Because the world is changing and everything he has taught me can be passed along to others. Because he really is the greater teacher.*

*I know there is grief so deep in you that it is hard to get out of bed sometimes. But we are so much more whole than we would be without him. There is lightness that permeates the darkness.*

*He may not say it, and I don't say it enough, but thank you. I love you, for all that you have done. I am happy to help. I am grateful to help. I have been preparing for this for as long as I can remember.*

*Don't worry, Mom, I got this. I got you.*

Siblings of kids with disabilities are amazing. I won't entertain any other thoughts on it.

They know patience and kindness and bravery. They know how to buckle their older siblings' seat belts and hold their hands when they cross the street. And they worry about their moms and dads.

The truth is, you can't tell the story of Cooper, and autism, without the siblings.

## ADRIAN

"They did not agree to this. You have forced them and they are hostage. Just *what* effect do you think that this is having on your *own* children?"

The question was rhetorical and meant to shame me. To be filled with guilt about the life our family had been gifted. After all, Amos's three older siblings hadn't signed up for special needs. But still, I asked myself the question: What effect do I think having a special needs sibling is having on my children?

Thomas is eighteen and the oldest. He's my most sensitive child and has always reflected on the brother whose path is far different from his own. His feelings often spilled into the safe space between us and I found that his words seemed to contradict each other more often than not, which seemed a sure sign of love. There have been moments of hurting along the way for this tenderhearted son of mine. He is the one who cried when he found out Amos would be in a special preschool class at our small-town public school. What this placement meant, he wasn't sure, but it was just enough to be worrisome. His reaction bit at my own throat and smarted my eyes. His tears mirrored the unusual pitch in my voice, careful but unable to hide my hurting heart.

I also remember the evening Thomas was working on a school assignment and I was cleaning up the kitchen. They were to come up with a project to commemorate the hundredth day of school and ten-year-old Thomas was threading Froot Loops on a cotton string.

"Mommy, if you could have a hundred of anything, what would it be?"

It was an innocent query that punctured the unusual quiet in a chaotic household. Being that my oldest son is famous for asking questions and I had not settled into the role of willing participant in quite a long time, I wiped counters and settled into the conversation.

I posed the question back to him, and within moments, his younger brother and sister had reappeared and quickly chimed in with their best ideas. The first responses centered around houses—chocolate ones—mansions and castles. Eight-year-old Russell—who thinks three steps ahead—smugly announced magic wands because then he would only use one wish and could give the remaining ninety-nine away. I pondered my own wish. Though pretend, wishes are fun to think about. They are windows into the heart's desires.

"Words," I said. "For Amos to have one hundred words."

A familiar silence echoed around me and I thought of the language I longed to hear from Amos. His silence had not gone unnoticed by anyone in our house and the three expectant faces were thoughtful and unusually pensive before my oldest son spoke.

"I didn't think of that. That would be mine too. Really hard words after he did our family names and then places we go—like *park* and *Mamie and DB*, *chicken nugget* and *doughnut* and *cookie* and *cupcake* and *car* and *book*." And because he was not such a good counter yet, he ended with "I think that's a hundred."

Amazing how the value of simple things is rarely considered until a there's a glaring absence of them. The most wonderful things in life cannot be bought, no matter our currency. At that moment, I saw a brother who believed words would be the greatest gift; it was such a selfless acknowledgment. I had never as keenly understood what it meant to say love can move mountains.

Russell comes next in the lineup, and at sixteen years old, he is sandwiched between his older brother and younger sister. He is not a natural nurturer, but has always been Amos's fiercest defender. By the time Amos was three years old, our house was a revolving door of children. I overheard a friend ask Russell why Amos was wearing a diaper. An honest question from a nine-year-old boy and asked without a speck of maliciousness.

I heard my son Russell pause before he replied that Amos was just a baby. *Ohhh,* I thought to myself, *it has begun.* It was not a total untruth. Amos was just three years old and a couple of his older siblings had also struggled with potty training at that age, so why did I grimace when I heard my son call his three-year-old brother a baby? He did look like a baby with his white-blond hair and the way he walked a bit wobbly, still falling over. Maybe it was the way his small self still vibrated with the infectious chortle or the fact that his words were very few. He was not a baby, though, and my own face grew hot.

Later on, I asked Russell about his reply, and his honest answer caught me off guard. He had said the first thing that popped into his little boy's mind. He asked what he should have said instead. "A really old baby?" he guessed.

"I'm not sure," I replied, and I wasn't. I didn't know what to say or what to tell him to say about the three-year-old who was far from potty training. Funny how a parenting stage like potty training, which you remember dreading, morphs into a wish that you long to come true. I told him to just say what was in his heart and said that I would try to do the same thing.

Our only daughter, Blair, is fourteen years old and the last of my three teenagers. It was Amos who made her a big sister, and she was immediately besotted, even though he was a far cry from the "sister baby" she had insisted upon. She loves him in the purest way and I'm reminded of the love I had for my own brother. Though my daughter adores all three of her brothers, it is Amos who captures her whole heart. When I unfold the love notes she wrote years ago, my role as mama pales in comparison. She loves him without expectation and with resplendent adoration.

*To Amos,*
*I love you to pieces because you are so funny and cool.*
*You are my baby brother and I love your glasses.*
*And I like being beside you on the trampolin so much.*
*And I am happy you leard how to walk.*
*And I'm so happy you are brother.*
*I love you so so so so so so so so so so so moch.*

That is love, the real kind, the kind that travels without expectations. Love that always looks for the good, the glass that is half-full, the other side of the rainbow, and the end of the tunnel. I've learned how to love bigger and better and stronger from my own half-pint and her choice of joy leaves me marveling that such natural fortitude exists in my universe—the love of a sibling.

Amos's siblings have been witness to a life that is not easy or predictable or commonplace, and they have become amazing humans. They have become amazing humans because of their brother, not in spite of him. They have always been gentle with him, maybe because he's the youngest or maybe because he's always been special. Never ever an unkind word, glance, shove, nudge, or even a light warning pinch. I remember how afternoons at the playground offered such a stark contrast to the gentleness at home. Amongst child strangers, no one slowed down to let him catch up. I remember thinking that no one follows the theorem of survival of the fittest quite like small children. Those typical children seemed overly harsh to me now. They pushed him away from their toys and tossed a stern NO at the boy who longed to play but didn't have the words or skills to make it happen.

There is solidarity amongst siblings when it comes to Amos. He is the world to which we all belong, not by choice but by the gift of happenstance, and no one has been more surprised than me to see the love and kindness they offer him without my prompting. Even in the early years, they looked for ways to be helpful. Many a morning I would arrive downstairs to find him sitting on the couch watching his favorite cartoon that his older sister had turned on for his viewing pleasure. Ten-year-old Thomas would remove Amos from his crib and give him a cuddle while I made breakfast and packed lunches. After school, eight-year-old Russell would take a packet of popcorn, microwave it, and then put it in a bowl for Amos with nary a word from me. I saw his siblings offering help when they weren't asked and growing in ways that came from being needed.

Time and time again, we've been challenged to love and accept even when things don't go our way. Amos wasn't the baby I was expecting, but I've never once wanted to trade him for that mythical portrait of perfection I had conjured up in pregnancy. He's always been enough and we have learned to acknowledge the hard and celebrate the small successes—which are not so small when you belong to a special person—like being willing to try a new playground swing.

Amos has always adored to swing and is perfectly happy in the baby swing and unwilling to try the one for big kids. His siblings long for him to graduate to the larger swing, which signifies independence. Every so often, I muster the nerve to coax him onto the big one, but he frets and fears its instability. He makes such a ruckus that I concede defeat and move back toward the swings that he is rapidly outgrowing. As he gets older, more is expected of him and we pretend it doesn't matter, but we feel the differences that seem to become more glaring. Though he may be unaware and unconcerned about who might be watching, his siblings know and are fiercely protective. But Amos has never been prideful. He will strip off his bathing suit at the pool without a second thought and tote his well-loved blankie to restaurants and soccer fields. And yes, he loves a swing meant for toddlers.

It was early evening, and because we were visiting grandparents and had four active children, many of our days ended with a romp at the playground. It had been my intention to keep a casual eye on the big three while I pushed Amos in his favorite traditional though now too-small baby swing. His siblings soon tired of playing tag and found us. They exclaimed over a nearby newfangled swing. This type of playground swing didn't exist in our small town. It was heavy plastic and dark gray and meant for two people. One end resembled a traditional swing and the other end was a seat in which the occupant would sit across from the person who pumped the swing. They collectively badgered me to deposit their baby brother in the seated end. I was curious myself, and within moments of my agreement, they loudly called dibs and argued as to who would get the first turn in the place of importance across from four-year-old Amos.

"It's not a baby swing, Mom!" crowed my middle son, Russell.

In that moment, a light switch flicked for Amos's siblings. They stopped hemming about Amos learning to use the big-kid swing and began to take turns with Amos going on the tandem swing. They happily monitored and admonished each other, too high, too fast, not fast enough, too slow. In that glorious moment, no one was perfect except Amos.

They would ask him if he wanted to get out just so they could bask in his firm reply of "No out!" and I got it. There is something so rewarding in a real answer—even when the question is rhetorical—when you love a boy of few words.

I never did get a turn to ride with Amos in that swing.

# CARRIE

"That's not the way we remember it," Charlie said, answering the question I just asked.

It was the middle of August. We were sitting outside eating lunch at one of our favorite burger places. We'd dropped Jack off at his college program a month earlier, so it was just me and the other four kids. We were still adjusting to his absence—this hole in our family's landscape. He always filled any space so acutely.

They turned to each other and started talking about when they were little. They brought up the time all five of them had the stomach bug and we let them sleep on the living room floor in sleeping bags.

Rose reached across the table for the ketchup, her curly hair catching the sunlight. "Remember the carrot fight?"

Joseph leaned back in his chair holding his burger in his hand. "I mean, how old were we then? I was maybe eight?"

They each recounted their surprise when one night after dinner, Joe and I started pelting each other with baby carrots. A bag of them sat on the counter while we cleaned up, and for some reason I picked one up and tossed it at him. Before we knew it, all five kids were crouching around corners and hiding, armed with orange.

Sitting at the picnic table, I leaned into their chatter. Listening to them, I was reminded of the term circling the internet used to describe brothers and sisters of diagnosed children. *Glass siblings*, they're called, because they are thought to be invisible—as transparent as glass.

For as long as I can remember, I've carried guilt around like a bucket of paint threatening to overflow. I always felt guilty that Jack took up too much of my time—that autism reshaped our family in ways I couldn't figure out how to change.

A family is a stage where we each choose our roles. In our house, autism provided the music to which we danced: violent drums one day, melancholy flutes the next. Practically speaking, this meant we sometimes had to leave the movies early if the theater was too loud. We endured stares in public, especially as Jack grew taller and his stimming became more noticeable. Kids whispered about him at school and on the bus.

"It's not fair!"

This phrase was hurled at me by each of my other four kids at some point—over homework assignments, chores, behavior.

"It isn't fair he doesn't have to do Math Facts!"

"It isn't fair he doesn't have to snow blow the driveway!"

"It isn't fair he gets to walk around during church!"

Gently, I explained there is no such thing as fair. I pointed out that we all have our own mountains to climb. We ask everyone to do what they are capable of doing. I also reminded them they had a responsibility to reach out and grab life with both hands—whatever that looked like. I reminded them their brother had a diagnosis that he did not ask for, and somehow, some way, they missed the genetic component.

And although Jack is the only diagnosed child, it's fair to say there are certain qualities that show up in my other kids. I often compare autism to a jar full of jelly beans. Each child reached in and plucked one out for themselves, while Jack took handfuls of color.

People are always curious to know how each of my kids interacts with Jack. Before I can fully capture that, I have to explain that, although all five of my kids were born to the same set of parents, grew up in the same house, and for the most part lived by the same rules, they could not be more different.

I guess it's best to start at the top down—oldest to youngest, if you will. After all, my firstborn son is the one who has lived alongside autism the longest. He is the one tasked with making sure his brother has somewhere to go on Christmas Eve once Joe and I are gone.

Joseph was thirteen months old when Jack was born. He wasn't even walking yet. Autism has been the timpani of his background since the day he pulled himself up from the rug and took a few tentative steps across the living room.

The first to leave the nest, Joseph is twenty now. He lives in a city that's a plane ride away. Yet in many ways, he helped shape his brother's life the most—particularly Jack's steps toward his own kind of independence.

Jack has always looked to Joseph for the next step, whether it was riding the big bus to school, or making First Communion, or heading off to college. It's like a brotherly beacon of light, as the younger one carefully watches his sibling's life begin to unfold and decides, *yes*, he wants this for himself.

My middle son, Charlie, knows Jack's heart. I don't know how else to describe it. He understands autism speaks a listener's language, and he has always been fluent. In other words, he is patient. He waits for Jack to find the words—he doesn't rush him.

Then there's my daughter, Rose. Once upon a time, coal miners released canaries into the mine shafts to test the air quality and oxygen levels. Known for their gift of song, these small birds are much more sensitive than humans to the deadly carbon monoxide found underground.

They carried these canaries down in special cages. Once inside, they would open the door and listen for the delicate melody. A sudden halt in the music would warn workers to evacuate the pit. The coal miners would rescue the birds by closing the cage door and opening a valve to pump oxygen inside. When I first read about this, I instantly thought of Rose.

I share about Rose the least on social media because she is very private, but she is an integral part of Jack's story—our story. Our fourth child, we were convinced she was another boy, until the nurse in the delivery room made the announcement. She joked that she could have knocked Joe over with a feather, he was so shocked.

For as long as I can remember, Rose has been Jack's "person." From the time she was a very little girl, she could read his energy better than anyone else. And when puberty descended upon him, and he bit and screamed and thrashed his way through sixth grade, she used the crocheting kit the Easter Bunny left her to braid long strands of yarn together, which she presented to him one morning before he left for school. She suggested he pull on them when he felt angry. He carried them with him for years.

Outwardly, it is a seemingly lovely connection. Yet often, I worry she forgets her own oxygen—her own air. The stress of a special needs sibling is at times a heavy weight upon her shoulders.

My youngest son, Henry, and Jack have probably had the least symbiotic relationship out of all the kids. If I had to guess, I would say this is because Henry was very loud when he was younger. He didn't talk; he shouted. Even his toys were loud—he had a giant Mickey Mouse doll that stood over two feet tall and broke into a song and dance when you tapped its hand. One time we found Jack trying to duct-tape Mickey's mouth shut. The metaphor was not lost on us.

At fifteen, Henry is mellowing out a bit. Now that he and Jack have some space—and no longer share a room—I see them making tentative steps toward a stronger sense of brotherhood. Shared texts, a mutual interest in pop culture, and a love of Wendy's. It is a most beautiful thing to watch.

As a mother, I hoped my kids would get along. With autism in our life, this felt especially important, as I know that, one day, they will need to lean on each other. This is simply our reality.

Jack is the second oldest, and there is a point in time when each of his younger siblings passes him in a milestone or emotional development. In our house we call this *leapfrogging*, and it is painful to witness. The landscape of our family is constantly shifting beneath our feet, as the siblings hop over him.

Though the benchmarks changed over the years, the small paper cuts were the same. Driving was a particular sting, because as of now Jack doesn't have a driver's license. First Charlie, then Rose took their turns at the Department of Motor Vehicles. Both assured Jack they would take him anywhere he wanted to go, and to this day they've kept that promise. Late-night runs to the grocery store for ice cream, trips to the movies, even just a chance to drive with the windows down as his favorite song plays on the radio. They never say no.

Still, he wants to be the big brother.

At a table with burgers and fries, we were briefly beautiful. I smiled to think of all the things I wanted to be perfect for them—matching pajamas at Christmas, constant familial harmony, picnics at the park in springtime.

The truth is, none of it mattered. Kids remember the bloopers, the laughter, the carrots sailing through the air.

Still, deep down, I always wondered what this life alongside autism was like for them.

I never asked them. All those years, I didn't know how. Finally, beneath the summer sky, I found the courage to ask the words that weighed upon me so heavily for years.

"Do you ever feel like autism took too much away from you?" I asked, and they answered.

*That's not how we remember it.*

Jack eventually learned how to use the snowblower. Charlie taught him.

# 6
# Building a Community

## KATE

"How did you find your autism community, Kate?"

I was the keynote speaker at a caregivers retreat and had just shared our journey, as I do quite often these days, from the beginning to the present, with moms walking a similar path to mine. There was laughter and tears and that hum that only happens when a group of like-minded people get excited. That's my favorite part of it all. Watching my words bring parents together.

During the question-and-answer portion that followed, a woman to my left indicated that she had a question. I had noticed her earlier, nodding, smiling, even tearing up. But that isn't why she caught my eye. It was the woman behind her who lovingly had a hand on her shoulder during my entire presentation.

Her question was simple.

"How did you find YOUR autism community, Kate?"

I knew why she was asking. I had made a grandiose statement midway through…a statement that I make sure to say in every presentation I deliver to moms.

"Mamas, find your autism person. It doesn't have to be a big community. You just need one person that you can text at 4:00 a.m. or call after a hard day, without judgment. Look around this room. She is in here. I found mine and you will too."

The reason I drill this point into caregivers is simple.

We can't do this alone.

I can say with certainty that if I had in the beginning what I have now in terms of community, my early days of autism would have been entirely different. I know it's possible to connect moms, even with all the barriers they face. They just need a gentle nudge to open up and share.

Knowing my community answer was layered, I deflected.

"Great question. Do you have a community?"

She turned to the woman behind her and said with love and pride, "I don't have a community, yet. I just have one person. My mom."

It was one of the most beautiful exchanges I have ever seen. As the two of them shared a bit about their journey, the grandma and the mother, I felt a tug at my heart as I watched this young mom in the beginning of her autism journey. She had mountains to climb, but she wouldn't be climbing them alone.

When Cooper was diagnosed, not really that many years ago when you think about it, there was none of this. No retreats. No support groups that I knew of. No one was even talking about autism. Even the books were different. More clinical, less human. It's so different now. Social media has changed everything.

There is a quote that says, "No one supports you like a social media friend you've never met." Truer words have never been written. A social media friend will cheer on your victories, cry with you during tough times, and send support across the digital divide, all without ever meeting you in person. Online relationships have removed so many barriers when it comes to finding community.

In the early days of autism, I was desperate for a connection. Except, I couldn't find it. We weren't welcome at the mommy-and-me groups, and at the playgrounds I was running and climbing, not standing and watching with the other moms. We had been kicked out of day cares and our preschool program looked a lot different from the one I had imagined. I had no opportunities to find parents who had a child with a disability. The ones who understood our secret world. The ones who I didn't have to defend our life to. The ones who have cried the same tears as me and just get it.

It's important to know, though, that I wasn't alone, not in the literal sense. I had a great family and wonderful friends. Many that I'd had for my whole life. I had my husband, too, who was very much involved. But early on, I learned an important lesson. There may be people in your life that you love, friends and family who love you and your child, who simply cannot be what you need them to be when it comes to your child's disability. And they aren't necessarily bad humans. They just can't be part of your autism support system.

I began pushing the people in my life away. I stopped answering text messages and returning phone calls. I couldn't pretend anymore that my son was fine, which it seemed like some of them needed. But I also didn't want anyone to see the severity of our situation. I was worried about being judged as a mom. I was also tired of defending our life. It was easier to pull away.

And after one Christmas, while sitting in the car with Cooper as he watched Barney for the hundredth time on a DVD player, I knew I was alone. I was staring out the window as the snow fell, observing my family standing around the Christmas tree. I wondered if they forgot about us. And if it was easier without us.

I realized that isolation is so much more than being physically alone, because you can be alone in a room full of people. People who love you. Isolation for me is living a life that no one understands.

For many years, I navigated it alone. I masked when I was in the neurotypical world and found comfort yet a nagging loneliness in the autism world—all while wondering where Cooper and I truly fit in.

Sharing on my blog *Finding Cooper's Voice* saved me. I vividly remember smiling so confidently as I pressed Publish on my first post.

For many years I wrote, pouring my heart out for strangers to read. I wrote about when Cooper was misdiagnosed deaf, the guilt I had surrounding Sawyer, and when Cooper was diagnosed with autism. I wrote that I was jealous of my friends whose babies were developing typically. I wrote that I wanted to give up. I wrote the words I couldn't say out loud. I shared the feelings I couldn't acknowledge.

In 2017, I pushed Publish on my Facebook page, also named *Finding Cooper's Voice*, never expecting to accumulate a following. My purpose was simple, really. I wanted to find other families like mine. Siblings for Sawyer to connect with. Dads for Jamie to talk with. And a child like Cooper. I wanted a community.

As time went on, my mission came into focus. I wanted to create a safe space for families of children and teens with special needs to come together to laugh, cry, and support each other, both virtually and in person. I wanted a place to celebrate Cooper drinking water from a cup for the first time at age six or buckling his seat belt for the first time at age ten. I had tried joining other groups. But my questions, frustrations, and celebrations were met with either crickets or judgment. Where were the parents like me supposed to share?

I knew in my heart that I wasn't the only mother who felt the way I did. I believed my story was the answer to someone's problems. And yet it still blew my mind when I reached one million followers. Which, I know, is probably not all that big of a deal in the real world. But there was a time, years ago, when we couldn't go to church, or to parks, or even to school. We seemed to disappear behind fences and locks and alarms. I began having this irrational, yet rational, fear that no one would ever know my son. He proved me wrong, of course. As he typically does.

And yet I still needed more. I needed real-life connection, especially as I started to look to the teenage years and eventually adulthood. I needed friends who walked the same path as me.

"I built it," I said to the crowd. "I built my community piece by piece because we didn't fit in anywhere, even in the autism world. And when I realized that, it nearly broke me."

It all changed in 2019. Cooper had gone to my mom's house for the weekend, his most favorite place on earth. They watch *Family Feud* and *The Price Is Right* and bake cookies and rest. He loves to go for two sleeps and two sleeps only. Then it's time to come home.

While he was gone, Jamie and I took Sawyer and Harbor to the beach for the day. Without Cooper, we had a flexibility that we weren't used to. We spent the entire day relaxing and playing. Midway through the day, as I was building a sandcastle with Harbor, it dawned on me that I had never sat and played at the beach like this before. Cooper was a runner and needed constant supervision. He was also notorious for throwing people's unsupervised personal items into water. If you had perused my Venmo receipts during that period of life, the notes would have said things like "shoe" or "cell phone."

When we got home that night, I shared a post to my Facebook page. A beautiful photo of me playing with my two younger boys while the sun set behind us. The text explained how for the first time I was able to take off my autism hat and just wear my typical mom hat. The first few hundred comments were wonderful, as they usually are. As I read further, I started seeing comments like "Why don't you love Cooper?" and "Why do you hate autism?"

That night I told my husband I was done. I had carried the advocacy torch far enough. It was someone else's turn to carry it on the next leg of the race. It is an act of bravery to share one's experience and feelings. Especially out loud. And I was done.

In an odd twist of fate, Facebook reached out to me and asked if I wanted to start a paid online supporter group. As a person who greatly struggles with imposter syndrome, I initially said no.

What is that phrase? "Build it and they will come"?

I filmed a video sharing about bullying, shaming, and isolation and uploaded it to my platform. Overnight, *Coop's Troops* was born. At first it was a place to simply ask questions. Today, it is a community of moms and dads and others who want to give and get support on this often lonely and all too often unfairly judged journey.

Shortly after the group was created, the need for in-person connection continued to ring in my ear. I needed it for me and for my other children and for Cooper. We all needed community in our own ways.

I tried bringing Cooper to different sensory-friendly

events, but we never fit in. His needs seemed to be so much more severe than those of others in attendance, and once again, I felt so isolated. Even within our own community. But I didn't give up.

I hosted a caregivers retreat for hundreds of moms to come together. From there, I started an in-person support group for parents. That led to private monthly events for families like mine where no one bats an eye if Cooper's swim trunks come flying down from a water slide. Every month a different event. From there, a Miracle League baseball team. The dads coaching and pitching. The moms laughing and running bases. Even doughnuts after the games. And an end-of-the-year pool party.

We aren't alone anymore. Figuratively or literally. A non-stop chat on our phones. Weekly lunches. Coffee dates. We cry. And we laugh a lot. The big, deep belly laughs that hunch you over.

Someone once told me that by me sharing my story, I gave them permission to share theirs. That sentiment changed me in a profound way. Because I wasn't doing anything amazing. I was simply sharing my life.

I love helping mothers who carry this unique grief because I carry it too. And I always will. I know their fears. I know their struggles. I've sat in the dark with them. We might have lain on different bathroom floors as we wondered "why my child?" but we walk the same path, and there is something beautiful about wearing the same scars. They bring us together. They give us a connection that is unspoken and undeniable. We wear our armor proudly. The parts that have changed us the most are usually the ones that make us want to be the most helpful to others.

I can say with absolute certainty, and there aren't many of those in this life, that I healed by helping and connecting others. This community saved me. I am no longer alone in this secret world. I am surrounded by people just like me, the ones who get it. Who see me. Who let me grieve. Who drop a coffee on my doorstep. Who don't try to fix it. Who know to just listen.

And on the days that I still feel alone, I know that all I need to do is send a text to my people, and the weight will feel just a little bit lighter.

Because we are never alone in the struggles we face. We just have to find each other.

## ADRIAN

I certainly never wanted to join the autism club, much less build a community in the disability arena. Funny enough, the community building began before the autism diagnosis. I was drowning in questions and fears, and the only way I could figure to unravel those feelings of dread and loneliness was to share them. I couldn't bear the thought of being the object of discussion in our community of my neighbors and friends whispering about the child who wasn't like the others.

In those days before Amos, I watched families who had children with special needs and felt a bit of pity and a tinge of unconscious relief. It looked so hard from the outside and I was happy to stay in my comfort zone of "normal." I never even had a personal relationship with someone living with a disability. I attended private school and lived in a land of typical children. When I did encounter one of "those" families, I tried to see myself in their shoes. I imagined what it would be like to belong to the young woman in a wheelchair at our church, her hair carefully coiffed like her mother's. What must it be like to love someone so much that their disability was secondary? I had no idea and felt relief that it wasn't *my* story. How could I have known what lay ahead?

I was so scared when I realized I was walking the plank toward the unexpected life. Amos was like those strangers I had studied, people I thought were nothing like me or my family. In a blink, my "normal" life ceased to exist, and because I was scared, I took a leap.

I told my husband I was starting a blog and calling it *Tales of an Educated Debutante.* He promptly said that it was a terrible name and its fate was sealed. Funny enough, the name was steeped in irony. Though I was educated—I had earned a PhD—my being a debutante was a title earned not by heritage. My parents were Yankees and North Carolina transplants. My invitation to be a debutante was owed to my parents' contributions to the community. A recognition that the young couple from Ohio had carved out a place of belonging in the South. Though the word *debutante* conjures up images of gentility and perfection, I would reframe the definition. My blog would be a platform for transparency and authenticity. I would break the expected mold and spill the secrets that would drown me if I didn't share them with the world. Always up for a challenge, I created a public page on Facebook and began to write. I divulged my heart and shared most every moment that left an imprint. There were so many in those early days, as I grappled with belonging to a child with a disability and becoming a mama bear in a way that hadn't been expected of me with my first three children. They were circles that rolled perfectly right into our world, whereas Amos was a square that never seemed to blend in, his edges always too sharp to fit, his differences always glaring.

I had been writing for a couple of months when I shared what happened on a routine grocery store trip. I hadn't even made it into the grocery store when we encountered an older couple in the parking lot. They smiled when they saw Amos's blond mop of hair and blue glasses and spoke to him immediately. I heard them say hello and ask him his age. He was turning three the next month and looking less like a baby and more like a little boy every day, so it made sense that they would speak directly to him. I hadn't known how hard it would be to witness these interactions between Amos and those who were unfamiliar with him, listening to them talk and ask questions while he remained silent. The boy who had not yet learned to answer questions.

I remember looking intently at Amos, internally begging him to wave hello or offer some sort of utterance. Nothing. Not a word, not a sound, not even the hint of a smile. I wished he were just an ordinary kid with bad manners and I could play the role of an annoyed mother, laughingly shrugging off her young son's rudeness. At that moment, I wished for it so much that we nearly went back to the car, but our family was counting on meals for the week and snacks for lunch boxes.

I'm not exactly sure what I said other than "He can't." I rambled on with a few more sentences, and if the surprised couple had been able to make sense of my halting words, they offered no sign of comprehension. They stared blankly at me for a long moment and then continued walking.

Talking about Amos's lack of speech was getting harder for me and I was feeling exceedingly vulnerable and defensive over my youngest child. With his birth, a sensitive side had blossomed in me and the tough woman I had previously been was left not knowing what to say or do in these situations. I wanted to be kind and say and do the right thing, but I didn't know what it was. Life was getting harder and harder as his lack of speech affected his behavior. To survive, I began to share and tell and preach and bemoan and shout all things autism and my experience as a parent. There are many of us who have squares in our circle worlds, and still, it's a lonely path. It could be anxiety, autism, or ADHD, a genetic disorder—rare or commonplace, a cognitive impairment, and then there are some of us who hit the piñata and got all the things. We learn to catch the snippets of joy and we know what it is to feel helpless and inept. Most of us didn't order a child with special needs. Those deliveries arrived and our scared selves fell in love. My community has been built on a foundation of truth and vulnerability, sharing my heart's desires, moments of absolute joy and dark sorrow.

It certainly wasn't my intention. I began writing to save myself, not relate to other people. I had to confront the feelings that came from accepting an unexpected life. Life's not a restaurant, I began to tell myself and try to believe it. As I shared moments steeped in reality, families came out of the shadows—divulging what it was like to long for a diagnosis, to struggle with forms at the pediatrician's office, or wait months for a needed doctor's appointment. Ultimately, how to come to terms with having a child who was not the one you ordered.

So many reached out to share that they saw me or that they felt I saw them. I heard from mothers and fathers and grandparents and siblings. I listened to people who had walked or were walking in my shoes and processed valuable information that would lead me along a path of acceptance and love. I shared the highlights on my blog so that others could be inspired and even learn the basics like how to apply for a waiver, what to do in an IEP meeting, or how to plan for a plane ride. Before I knew it, I was immersed in an unexpected and beautiful community.

It has lifted me up and made life better. I remember sharing my fears about flying with Amos during the pandemic. He was unable to wear a mask and had been vaccinated and we longed to see his grandparents after a long year of isolation. We made reservations on Delta, which was the only airline that allowed exceptions to the mask policy for people with disabilities. But still, I worried and so I did what I had learned to do. I wrote the airline a letter and acknowledged my own anxiety about flying with a child with autism. I shared how my mind was skipping to a scenario where I imagined myself crying after being refused admittance onto the airplane.

I didn't have to send this letter; I could have just waited until we were at the airport. But I didn't know if it would be an awesome or terrible experience, and if we don't reach out a hand, people don't know we're drowning. I laid all my cards on the table and it paid off. The next day at the airline counter, our family was greeted with love and compassion and acceptance. Still a wee bit worried about the kicking of seats or raucous laughter, but those concerns were minute and I was filled with gratitude. I remember people responding—"That's great for you, but what about the other families?" I would tell them that there's never been a moment that I don't think about my community and I hope that by reaching out a hand to the world, the world will learn to more often look for those who need a hand. We have to start somewhere and my son Amos is a jar of lightning bugs on a dark summer's night. He sat on that pilot's lap, plopped his cap on his head, and pushed buttons as I held back tears. Kindness fell like rain and I imagined a world where this sort of thing wouldn't be worth noting because it was so commonplace.

Someday, Amos, someday.

The world wants to help and to fix and to offer advice and make it all better—like a mother blowing on a child's scraped knee. Families like mine want the same thing, but there is no wishing away the hard with an easy solution. Our children will always be squares and we balance a life of molding our sharp corners to fit this round world AND fiercely advocating for those marvelous squares. It's quite a dilemma to know when to push and when to protect, and no one knows better than us.

Amos's birth was our path to membership in this community. Any club that requires so much is bound to have merit. I am thankful for my own golden ticket, three-and-a-half-year-old Amos, the spark that lit the fire of knowledge of a life worth living. We have been gifted a behind-the-scenes perspective of what really matters in life.

"It does get better and it always hurts," a mother wrote to me. She explained she was planning her son's forty-third birthday party. I was more annoyed than appreciative when I read those words. In the beginning, I was unwilling to embrace my journey and accept my gift. Seven years later, I can offer a sincere thank-you and no longer struggle to digest those kind of words. Looking back, I am wowed by the strength and camaraderie offered by a stranger who had accepted her gift and was reaching out to me in encouragement. We both received gifts that we never asked for, never desired, yet neither of us would consider exchanging our precious children. Not even for one tiny second. We have learned to accept them for what they are, and like all true gifts, they come along by surprise and we are left wondering how we ever went without them.

Though Amos learned to talk, trips to the grocery store got harder rather than easier. By the time he was four years old, he would not ride in the cart or even walk in the direction I was going. My goal became to get through as quickly as possible and convince him not to open every item we placed in the cart. One particular day, I had him sequestered in the cart (he could last through the fruit-and-veggies section). I had brought a bag of Goldfish, but he demanded fresh green grapes, a bite of a green apple, and a banana, of which he ate the whole thing. My oldest son was horrified with this scene and my next son was quite sure Amos would be labeled a thief. Though they waited for what they believed was an inevitable arrest, I was too exasperated to protest.

As we were checking out, the manager came up to us smiling brightly and asked how we found everything. We'd seen this man before, and he was always friendly. I felt an obligation to speak up about the snacks Amos had eaten as my older three children shuffled nervously. I explained that although he was almost five, he had autism and grocery store trips were hard for him.

"He had a banana and some grapes and he wasted an apple," my daughter chimed in loudly.

I didn't expect the man to rant and rave about it, but I also didn't expect his response.

"He's welcome to as many bananas as he likes, and apples too. I'm glad he's here," he replied with a smile, and I knew he meant it.

I told him thank you, which seemed grossly inadequate for the amount of gratitude I felt. I had needed to feel like we were welcome in the world that day and his kindness took my breath away.

"That man's nice," my daughter said.

"Yes, he really is," I replied.

Our village.

## CARRIE

About six months after Jack was diagnosed, I went for a walk with a friend in the neighborhood. We each pushed strollers—hers with her own little boy, mine with two toddlers sitting side by side. Three-year-old Joseph walked next to me, sometimes skipping ahead in his new blue sneakers. It was early spring. Tiny green buds dotted the leaves.

Now familiar with concepts like *joint attention* and *expres-*

*sive language*, I pointed things out constantly, trying to engage Jack in the world around him. I gestured at the birds in the sky, the neighbor's little dog, a plane rumbling overhead. I named them all: bird, dog, plane. He stared blankly ahead.

My friend glanced over at me quizzically. I forced myself not to mention the red car at the stop sign in the same singsong voice I'd used for previously acknowledged neighborhood accoutrements. It probably wouldn't matter anyway. He barely turned his head when I spoke. Yet somehow, over the last six months, I'd morphed into some kind of talking doll who spit out words constantly. If a person could be pulled from autism's inner sanctum by having someone constantly talk at them, well, I would be the one to do it.

As we stood at the corner of the street and waited to cross, Jack began to hit his head with the palm of his hand. My friend looked at him and then back at me. Gently moving his hand down, I explained it was part of autism. Sometimes he did this when he felt overwhelmed.

"I still can't believe the doctor said he has autism. That must be so *hard*!"

I nodded, thinking of just that morning when he screamed for twenty minutes straight when a pillow fell off the couch. It *was* hard.

"I mean, no one wants to know something is *wrong* with their child."

I glanced down at her perfect little boy sitting calmly in the stroller, and I felt a sense of loneliness descend upon me like a cloud. She meant well. I know she did. It's just that unless you are in the blizzard yourself, it can be difficult to comprehend the weight of the storm.

This was May of 2006. We accessed the internet through a dial-up connection that made a series of beeping noises. Cell phones were huge and clunky. Texting involved a complicated system where you tapped the numbers of your phone to correspond with letters and, if you were lucky, spell out a word. And although Twitter had launched two months earlier, Facebook wouldn't announce the novel idea of an online community for quite some time. It would be years before I connected in any meaningful way with a family who looked like ours. I felt isolated and alone much of the time.

This was further compounded by the fact that people understood very little about autism. The only books I could find on the topic were clinical. I longed for the story version—preferably from someone a few years ahead of me on the journey. I wanted to talk to the person I thought of as the "old mom"—one who could give me some glimpse as to what to expect next. Instead, autism seemed almost taboo. It lived in the shadows.

In the meantime, I soldiered on through the social stuff that comprises early motherhood: birthday parties, backyard barbecues, and playdates.

Playdates were perhaps the worst for me. The great theater of American Child-Rearing, where our dramas played out on the living room floor of one friend or another. Surrounded by diaper bags and sippy cups, our children played with blocks or dozed on blankets as we compared notes on milestones like potty training and who said *Mama* first. For perhaps the first time in my life, I felt fully on display.

For starters, Jack never *played* with anything. He took vacuums apart. He broke knickknacks. He snuck upstairs into the master bedroom and wormed his way into king-sized beds. He had no boundaries—opening refrigerators and helping himself to whatever was inside when he was little, asking personal questions or announcing every thought that came to his mind as he got older.

"My mother would *never* let us keep our house this messy." He shouted this gem after observing a lot of shoes strewn about our neighbor's mudroom. Let's just say it was a while before we were invited back there again.

And the milestone comparing, well, that was a whole other thing. Jack had very little language until he was about four. *Mama* wasn't his first word, or even his second. I didn't have much to share in the way of triumphs, simply because ours looked so very different from the average family with a toddler. Few people in our social circle understood the joy Joe and I experienced the first time Jack used the sign for *more* during dinner.

It's a part of our story that plays on repeat, especially as Jack gets older. A friend will announce something new and great her kiddo did—made the honor roll, got a driver's license, rented a tux for the prom—and my stomach does a weird little flip. It's not that I can't celebrate these triumphs for other people. I can and I do. But at the same time, I feel the sting of autism's paper cut, knowing Jack may never reach these for himself.

One thing I never quite got used to was the staring. From the time he was little, people stared at him—at us. I get it. His movements are a little different. He hops in place and flicks his fingers. And the meltdowns can bring an entire room to a screeching halt with all eyes on us.

There were a handful of incidents that made me cringe—like the time a man muttered under his breath about how discipline might solve the problem as four-year-old Jack threw himself to the floor in the grocery store because the packaging for his beloved Oreos had changed—but for the most part, people were very kind. There are many instances when someone would smile gently in my direction, which was like a soothing balm upon my breaking heart. One gentleman insisted on folding up the stroller when Jack was whirling around the parking lot.

The nicest thing anyone has ever done for me was at a ball field. It was some kind of showcase for Little League—the sort of night when entire families turn out and the bleachers are packed.

Charlie was playing. It was a warm spring evening. We packed up all the kids with the promise of dinner afterward and headed for the field. As soon as we pulled up, I got a pit in my stomach. There were cars everywhere. The parking lot was full, and we had to drive down the street to find a spot.

Jack was around ten at this point. He hated crowds. He kept his head down when anyone addressed him. He picked his nose, dragging out terrible treasures and, well, ingesting them.

There was a chain-link fence bordering this particular field. While Joe brought the other kids to the bleachers, I hung back with Jack near the scoreboard. That is, until Jack decided to take off running—charging through the field as players took their places in between innings.

I ran after him, calling his name and telling him to come back. He never even turned around, just bolted off the field and into the dugout of the opposing team. I caught up with him after a few minutes and stood by his side, trying to coax him into walking back to the car with me. He wrenched his hand out of mine and started walking away quickly. Out of the corner of my eye, I saw Joe begin to move toward us.

It was yet another instance where I felt on display. Although people's faces were somewhat of a blur as I ran past, I could feel the stares upon my back. When would we ever fit in? Why did every other family seem so normal compared to ours? Why couldn't I just sit, for once, and watch one of my other kids play a sport?

Finally, I caught up to Jack. As was often the case, his battery power seemed to run out and he was subdued, staring straight ahead while I tried to figure out the cause of his deregulation.

A woman appeared by my side. She was familiar—the

mother of a boy Charlie played with for a few years. She smiled at us gently and held out a bottle of water.

"I thought you could use this."

Gratefully, I accepted it and murmured my thanks. I turned away before she could see the tears in my eyes. This gesture—so simple, so practical—nearly leveled me.

A community is at once the easiest and hardest thing to build. You take a group of like-minded people who likely live near one another, and their interests create a sense of bonding. They participate in shared activities. Everyone feels as though they belong.

When it came to autism, I had trouble finding any such community. Back in 2005, when Jack was diagnosed, I was fairly convinced it didn't exist. Sure, he went to an integrated preschool with other diagnosed kids, but the only time I saw the parents was during the rush of the morning drop-off. The school didn't have a newsletter or an email chain to connect families the way my older son's day care did. It was one more way that made me feel like autism was taboo. Very few people in my life even wanted to talk about it with me. Family and friends squirmed when I brought it up—when I mentioned that perhaps there was no cure, and how the future looked so very uncertain for us. They wanted to reassure me it would all be *fine.* They would point out all the gains he was making—albeit slowly—and tell me I needed to relax. All while my heartbeat fluttered beneath my rib cage.

The publisher of my first memoir, *What Color Is Monday,* insisted I get on social media and begin blogging before the book was released. I was very hesitant at first. I couldn't see how a Facebook account could add much to my already busy life—and to be honest, I was slightly suspicious of people who talked about their profiles and news feeds. It felt like a different universe altogether.

And it was. For me, in the very best way possible. Reluctantly, I set up a WordPress account to blog. My first essay was a letter to Jack on his eighth birthday. It got a modest number of views—maybe a thousand, which far exceeded any expectation I had—and I decided I would post a new one every Monday. From there, I launched a public Facebook page to share updates about our family and Jack.

Writing healed me just the tiniest bit each week. It forced me to spend a few minutes after the kids went to bed and chronicle all that went on during the day. Meltdowns, IEP meetings, arguments with Joe. Then I'd fill in the black-and-white challenges with moments of color: a new word Jack said, our favorite pasta dish for dinner, a stolen makeup kiss at the sink while the kids watched TV in the other room.

It also gave me what I hungered for: a chance to see families who looked like mine. Families who were struggling to make room for siblings, navigating unwilling school districts, and trying to keep their marriages together amidst the chaos autism often brought. It was like pulling back a virtual curtain to discover—*aha!*—we are not alone in life's messiness.

When it comes to progress and goals, I have the tendency to maintain a balance sheet in my mind, often skewed to all of the things Jack's *not* doing. He's not sleeping through the night. He's not reading at grade level. He's not driving a car.

Seeing other families across the country fighting battles I knew nothing about also inspired a sense of gratitude in me. The balance sheet shifted just a bit, and I started to notice—and appreciate—all the things Jack could do, like sit through dinner, load the dishwasher, and switch laundry from the washer to the dryer.

I've been blogging and writing for over a decade now, with a new post every single Monday since I first started on Jack's birthday. I guess you could say I am the "old mom" now, and I feel a certain sense of responsibility to share my experiences with those behind me on this wild and ordinary path.

Although our community is modest in size, we continue to remind ourselves of one truth.

We are not alone.

You are not alone.

*Ball.* That was his first word.

There's nothing wrong with him.

# 7
# Exploring Grief

## KATE

Since my book came out in 2022, I have been doing a lot of public speaking. I can remember being in middle school, mouth dry, hands ice-cold, terrified to deliver a speech to my classmates. Today, I can't imagine a crowd intimidating me. Sharing our secret world of autism is my passion. But the travel part is hard, especially with little kids at home.

My younger three love to call me on the phone when I travel. They ask when I'm coming home, tattle on their dad, and ask for presents. They call whenever they can. Cooper, he doesn't call. He won't FaceTime when Jamie offers him the phone either. But I know that the second I leave the house, whether it's for a quick trip to the store or a longer event, he makes his way to the picture window facing the driveway and settles in. And he waits for me.

It doesn't matter if it's five minutes or five days. He waits. Sometimes for as long as it takes.

When I pull in the driveway, every single time, he is there. Smiling. Waving. And when I finally come into the house, hands usually full, he is always standing there, greeting me and eventually leaning in for a hug. There are equal parts beauty and pressure in being someone's person.

How lucky am I to have such love to come home to? And what happens if someday I don't make it home?

The other day as I sat on a runway waiting to take off, I had a flash of my plane crashing. Morbid, yes, I know. But the feeling was real, nevertheless. Cooper and I are both getting older. Just this year we discussed transition planning after high school at his IEP meeting. Their goal was to get us thinking about the future. I admitted to his team and myself that I wasn't ready. I am terrified of dying and leaving my son behind because I know that no one will love him like I do. I need more time.

As I powered my phone off from row 17, seat A1, I sent a quick message to Jamie telling him I love him and the kids. I thought about what would happen if I didn't come home. Would Cooper continue to wait? Would he understand? For a brief second, I let myself imagine a man waiting in the window. Taller than me. Hands dancing in the sunlight. Music coming from an iPad. Waiting for his mom.

Grief. My old friend. Although just as heavy, I carry it well these days. One of the most important things I can share with my fellow parents is that we cannot heal from what we refuse to acknowledge. It took me so long to learn that. Now I force myself to lean into the pain and the emotions that hurt and scare me the most. I felt the familiar pit in my stomach and tears filled my eyes.

I could write a whole book on grief. And no, I'm not an expert. I'm just a mom who tried to heal by being resilient and failed miserably. I've made a lot of mistakes in my special needs parenting journey, many publicly. Autism turned me upside down and inside out, but I'm learning and growing and embracing. I know now in the beginning I was just trying to evade my grief. I talk about my feelings whenever I can now. I share my fears for the future. I have uncomfortable conversations and I don't feel the need to put a bow on everything either.

Age thirteen has brought on an entirely new wave of grief for me as a mom. A secondary wave of grief. One that no one prepared me for. Grief usually is reserved for something you lost and is defined as "a natural reaction" to that sense of loss. How can I grieve for his "typicalness" when it was never really there? Grief is complicated to define in relation to disability parenting. Taboo to discuss, even. But I believe it should be shared with every parent when the diagnosis is said out loud in relation to their child. The folder we received after Cooper was diagnosed was blue. It had a list of clinics and definitions and resources. There was nothing of value in that folder. What it should have had was a pamphlet describing the five stages of grief—denial, anger, bargaining, depression, and acceptance—and encouraging parents to find someone to talk to about their feelings. That's what parents need. Because the truth is, Cooper has always been fine. Because he had me and his dad to advocate for him. It's Jamie and I, the parents, who need the support. We were given this life-changing diagnosis for our child and expected to be experts immediately. We were not.

I have learned in my own grief journey that it's hard to heal from things that no one lets you talk about. Grief makes people uncomfortable. They feel the need to try and fix it. Or tell you how it could be worse. Or even rush you through it. I've heard it all. Each response of *"at least it isn't cancer"* or *"but at least you have other children"* silencing me a little more each time.

The most damaging thing I ever did to myself was to deny my own feelings to make everyone else comfortable. Maybe it's a generational thing or even a female thing. I don't know. But I learned early on that the people in my life didn't like me sad. They wanted me to be fine, to get over it, to carry on. As a result, I lived in a place of perpetual grief for many years without even knowing it.

I went to an event a while back, to honor and celebrate special needs moms. It was one of the first times I realized how lucky I was that my son just had autism.

One of the moms spoke about the moment her daughter passed, and they finally shut off the beeping machines. She said there were days, weeks, and months leading up to that moment where she prayed for the beeping to end because it was driving her mad. And then when it ended, she desperately wanted it back. She spoke about the silence and how much louder it is than a continuous beep.

Another mom, who I will never forget, spoke of her son and his multiple suicide attempts and how she eventually lost him to his pain. The sentence that haunts me to this day: "I couldn't convince my son to want to live."

The mothers who spoke defined their grief in ways I was thankful I had never experienced. My son wasn't medically complex. He wasn't dying. He could run and eat, and we didn't live our lives at Children's Hospital. He just had autism. I was lucky. But why didn't I feel that way?

I learned, after sharing my story with a therapist, that grief does not need to be caused solely by the death of a loved one. It can be triggered by any event that involves an identity-altering type of loss. I wasn't grieving the loss of my son—I was grieving the loss of the experiences and the life I imagined for my child, myself, and our family. But I would always choose Cooper. A million times over. I wouldn't forgo the grief if it meant that I had to lose my boy.

For way too long I lived in the space between grief and growth, trying to make sense of why my son had autism. And I didn't like how that space made me feel.

The hardest question we can ever ask is why. Why my child?

I fixated on the why for years. Obsessively, I would go over everything I did or didn't do during the months that turned into the years that got us to the point we were at. I would justify and find reasoning that soothed my heart. But I always found myself back at why.

Why my child? Why our family? Why me?

Why do some kids have autism and some don't? Why do some kids improve? Why are some severe? Why do some get to talk? And on the loneliest nights it was why are some families chosen for this life, and some aren't? Why were we picked?

I even imagined the moment I entered heaven, and a quick conversation with God where I got to ask one question. I knew exactly what I would ask.

"Why Cooper?"

We can't heal from what we refuse to acknowledge. I use that phrase a lot. Admitting that my son has autism wasn't hard for me. I could acknowledge that part. I could acknowledge that he didn't talk "yet" and that he was different from his peers. What I couldn't do was acknowledge that autism was forever. And that my son may never talk to me and will eventually live in a group home and that he will have to live without me.

I thought for so long that he would get better. That he would catch up. But he hasn't and I know he never will. His severity is crushing to me. In the beginning, his neurotypical peers left us behind. Today, it's his autistic peers. Sometimes it feels like we are frozen in time while the rest of the world continues to advance. And deep down I worry that I am not strong enough to do this for the rest of my life. That makes people uncomfortable when I share it. Just like when I talk about grief and his life after we are gone. My mission is to get comfortable having uncomfortable conversations.

I'll be giving him a shower, reaching my hand in to wash his hair, and I'll look up at him, eyes squished shut, throwing his head back, smiling, squealing, and I'll wonder how this happened. And who will do this with such love and care after I'm gone.

Or he'll be having a meltdown, self-injuring, and screaming over a walk to the park or a crinkle in his paper, and I'll drop to the ground to hold his strong body. I'll wrap my hands around his face, pull him in, and help him breathe, and I'll wonder why. And whether I can ever die because no one will be able to care for him after I'm gone.

Or I'll be helping him with his shoes, and he'll grab my face, turning my cheek to look at whatever is on his screen, Barney or a favorite train, willing me to see how amazing it is. The same scene for the millionth time. Year after year and I'll smile, of course, and act as if it's the best train or the funniest Barney. But inside I'll wonder why. And how. He's thirteen. It shouldn't be like this.

I know now that for years I was pushing my emotions down in order to survive the hardest time of my life. Jealousy, fear, worry, sadness, anxiety, and anger tormented me the most. But anger was my favorite. Which was so confusing to me because at my core I am not an angry person.

I am a happy person. Annoyingly happy, really. I always have been. I see the good in things. The silver lining. I believe it will get better. But the years of special needs parenting, with not much help, and fighting for every basic right for my son, had hardened me. But instead of feeling the feelings as they happened, I packed each of them away in an imaginary backpack that I carried with me at all times so I wouldn't have to acknowledge them. One that I refused to unpack.

So, I kept myself busy. I kept moving and going and doing more and more. We had two more children. We moved a few times too. Even got a puppy and a boat. I wrote a book and started hosting events.

*Feeling the need to be busy all the time is a trauma response.*

People who have experienced trauma in some shape or form respond in different ways. Some shut down and withdraw from situations. I was the opposite. I was doing whatever it took to avoid acknowledging the forever of Cooper's autism. I lived in overdrive, constantly.

My backpack eventually turned into two and three and four backpacks. One for anger. One for jealousy. One for sadness. One for fear.

The weight was unbearable. Until I was hunched over, unrecognizable to myself. I remember the day I stumbled and fell.

It didn't happen overnight, but eventually, I forced myself to sit down, think, and acknowledge the realities of a lifelong disability for my son. I unpacked each bag, slowly and methodically.

I let myself be jealous of other families. And be fearful about the future. I worried about someone hurting him. And I felt sad that he had never played with his brother. And I let myself be angry at the world for the hand we had been dealt.

It took months for me to unpack it all. And I'll be honest, some of the people in my life didn't like me much at that time. But I didn't care. Growth is uncomfortable and I was becoming the person, the mom, Cooper needed me to be.

In my first book, I reference acceptance as a destination. A place that parents are desperate to reach. I think I even called it autism island. Once reached, we get to be happy. I thought I was there for many years. Our hardest years were ages four to eight. From eight to twelve I found peace. Age thirteen has found me in a place of grief again. I find myself catastrophizing at 3:00 a.m., in the car, and the shower, too, about life after I'm gone. Who will love him? Who will protect him?

I now think of acceptance as a moving target. With each new season, it moves again, just out of my reach. I think it will be this way forever. But we get to be happy too. We learn to live with grief, to carry it with us, and have a wonderful life, as we seek that elusive island.

Today when I encounter moments of grief, a boy his same age talking, a school dance he is unable to go to, a brother riding his bike to a friend's house, a younger sister speaking in complete sentences, my first reaction is to pack them up, shove them into that backpack I carry, and keep going. But I don't do that anymore. Because I know it will just set me back.

Instead, I sit in my feelings. I let them wash over me in the most heartbreaking ways because I know there is beauty and joy mixed in. I've learned over the last few years that belonging to a person with autism is never just one feeling. It's a combination of unbelievable joy and worry and longing and wishing and hoping. And none of the emotions are wrong. We get to feel all the things at once. Guilt-free.

I read somewhere that grief is just love. For me, as a mom of a child with a disability, grief is all the love and worry I carry for him. It's all of the experiences I want for him to have but he cannot.

Today, after years of working internally, I know there is absolutely nothing wrong with me or my feelings. Grief is just complicated.

As the wheels touched down, I heard the familiar ding of a message, after turning on my phone.

My husband…

"Cooper has said 'M-AW-M' 475 times since 8:00 a.m. He's waiting for you, Mama. You better hurry up."

## ADRIAN

Twenty-five years before autism, I loved another beautiful boy. His name was Adam and he was my only sibling. Like most big brothers, he was the center of my universe. When he began to feel unwell, our family saw doctors, and when six brain tumors were unearthed on a grainy black-and-white image, the hospital became our home. For months, they searched for a diagnosis—my dad and the doctors—and still, nothing. It wasn't until the beautiful boy was loaded on a medical flight and taken to a faraway city that a new set of physicians told my parents it was cancer. There was nothing to be done except to bring him home, secure a room in our small-town hospital, and sit vigil until that hot July day when the clock struck noon.

I had just turned fifteen years old and there would be no more memories made in summers spent at the beach or on Christmas morning. Our family of four had imploded and we were left to grieve. We know that parents grieve for their offspring, but the genetic and familial tie of siblings, those people to whom we are most closely connected, is also a lightning grasp. Only, I did not grieve. Many think that there is no choice but to move forward, but that's untrue. I know because I didn't. Instead, I chose to swallow hurt and pain and longing because I was afraid it would destroy me. I didn't know that it was important to lean into the pain. It seemed easier to ignore and move on.

I had certainly tackled life—married a boy from college, finished my PhD, and had four children. I was happy, but there was something that I couldn't shake. It was grief. I was drowning in it and had no idea until autism came along. I did what I had always done when things got hard—I tried to run away. Only this time when I attempted to swallow the hurt and fear that echoed with Amos's autism diagnosis, I couldn't. I had been shoving the pain down for so long, and now the jig was up.

I knew that I had been held captive by grief and I wasn't going to let it happen again. I wasn't quite sure how to start, but found that tears came first. I hated crying, detested weakness, and felt ashamed of mourning a son I love, but I had no choice. I wasn't going to make the same mistake I had twenty-six years earlier. On that hot July morning, I chained my vault of emotions and discarded the key. And today? I have bucked against the urge to run away from my feelings. This time, I would face my fears and acknowledge the feelings. I committed to walking alongside Amos and navigating this new normal.

*You used to write*, a voice whispered in the innermost recesses of my mothering heart. That, too, had abruptly ended with the death of my brother. My last writing had been in a yellow notebook where I detailed the journey to my brother's cancer diagnosis, a family's search for answers, and the ending that was far from one in my beloved book of fairy tales. After Amos was diagnosed with autism, I began to write again. I grieved in a way that I had never allowed myself. I grieved first for my brother and then for myself. I stayed up late, tucked by the fire, wearing a pair of Adam's now tattered socks, and shared my heart on paper. Tears streamed down my face and I allowed myself to feel those feelings that I had shoved aside in a feeble attempt to survive. I grieved autism and the loss of a dream. I had been following a well-executed plan, and suddenly, life had imploded again. Only this time, there was no death sentence. This diagnosis, though hard and scary and unexpected, wouldn't end with the lowering of a mahogany box into the ground. Yet I grieved and felt ashamed for grieving. I was unable to reveal those feelings even to the people I loved most in this world. It was just too raw for me to broach the subject aloud. I worried that the tornadic feelings surrounding Amos could be misconstrued as shame for him. That feeling was certainly far from my heart. I could adore no one more, and I would go to the earth's end to offer more or better for him. I love him, yet I have wept and gulped sobs in almost every place on earth—grocery store, playground, church, car-pool line.

The bubble of safety that I had maintained in the two dozen years since my brother's death drifted away with the arrival of Amos. Surprisingly, the grief of a death was more manageable for me because it had a beginning and an end. This grief was unfamiliar and sprang tentacles to an endless supply of new concerns to plague the mind. Real life is messy and it doesn't take a pause for any of us, not even mamas grieving a diagnosis for the little people they call their own. Real life is a whirlwind of feelings, thoughts, discarded expectations, grief, loss, disappointment. Real life is marked by the unknown paths that we will tread tomorrow, and I am reminded that motherhood is not for the faint of heart. Be thankful, the heart whispers.

And I am thankful. I am thankful for a husband who loves and requires very little in return. I am thankful for parents who would give me the moon if I asked. I am thankful for siblings who love and adore and seem to take their mysterious brother in stride. I am the one who seems to struggle the most. Maybe that's the job of mamas, or maybe it's just me, an imperfect soul in a sea of millions. It's quite disconcerting to adore someone so much, yet find yourself crying over their very personhood. To be sad and thankful simultaneously is a strange paradox and has been difficult to navigate.

Autism was here to stay and I had to make a choice. I could swallow the hurt and ignore that familiar river of grief or I could meet it head-on. I loved Amos and needed to do right by him, and so, I grieved. Some days, I still do. My heart stings when I see boys his age swing bats over their shoulders, sit on benches, swiftly change into cleats, and magically tie their shoes while carrying on a conversation about weekend plans. I may grieve, but I don't hold those feelings inside. I acknowledge and accept. I also remind myself to have perspective. Grief is necessary for cancer and acceptance is necessary for autism. I challenged myself to feel the feelings this time around. I had a lot of catching up to do in those first couple of years, and it felt like I would never unearth all the grief that had been weighing me down. Slowly, a lightness came, and somewhere along the way, an old friend found me once again.

It was joy—the elusive emotion that had been buried deep within my soul for so many years. I didn't know that joy was even a possibility after I lost my beautiful brother. Of course, fate decided another beautiful boy would carry me home again.

## CARRIE

Jack has never once hugged me.

When he was an infant, he squirmed and thrashed in my arms. As he got older, he never came to me for comfort. If he fell and scraped his knee or pinched his fingers in a drawer, he rejected my attempts to soothe him. Even now, whenever I try to embrace him, his whole body stiffens.

Can you imagine your own child resisting your touch?

I often describe autism as heartbreak by a thousand paper cuts. This phrase first occurred to me when I watched Joe embrace four-year-old Jack in a deep bear hug. Jack leaned into him without pulling away. It's always been this way—he enjoys affection from his father more than me.

Seeing their ease together stings. I don't know how else to describe it. It isn't jealousy, exactly, just a tiny stab of hurt that I wrestle with occasionally.

The grief never quite goes away, unfortunately. I wish I could say I've healed completely—that little things about this diagnosis don't bother me. For me, that hasn't been the case.

I can be driving through town when I see a bunch of teenagers his age bouncing a basketball, and my heart squeezes together. I wonder who he could have been, without autism controlling his arms and legs. Perhaps, at six feet, five inches tall, an athlete.

One time I saw a girl notice Jack when we were in the grocery store. She was right around his age, maybe eighteen or so, and she was standing with a group of girls who were similarly dressed. Oversized hoodies, leggings, and the Converse sneakers that seemed to have come back in style.

And why shouldn't she notice him? He's tall. With thick brown hair and blue eyes, he's handsome. And he was wearing his snappy new scarf that he picked out himself.

In the middle of the aisle, surrounded by the latest flavor of Oreos and other assorted cookies, he began to lightly hop in place. He flicked his fingers once, twice. He cleared his throat loudly—his version of verbal stimming. I saw her face fall. She looked down at the ground and shuffled her feet. My stomach sank.

Autism grief is something that never quite disappears. It slides into the background for a while. Then it rears its ugly head when you least expect it. I think of it as love without a landing spot.

Dr. Michael Beckwith quotes, "Pain pushes until vision pulls." The pain of the paper cut's sting, the pain of watching Jack's siblings leapfrog over him, the pain of having so many uncertain parts to the future—this is my reality.

Yet the vision remains cloudy. Constantly, I search for the crystal ball into the future. Where will he go once this program is over? Where will he live for the rest of his life? How will he afford an apartment, or pay life insurance? I am propelled by the pain and the fear, but I can't quite see where we're going.

Last summer, grief visited me once more.

"I'm not close with my mother." Time and time again, I offered these six words neutrally, the way one might offer an opinion about whether or not they like cucumbers.

I had planned on talking about our estrangement exactly zero times. The twelve conversations in as many years, the fact that she met my youngest son perhaps twice, or how I never listed her as my emergency contact on medical forms. She wasn't who I called when I had a bad day or got a book deal.

Then she died. And those six words became my mantra. "I'm not close with my mother."

Once she passed, I said them at cocktail parties, book club, during dinner with my in-laws. I always kept my voice neutral. I made sure my shoulders were relaxed. I didn't want to invite further conversation. After all, what kind of freak, or weirdo, or misfit, doesn't talk to her own mother? How unlovable could one person be?

I pretended they were meaningless—as though they cost me nothing at all to say. It was a benign answer to a somewhat loaded topic.

Once in a while, I wished I could talk about it. I wished I could talk about the dysfunction, the shame, the little band of family held together by secrets. But how? Who do you tell?

How do you explain the way these memories are punctuated by pure goodness? You see, our family was a beautiful idea. We had dinner around the table at night. We went to Sunday school once a week. Our report cards had good grades. In the summer, we drove to the ocean and jumped in the waves.

We were a beautiful idea, but we were a mess in the nighttime. We were smashed plates. We were chaos and eggshells. We were unaddressed mental illness shrouded in a fierce kind of love.

If I was on a game show as a child, and someone asked me *what is a family*, I wouldn't have known how to answer. From a six-year-old's eyes, I would have said a family is a father leaving a mother on a gray day in springtime. I would have explained the suitcases on the front porch and the visitation rights, the court orders, the screaming matches on the front lawn while the neighbors watch helplessly.

I would have shared about the slippery terrain upon which we tread every day as children, thanks to an untreated condition known as borderline personality disorder.

Her passing was unexpected. In the middle of July, my brother called me with the news that she was admitted to the hospital and explained that the prognosis didn't look good. Her COPD (chronic obstructive pulmonary disease) had skyrocketed, and they had no choice but to intubate her.

Ironically, I was on my way to drop Jack off at a summer camp to which he was vehemently opposed. After a rough start to his college experience, his residential team suggested we address his severe anxiety through a different kind of program—one that focused on getting him off technology and immersed in outdoor activities.

I drove down Interstate 84—the corridor of Connecticut and New York—and alternately received updates from my brother and soothed Jack's fears. After a nearly eight-hour drive, I steered us down a long, winding back road to the summer camp. Dark gray clouds gathered thickly overhead. The camp director by our side, we rushed to unload the car before the sky unleashed its pent-up rain. I walked away as it started to drizzle. I held my hand over my mouth to stifle a sob. Once alone in the car, I openly wept.

Like most people, inside my heart is a glossary of nonwords. Some moments are impossible to capture, no matter how many syllables you cobble together. These nonwords, they are an experience bigger than language can hold. Leaving my son behind as I drove to my mother's bedside was one such experience.

The following morning, after a sleepless night at a hotel, I drove to the hospital. Under a midsummer sky, I walked into the main entrance. Beneath my rib cage, I knew once I left, I would never be back again.

She looked diminutive—a stark contrast to her presence throughout my childhood. Although petite in stature, she always loomed large. I clasped her tiny hand in mine. With complete candor, we agreed we did the best we could. Beneath the glare of fluorescent lights, for just a moment, we were briefly beautiful again. Three days later, she died.

*What's wrong with me?* Every now and again, this was what I asked myself. So often, I wondered if I let her go too easily. I wondered if I gave up—if I should have tried harder. Never once did I consider how easily she let me go. I try to capture the sensation of never having a mother again, even though I was never sure I had one in the first place.

I know nothing about her, I insist to myself.

Yet I know everything. I know her favorite song, the perfume she always wore, the way she liked her macaroni salad with extra mayonnaise. I know the shape of her hands, her sudden smile, the tilt of her head.

*Estranged.* A word with a bad consonant-to-vowel ratio.

Autism and borderline personality disorder. Are the two connected? It's hard to know. All I can say is there is a complicated loss mixed up in both: the son I never expected intertwined with the mother I always wanted.

Every now and again, she surfaces into the periphery of my mind. A book we both enjoyed, sitting still and dusty on the shelf. A song by her beloved Rick Astley on the radio. The smell of cigarettes mingled with strong coffee. Her green eyes reflected in my oldest son.

Do I wish I could change it? Not necessarily. I wish I had savored the softer moments between us, perhaps. I wish I held on more tightly to the smiles over chocolate and whipped cream—the salty waves beneath a cloudless sky. I wish mental health was more than a concealed whisper amongst her generation. I wish medication and therapy had been a part of the conversation.

Who am I without her, my invisible, perpetual antagonist? For it is against her emotional tide that I swim, hoping I didn't inherit the same capacity for riptides. When my maternal ghosts haunt me, and I hear a familiar shrillness in my own voice, I remind myself. I have built something new. I have built something different.

At night, I toss and turn while Joe sleeps next to me. I remember my childhood home, now sold. I recall the odd details from each room—how the late afternoon sunlight fell across the carpet in the dining room, or the blue wallpaper she hung in the kitchen shortly after her second divorce.

Now a new family will move into these rooms. I consider money I never expected, and perhaps don't deserve. How will I spend it? What is the right thing to do here? How can I continue her legacy, whatever that may be?

I consider how, despite two different diagnoses—borderline personality disorder and autism—their vulnerabilities presented very similarly. Extreme anxiety, paranoia, a tendency to misread the intentions of others.

I think of the hundreds of messages in my inbox, chronicling similar familial fractures. Again and again, daughters and mothers and fathers ask me what to do—how to mend the broken bonds. *Find something,* I urge them. *Something to keep you connected, no matter how small.*

For us it was books. Over the years I sent her novels I thought she'd enjoy: *State of Wonder* by Ann Patchett, *The Poisonwood Bible* by Barbara Kingsolver. She sent me her favorites for Christmas and my birthday. *Family Pictures* by Sue Miller. *The Shell Seekers* by Rosamunde Pilcher. I've read them so many times their covers are threadbare. I guess you could say inside each story, I was looking for a piece of my own.

When I went back to the house for a final time, every book I sent was there, lined up on a shelf next to every article I had ever written. My breath caught in my throat. She remembered me. She thought of me. My mother.

*We did the best we could.* This is the sentence I thought over and over again as I ran my fingertips down the row.

At night, the clock ticks on the bedside table. The numbers climb toward morning.

From inside grief's cloud, I consider ways in which we heal from things out of our control—how deeply neurodiverse brain wiring has affected the trajectory of my own life on either side: as both daughter and mother.

Joe turns over in the bed and pulls the cover up over his shoulder. He mumbles something in his sleep. I make a decision—a plan.

The next morning, after everyone has left for work and school, I pick up my phone. I think of my tall boy. I think of my mother and her green eyes. I think of sunshine, blue wallpaper, and an unexpected sum of money.

"Good morning, yes, I'm looking for a Realtor. I'd like to look into buying my son an apartment."

Pain pushes until vision pulls.

She hated to be hugged.

# 8

# Caregiving vs. Motherhood

## KATE

"Is there any stress at home?"

You could have heard a pin drop in the exam room when the doctor asked the question, the only sound being the crinkle from my paper gown. I averted my eyes from hers while fidgeting with my hands, probably appearing guilty.

"You seem like you are under an incredible amount of stress, Katie," she pressed, using the name on my birth certificate. "Is there anything you want to share with me?"

I know she was just doing her job, with a little bit of kindness mixed in, but her questions felt accusatory.

I hadn't been to the doctor in years, with my last appointment being my six-week postpartum follow-up after the birth of my second son. He was starting kindergarten soon.

I didn't have time for medical appointments. I was too busy working, running a household, and caring for my children, one having severe autism. But something was wrong with me and I couldn't deny it any longer.

A chronic cough. Extreme fatigue. Weight loss. Fever.

Despite my best efforts to home remedy, nothing was working, and after six months, I was worn down. And as a special needs mom, I was scared. Scared of being sick. Scared of dying. Scared of leaving Cooper. I needed to figure out what was wrong with me.

"Katie, as your doctor, I have to ask—do you feel safe at home?"

Laughter erupted from deep inside of me. This doctor was way off. But I could tell by the look on her face that she was serious in her questioning. I watched as she scribbled something onto her notepad.

I straightened up, trying to see what she wrote.

"AUTISM." It came out louder than I expected.

I cleared my throat and said it again. "Autism. My son has severe autism.

"He's…um…only six," I continued. "He doesn't sleep and he was just kicked out of kindergarten. It's really hard and no one seems to understand."

I rarely talked about my home life with open honesty. When I did, I felt like a failure. I felt like a bad mom. Or that I was being judged. I also didn't want anyone to know how significant my son's needs were. I felt like a traitor to him if I complained. But worse yet, what if I did ask for help and no one believed me? It was easier to stay quiet, it seemed.

Autism wasn't new to me. I could say the word without tears coming to my eyes. I was settling into the role of special needs parent. But it also wasn't getting any easier. The hard parts—the aggression, the self-injuring, the running, the screaming, the rigidity—were my new normal. Cooper was getting bigger, his needs getting greater, as well. I had pushed everyone away in my life. I had stopped answering texts and returning phone calls. And most recently, I was having thoughts that maybe I wasn't meant to be happy. Maybe this was it.

I felt that this new doctor was waiting for more.

I told her about autism. About Cooper, my yellow-haired, misunderstood boy. About the locks on the doors and the permanent bruises on my legs from his kicks. I spoke of the pressure. The isolation. The never-ending worry. It felt strange to speak so honestly, so openly.

I felt guilty telling her so much. This stranger. But up until this point, I hadn't put the whole entire story together for anyone. Not my mom, or my friends, or Jamie. After a minute or so of me sharing, I paused, and then said, "But I love my son so much."

I was crying at this point, my body hunched over. I couldn't make eye contact with her, out of shame. I felt her hand on my shoulder.

"No one is questioning the love you have for your son, Katie. That is evident. It practically radiates from you. But your body is telling you something and you need to listen. Before it's too late."

I felt seen and heard for the first time. I left with a pamphlet on combating the stress of being a caregiver.

Be physically active. Learn new skills. Get more sleep. Drink more water. Find a support group. Pay attention to the present moment.

And the final tip...the real secret to improving one's mental health...change your mindset. Tell yourself you are happy. Eventually, it will come true.

What a joke, I remember thinking.

But I was intrigued by the term *caregiver.* I had never heard of it before. The cover of the pamphlet showed a woman probably in her fifties alongside an older woman. Her mother, I assumed. The headline read, "Stepping Successfully into the Role of a Caregiver."

Was that me? Was I a caregiver? My gut told me no.

Yes, my life was different from that of my friends with kids the same age. There was no denying that, but could a mother be a caregiver?

As I crumpled the pamphlet into a ball and tossed it into the garbage, I put the term *caregiver* out of my mind. I was a mother, doing motherly things, nothing more.

Cooper is thirteen years old now, and supporting caregivers has become a mission of mine. Because I am one. And will be for the rest of my life. I don't want any mother to ever feel as alone and isolated as I did in the beginning.

It is important to recognize how challenging the caregiver role is because it can consume us without us realizing it. I know it did for me. I often say I turned invisible at times, consumed by my son's disability. I was unrecognizable.

There is an urban myth I often think about. It says if you put a frog in a pot of boiling water it will instantly leap out. But if you put it in a pot filled with pleasantly tepid water and gradually heat it, the frog will remain in the water until it boils. Morbid, yes. But stick with me.

Allegedly, the frog is not able to detect the gradual increase in temperature until it's too late. In essence, when our living conditions deteriorate gradually, we adapt to these conditions instead of getting rid of them, until we are no longer strong enough to escape. The boiling frog syndrome may occur in our relationships, our lifestyle, our work, and countless other scenarios.

I'm afraid of becoming a frog. And caregiving turned the temperature up.

We love our children so deeply that there is nothing we wouldn't do to ensure their well-being, safety, and happiness. But late at night I found myself wondering...at what cost? We love our children so deeply that the lengths we go to in order to ensure their comfort become our new normal. But our norm is not the norm. This is why we have to share our stories. The roles of mother and caregiver are intertwined, neither able to be separated from the other.

We are mothers first and will do anything for our children. Part of that needs to be loving ourselves too. We are no good if we don't save ourselves first.

## ADRIAN

I dreamed of motherhood as a little girl, but caregiving? Not so much. Caregiving is the hamster wheel of motherhood—belonging to a beautiful square in a world that is fraught with roundness. Being a caregiver was never even a casual blip on my radar. I had three typical children; caregiving didn't apply to me.

I've been a mother now for over eighteen years, and I've learned four times over what it means to lose your heart to love. I know now why my mother couldn't sleep until she heard the clicking of a door signaling my late-night arrival. There's nothing I had longed for more in life than to have a gaggle of children. I happily anticipated messy chaos amidst a house full of laughter and bickering, friends and fun. When our first three arrived in three years, my childhood dreams were realized. I played the role well. I dressed my ducks in matching garb, and for the most part, they followed societal norms—weekly visits to the library, meals in restaurant high chairs, and afternoons spent in strollers, chubby hands clutching a clear bag of Goldfish or a white powdery doughnut.

Those first three tumbled about our expansive sea of green like unruly puppies. They squabbled over trucks and shovels and played king of the mountain—each vying to stand atop the sand pile in our yard made generous by a not-so-shiny red dump truck. I sat beneath the coolness of the shade in the summer sun and gathered pecans from the trees on the chilly days of early November. I lived easily, basking in the traditional ease of motherhood and oblivious to the arrogance that must have radiated from my clueless self. I believed with all my being that my children were clever creatures because I was the right kind of mother.

I giggle as I write that now. My own ignorance was impervious to life's lightning bolts. The birth of Amos enlightened me. The change in my thinking began around his first birthday. We had been visited by an early interventionist—at my request—and I welcomed her input and assistance with the child whose development seemed a bit behind. My first three children had not been speedy developers in the area of motor skills either, and I had been able to shrug off the nagging thoughts that became inextinguishable as his first birthday loomed.

Amos's dad was at work and his siblings were at school, so I singularly welcomed the unfamiliar face inside the home that had once been owned by a signer of the Declaration of Independence. I led her to our family room—we had decided that a dining room was a waste of space with four children—where Amos lay on his back surrounded by toys on a cream blanket that was hand stitched with a happy clown holding a handful of balloons. I still have that blanket. I smiled brightly and introduced her to my last baby. She stood unmoving and smiled as she studied the ten-month-old baby who could not yet roll over or sit up on his own. She asked casually, "What can he do?" Her eyes grew wide at my silence, and she said quietly, "Is that all he can do?"

My orderly world was lost forever.

I sat cross-legged beside that happy blanket, and as I fielded her well-meaning questions, my thumping heart crumbled. How could I have not known? Why had I waited? Why had I shrugged off the thoughts that had first crossed my mind when he was ten days old? I had so eagerly grasped the empty promises of the doctors who came before her, and the reckoning was swift. *He will never catch up*, my mind screamed as his baby hand clutched my own.

In a matter of seconds, I was transformed from a mother into a caregiver. Being thrust into this role has taught me so much about how little we can control who our children are born to be. After all, if I were to take credit for that well-behaved parcel of three, I must also claim ownership of the child whose very soul bucks the traditional system.

Not so long ago, I found myself standing amongst a group of women at a Christmas cocktail party. We exchanged stories and a few lamented laughingly about that hopeful day our errant teenagers would be missed. The laughter was alienating and I felt trapped by my own whirring thoughts. I silently pondered my own nest, unexpected and yet strangely familiar. A nest that will never be truly empty. I think back to the time when age was still measured in weeks and how I longed for Amos to smile. He was twelve weeks old and I remember the joy that came as he learned to share his evident joy with the world and me. I was so pleased with what he had finally learned, never guessing that it was the beginning of a journey that would markedly change me as a mother.

It would transform me into a caregiver.

Because of this role, I've become more accepting. I smile more than I frown, and I hug more than I judge. Becoming a caregiver lightened that perfect load that had once held me captive. ALL mothers bring their own special color and light.

Some moms cook elaborate meals and some teach their

kids to make mac and cheese in the microwave. They're both awesome.

There are moms with jobs outside of the home, and moms whose job is to raise the kids. Again, both are extraordinary.

Some of us homeschool, others have kids in public school, and some go to private. Does it really matter?

Lots of kids go to camp and lots don't. Who cares?

There are houses where televisions don't exist and then there are those where kids have their own. Why must we chime in?

Breastfeed, formula, or strictly pumping. Can we just say that what matters most is a happy mama and a fed baby?

There are families with one child or a half dozen. Have as few or many as you like—it's all right.

Some kids need regular medication and some are healthy as horses. Parenting is about way more than who gets sick or not.

Some of us teach tiny people to swim like fish and others rely on floaties. I say, just have fun.

Athletes or moms with a bit of pudge, as long as we play, who cares?

Some are young and some are pushing fifty, but we all struggle and laugh.

Some of us keep an impeccable house and others use leaf blowers rather than vacuums.

A few of us have very little and there are those who have more than they could ever spend.

Hugs and kisses don't cost a dime.

Do whatever you want as long as you love big and remember there's no second place when it comes to motherhood. Caregiving is just another way of being the best mother you can be for your child.

Caregivers are a special species, created through a life shrouded in heartache, awe, and love, on a path hidden far in the hills of all things unexpected. Loving is way more of a cliff jump when it involves baby birds that plummet. It's taken every ounce of toughness that I didn't know I had and has shown that love defies all.

When Amos was about three years old, we went camping for a long weekend with friends. We hauled children, packed and schlepped bags, fixed makeshift meals, and spent hours combing the beach and swimming. When we arrived home, I was tired. I gave myself some well-deserved freedom to sheepishly admit it, and my husband, Thomas, made pancakes for supper and took over bedtime.

I had just settled in a tub filled with bubbles and closed my eyes to ponder the events of the coming week. It was only a few minutes before I heard the urgent crying. Sobbing, really. Amos. At three, he was still without proper speech. I rose quickly. My heart hammering, I shoved my arms into my robe. Quickly, I went into the bedroom where Thomas was changing Amos's diaper. On the bed, my son was howling.

"What in the world?" I asked.

"He couldn't find you," he said.

Of course. He couldn't find me and he needed me. For what, I didn't know, but I gathered him in my arms to rock him in the old nursing chair where I had handled babies for thousands of hours over the course of my motherhood career. When Amos quieted, I laid him atop our bed and finished putting on his pajamas and told him it was time for night-night.

When you're a caregiver, tears are a sign of bravery, admitting weakness is a sign of strength, and you know love is the biggest risk you'll ever take except being loved. I can't think of anything better in this world. Who have I become? I ask myself and find that I rather like this new person. And as for my role of caregiver? It's a title awarded to the bravest and the strongest and the toughest of mothers—humans tasked with making this world a better place—even the ones who didn't sign up for it.

Glad you're here.

## CARRIE

As Kate mentioned, there is a big difference between caregiving and motherhood for families living alongside autism. It's a world few understand.

I often refer to the caregiving side of things as *Autism Management*. Everything from the endless paperwork, medication follow-ups, making appointments, and researching independent living options.

The paperwork alone is enough to make me want to light my eyelashes on fire. Rows of boxes, rating systems, questions about toilet training and psychotic episodes.

Scales are popular. Not the lovely scales one plays on the piano, but the 1–10 kind. Or, even better, the *sometimes, often, rarely, never* kind.

*Does your child ever run from you in public places?*

*Sometimes.*

*Often.*

*Rarely.*

*Never.*

Motherhood, on the other hand, is the nurturing aspect of raising your child. It is Band-Aids on scraped knees, bedtime snuggles, late-night bagels with restless teenagers.

In my life, both are endlessly intertwined.

Caregiving.

Motherhood.

Caregiving.

Motherhood.

Like a child picking petals from a flower, I alternate between the two.

I have a giant blue folder in my desk drawer. I bought it when Jack was a toddler, shortly after he was diagnosed. Inside is a jumble of evaluations, test results, doctors' notes, and articles.

He's nineteen now, and still, every time I catch a glimpse of it, my stomach sinks. It's my boy, reduced to black-and-white words on paper. It is also a symbol of my role beyond motherhood—my role of advocate, caregiver, and manager.

It's a reminder of all I do for him that I didn't have to do for my other kids. And if I did do it for them, slowly they are outgrowing the need for me to handle certain aspects of their lives.

For me, the defining factor between caregiving and motherhood is the outgrowing. At some point, most kids outgrow the need for their parents to manage them on a daily basis.

Making appointments, medical decisions, financial management.

When Jack turned eighteen, my husband, Joe, and I obtained guardianship. It was one of the lowest points for me on this autism journey.

In many families, the eighteenth birthday is a big celebration. Elaborate parties are planned. Large gifts are purchased—a new watch, perhaps, or maybe even a car.

With Jack, we hired an attorney. We filled out more paperwork. We made an appointment at the courthouse.

The courthouse.

Power of attorney, supported decision-making, guardianship.

Like wispy smoke at a campfire, these words had been floating around in my periphery for a few years. But I couldn't grasp the permanency of them—I couldn't quite fit them inside our world. Yet before I knew it, the decision was upon us.

I often say there is a duality within my son—his physical age and his emotional age. Physically, at eighteen, he was tall and healthy and strong. Emotionally, he hovered around eleven, maybe twelve.

As a teenager, he didn't understand the concept of a checking account. He thought dollars just came out of the ATM machine because you asked for them. He was easily persuaded by advertisements and political campaigns.

We needed to protect him. We needed safeguards in place to make sure no one could take advantage of him.

It almost broke me.

We worked so hard to make him independent in every aspect of life. And now, as he was perched on the precipice of adulthood, we were about to take it all away.

What choice did we have?

Before we could blink, the day arrived.

On a tender green morning in May, we were due to arrive in court by 9:00. It was a dreary day. Rain came down in sheets. I woke early. I knew I needed to run, because running always makes me think clearly. We promised Jack breakfast afterward. Denny's, for their pancakes.

The night before, Jack's court-appointed attorney stopped at the house. He was a kindly man with a white mustache. He explained what we could expect. He asked me to leave the room so he could confer with my son.

*My son's court-appointed attorney suggested I leave the room so they could confer.* Where is this sentence in all the baby books I read? In all the articles I consumed about autism? Nowhere. This sentence is nowhere.

That morning, my feet pounded on the treadmill as I tried to get rid of my rising anxiety and panic. A few hours later, we sat at separate tables with our separate attorneys. Joe leaned his shoulder against mine. I think we were too afraid to look at one another, for fear we might dissolve.

At one point, our attorney stood up from his seat. In his hand he held the very paperwork I filled out—the boxes I checked and the words I wrote, trying to paint a picture of my son and his autism. Standing before the judge, he read my words all out loud. Every challenge, every vulnerability, every worry was spoken into the air around us. Jack's naivete, his challenges, his everlasting fight to succeed.

*Must be supervised when cooking.*

*Gives personal information to strangers.*

*Has difficulty understanding money.*

From across the room, I watched Jack's face change. He looked at me in surprise. My stomach sank.

In an attempt to safeguard his health care, his finances, his general well-being, we forgot to safeguard his most tender heart.

For the rest of my life, I'll never fully understand what that did to him.

Caregiver.

Motherhood.

Caregiver.

Motherhood.

The silky petals twirl beneath my fingertips.

So often, I just want to be the mother. I wanted to hug my son before he stepped onto the bus each morning. I wanted to watch his academic journey from the sidelines as a supportive bystander. Caregiving eclipsed all of that. His needs outweighed my maternal intentions.

Instead, I had to make sure he was regulated enough to even ride the bus. I had to rifle through his backpack after school for notes about his behavior that day. I had to sit with him in the afternoon and painstakingly get him through homework.

A reader once left a comment on my website, urging me to let my son grow up and become a functioning adult. She suggested I was a Helicopter Mom who did everything for him so he would always need me.

I am not a Helicopter Mom. I am a Forever Mother.

A Forever Mother is a caregiver who will spend the rest of her life taking care of her child's day-to-day needs. We arrange appointments, oversee medical care, and manage bank accounts long into adulthood. This is not by choice. Autism made the choices for us.

It can be hard to explain. So we don't. We don't say the words that sit firmly upon our psyche, like elephants in an elevator: *guardianship, group homes, family court.* We don't admit we are stuck on a roller coaster of highs and lows, hope and grief. We don't admit how much we think about what will happen when we die.

When I saw the comment, I just wanted to keep scrolling and forget about it. After all, I don't need to change anyone's mind. I don't care what people think.

Yet at the same time, I do.

This is the push-pull of autism advocacy. As much as I don't want to, I have to reach my fingers toward the red-hot flame of misconception.

I have to care because someone might stand in line behind my son at the movie theater and think he's dumb when he takes a while to order his popcorn.

I have to care because the manager of a restaurant might overlook his application for a dishwasher because he doesn't drive.

I have to tell our story. It's the only way to make space for him in the world.

Some days I feel like I'm screaming into the wind.

Caregiver.

Motherhood.

If I hold on too tightly, the blossoms turn to dust in my palms. Yet a single gust could blow them all away.

I once chatted with another mother in the grocery store. The conversation turned to college. She insisted her kids would only apply to Ivy League schools. Listening to her talk, I felt a surge of rage so strong, I had to turn away.

At nineteen, Jack is in what you'd call a program. It has staff from 7:00 in the morning until 11:00 at night. He works with an academic team and a social pragmatics coach and an expert in life skills. It is perhaps the very opposite of Ivy League.

There are days I feel like I am on the phone for hours. With the doctor to talk about changes in medication. With a therapist trying to make room in his schedule, or his neurologist to figure out new behavior.

Once I started having kids, I knew I would always be a mother in one way or another. After all, motherhood doesn't stop once your children move out of the house, or get married, or have children of their own.

When my kids became adults, I thought I might need to give gentle advice about marital woes or offer to babysit for the weekend.

And I'd chase the wobbly toddler or rock the sleepy baby and think back to the days when I was tired and unsure.

I am tired.

I am unsure.

Jack is nineteen now. He doesn't live here anymore. He's been in his residential space for over a year. Yet it's not as though he shed his trifecta diagnosis of autism, severe anxiety, and obsessive-compulsive disorder the way a caterpillar sheds a cocoon. He packed it all up and moved it with him. To some extent, I still manage it. I simply do it from hundreds of miles away.

I don't want to do this forever. This is hard to admit because it's shameful and embarrassing. Yet it is my truth.

From the time he was a toddler, Jack has used my nervous system to regulate his own. It is an enormous amount of pressure to remain calm when I'm around him.

It took his leaving to help me understand just how much pressure I was under regularly. I realize now that I was always guarding my own emotional state—worried perhaps I was talking too fast or gesturing too much, and it would send him into a spiral.

It was exhausting.

As many of us experience with a diagnosed child, there is a real fear in passing the baton, so to speak. Will people care for our kids the way we do? Will they keep him safe? Will they understand his movements, his speech patterns, his fondness for Disney movies and popcorn?

Dropping him off at his program was perhaps one of the hardest things I've ever done. It was a warm day in the middle of July. Our feet danced around the puddles from an early morning rainstorm. As a lemon yellow sun climbed overhead, the seven of us unpacked the car. We carried in all that was important to this boy. His new comforter, carefully chosen at Bed Bath & Beyond. A duffel bag full of shorts and T-shirts. I made his bed, like I've done thousands of times before. We folded the new towels. We slid his new shirts into the drawer.

There was a barbecue lunch. We met the people who will take this autism journey from here—the torch-takers of life skills and academic support and dorm life.

At some point, he walked one way. And we walked the other. Leading up to that day, people asked me if I was ready. The truth is, a mother is never ready. But it was time. Readiness and time rarely share the same clock. With all my heart, I want him to fly.

I don't want him to need me.

*For Mom. I am a good cook.*

The flowers are vibrant in color. I can only hope the roots are strong.

# 9
# Education

## KATE

"I feel like a fraud."

That's how I start every presentation I give to school districts these days. I always start the same way because I want the audience, whether it be special education teachers, general education teachers, or support staff, to know that I don't necessarily have the answers. Heck, I don't even know the questions half the time. But I am more than willing to have the discussion openly and vulnerably so we can each learn the unique challenges that the other side of the table faces when it comes to serving kids like my son.

"Hi, my name is Kate and I have four children. They are thirteen, eleven, five, and two. My oldest has a diagnosis of severe, nonverbal, level 3 autism. His name is Cooper and I feel like a fraud because I have no idea where my son fits into the world of education. And I'm scared to say it might be nowhere."

I know teaching special education is not for everyone and I'm sure it often feels thankless. I can say with certainty that I am beyond thankful for the people who CHOOSE to teach the kids like mine. I polled a group of special education teachers once and asked them what the hardest part was. I expected to hear about challenging kids or even more challenging parents. I was wrong. The most common answer was teachers feeling unsupported and ultimately unable to help their students. I think about the other side of the table a lot as we continue to navigate education for Cooper not knowing what the future holds.

I've always felt like having a child in special education is like playing a game with ever-changing rules. But it's a game of hearts too. And that's the part that breaks us as parents.

I read a comment once that said, "It's always about the special needs kids. You parents are always whining for them to get everything."

It was in response to a post I had made about how children with disabilities were forgotten during the COVID quarantine. A bold statement, yes, but also true. I called them the forgotten children.

The comment was made by a lady who looked to be the same age as me. She had kids; I could tell from her Facebook profile. She went on to say, in a not-so-nice way that I won't share here, that the kids like my son get everything handed to them.

I think about her comments often and how much misinformation there is about special education. But the reality is, unless you have experienced it, you probably would have no idea.

*There was none of this autism stuff back when I was in school.*

I hear some version of that statement often. It typically comes from someone older than me, and most often, not from a cruel place. More of a place of wonder. I gently tell them that there were kids with disabilities, there were Coopers and Jacks and Amoses; they were just hidden away.

It wasn't until 1975 that the United States Congress passed the Individuals with Disabilities Education Act, referred to as IDEA, which organized the right of all American children to a free and appropriate public education regardless of disability status.

I'm in my forties, and when I was in high school, kids with disabilities were kept behind closed doors. Yes, sometimes they'd be seen walking in the hallways or sitting in special seats at the school assembly, but that was about the extent of it.

Before Cooper, I had always thought of special education as a place you go. A set of rooms in a different wing of the school. But after reading an article by Elizabeth Terry on the Teach for America website, I've come to realize that's not true at all. Special education is not a place. Instead, special education makes up all the services and supports that my son needs to be successful in a school setting. And they are based on his individual needs.

The truth is, parents like me, we're not fighting for the Cadillac or to have the red carpet rolled out in terms of education. We are fighting for basic rights for our kids. A school to welcome them. An aide to help them. A bus to take them. The right to walk in the halls and eat in the cafeteria and for their photo to be in the yearbook so their peers don't wonder who they are at the end of the year.

These are rights that most parents take for granted. And I say that with certainty because I know. I have three other children who do not need special education services. There has never been a question as to whether they would or wouldn't be educated at our school of choice or be at our neighborhood school.

It takes incredible bravery and determination to have a child in special education. Because it often feels as if we were dropped into a building...one with posters of clubs and sports on the wall that my son will never be a part of, as if we were finally invited to the party but not allowed to dance. More than once, I've felt like an imposter as I walked the halls wondering if anyone even knows my son's name.

Cooper is thirteen years old and an eighth grader in a self-contained autism classroom with four other peers. The road to get where we are now has been exhausting. A constant tension. A push-pull. Beauty. Worry. Hope. Fear. Gratitude. Frustration. All intertwined together. It's as simple and as complicated as that.

I lie awake at night and wonder, how do we fit this square peg into a round hole? And daily, I wait for the phone to ring. My worry never stops, not for a second, when he is away from me.

The bravest act I have ever had to do is send my most precious, vulnerable thing into the world and trust it will treat him well and deliver him back to me in one piece.

Parents like me are often labeled as difficult, even angry. I wouldn't say that about myself, but I will say, I've been fighting for so long, for so little, that I don't know how not to anymore. Navigating the educational system with Cooper has changed me in so many ways.

A while back, while virtually attending one of Cooper's IEP meetings, a team of folks told us that he was too challenging for their school. The use of the word *their* stuck out to me. There were nearly a dozen faces on the screen plus

Jamie and me. Let that sink in… It took that many people to determine if my son could enter the doors of the building.

The presenter pulled up the agenda, the first item reading, "Positive things about the student." They needed an agenda item to remind themselves to say something positive about my son.

I felt as if the staff at the school didn't like him. They weren't even pretending anymore. The fear of him being kicked out and "what next" was keeping me up at night. Our phone had been ringing every day for weeks to pick him up early. A sigh of relief was breathed as they handed him over to us.

As they listed his challenges one by one, citing data and percentages and charts and graphs, it was hard for me to picture my son's face. I didn't know the boy they were describing.

I know he can be challenging. If pushed too far he can be aggressive, although at home we haven't seen any aggression in years. I know he can be silly. Over-the-top. Too much. Exasperating, even. But I also know that he absolutely adores school and if his IEP and behavior plan are followed he has good days. He even has two best friends. He adores hugs and waving to kids in the hallway. He is ready twenty minutes every morning before the bus arrives. He is smart, worthy, and deserving of an education.

The biggest issue with special education today is that because of the funding and rules and regulations, the education system seems to forget that they are children, not data. And that I am a mother. We are just people.

The words they used were void of his light and his potential. I often say his autism is woven through him and there is no separating it out. It's his color. It's where the light hits. But on paper it's not colorful. It's black-and-white. It's level 3 severe. He was reduced to a twenty-four-page document until there was no Cooper left.

One of the faces said some things that they should never have said. They were bad. The words she said, the way she described him…psychologically damaging to the other students and staff…and that I should take into consideration that others don't want to be there because of him…and I should put the other students and staff before my own son…

That's when the director cut her off. The faces of everyone around the table in shock, their mouths hanging open. The screen went blank. The Zoom ended. Just like that. No more words to be said.

The phone rang immediately. "Kate, I am so sorry. She should have never described Cooper like that."

I looked down at the report in front of me, the graph of his most recent behaviors staring up at me. But instead of seeing the black and white, I saw my son toddling into his first day of preschool, his backpack bigger than him. The first time he said *school*. And *bus*. And I wondered, how did we get here? Right here. This very moment.

As she spoke of a new placement and keeping him home in the interim, I found myself thinking, *What am I fighting for here?*

Am I fighting for him to go to school? To simply be in the building? Am I fighting for him to be included? Accepted? Invited? Am I fighting for him to learn? To be taught? To be babysat? Am I fighting for people to like him? Because it's hard for me to believe that he is that terrible.

Another realization: I wasn't winning the fight. I was just a mom. The entity of public education is too big. And I don't think I have the longevity to keep fighting like this.

That was the IEP meeting that broke me. But you know what? From broken comes a new beginning. A fresh start. A new school. A new teacher. A new possibility. A story to share with special educators that hopefully starts a conversation of how we can best serve these kids.

When I get a captive audience of teachers, I tell them exactly what I want them to know. I fill in the cracks with stories that make them laugh and cry. I bring my boy and our struggles and joy to life right in front of them. I don't tell his story with data; I tell it with light.

I tell them the time I was pulled aside by a teacher who told me that Cooper brought photos of me to school…interesting photos, she said. She blushed as she handed me a stack. Me as a naughty nurse on Halloween. Another of me taking a beer bong out of a plastic flamingo named Petey. And lastly, me birthing my second son. I learned to always check the backpack.

I tell them that he is loved and treasured. Back before I had a complicated child, I had a lot of assumptions about children and parenting. For one, I assumed that the bad kids just came from bad homes. I probably even blamed the parents. I was unbelievably wrong. I have a hard kid and the reason is autism; it's not bad parenting or lack of love.

I share with them the unique kind of grief that comes along with being the parent of a child with special needs. For me, the grief comes in waves, sometimes threatening to overtake me while at other times ebbing and allowing me the chance to breathe. School exacerbates the grief for me. It is a reminder of what could be and what isn't. I ask teachers to remember that they don't know where a parent is in that grief cycle on any given day. And a "how are YOU doing, mom or dad?" goes a long way.

I ask them to presume competence. Presumed competence is a strengths-based approach that assumes people with autism have abilities to learn, think, and understand. It's very hard to measure what Cooper knows, but I am certain it's more than we give him credit for.

I beg them to speak kindly around him and other kids with disabilities. Cooper hears everything that is said around him. I went on a field trip a while back with Cooper's class, and I was shocked at the discussions that were happening around the kids. People often assume a nonverbal or minimally verbal person, isn't listening. That is untrue. They hear everything.

I hit heavily on the vulnerability factor. If he is feared or not liked by those who need to protect him, he is susceptible to abuse, whether verbal or physical. Kids like my son are incredibly vulnerable to abuse of all kinds and it can happen anywhere and everywhere. So much so that I check his body daily for bumps, bruises, scratches, and marks. We have for thirteen years, and I assume we will forever.

I tell them that I never stop worrying, not ever. Every school day I wait for the phone to ring, still, even though we are in a good place. My anxiety never rests when he is away from me.

I remind them that the words they say matter. And how they say them too. Something they have said, good or bad, will run through a parent's mind forever.

"Cooper is fantastic, Kate. You need to know that."

I was at my son's fourth-grade conference and listened to his teacher, my mouth hanging open, as she went on to say wonderful things about him for what felt like an eternity. Until I finally looked at her and said, "Cut the crap. Give it to me straight." We both burst out laughing at my boldness.

"He's amazing, Kate. I could tell you every bad thing that happens in his day, but it's not needed. I'm only going to tell you the good news until I need to share something else with you."

She was one of the first people to ever say something nice about Cooper in terms of education. I will never forget her and how she healed parts of me that I didn't know were broken.

And finally, happiness above all. Of course, Cooper's education is important to me. But his happiness is something

I will not negotiate on. I know there is a lot of pressure on teachers to set goals and move our kids toward mastering them. And I am thankful for that. But his happiness is imperative.

I know my audiences often assume I am against public education. That is false. I am hopeful and thankful for every person who chooses to work with kids like my son and the schools who welcome our kids. Cooper has so many gifts to offer educators and peers. I know the challenges can be high, but I hope the reward is higher.

There is no textbook on educating autism. There is just a child. And love, hope, and determination. There is refusing to put them in a box. There is believing in them. Pushing and encouraging and motivating and meeting them where they are at.

"You are not a fraud. You are a mother who loves her son. Never stop fighting for him, Kate."

## ADRIAN

*The most important thing you can do for him is to be PTA president.*

—Geneticist, Columbia University Hospital

Education is my mojo.

If anyone was prepared to navigate the special education world, it was me. Quite by accident, though I don't really believe in accidents. I also underestimated the importance of love as it relates to education.

I majored in child development at Meredith College and went on to UNC–CH for a master's in education. The yearlong intensive program would train me as an early interventionist—a professional who worked with families and their children who had disabilities from birth to age three. I stayed an additional semester to focus on inclusion—the concept of educating children with disabilities amongst their typically developing peers. The year was 1997 and it had only been seven years since the Individuals with Disabilities Education Act (IDEA) had been revised to "ensure that children with disabilities be granted a free appropriate public education (FAPE) in the least restrictive environment (LRE)." In layman's language—children with disabilities have a constitutional right to be educated amongst their typical peers, even if it means they need an aide to do so.

Nearly thirty years later, IDEA is still a bone of contention between families and school districts. The concept of an aide is an expensive one and school districts shoulder the costs because the federal government still has never fully funded the original law of 1975. Though the terms of IDEA stated that the federal government would pay 40 percent of the average per pupil expenditure for special education, that pledge has never been met, and in 2023, current funding was at less than 13 percent. While a graduate student at UNC, I worked at Frank Porter Graham Child Development Institute (FPG) as a research assistant and focused on research related to education for children with and without disabilities and access to high-quality childcare for families.

Upon graduation, I was accepted to a PhD program at NC State and earned a full scholarship where I would complete the requirements for a doctorate in Educational Research and Policy Analysis with a specialty in Curriculum and Instruction. After graduation, I continued to work for FPG as a researcher, and when our first child was born, I became a full-time mother. There you have it—I strolled off into the sunset to raise children and someday I planned to reappear, maybe teach at the local community college or pick up another research project. I couldn't have known that my fourth child would demand every bit of my education, knowledge, schooling, and even then, navigating the education system for Amos has been the hardest thing I've ever done.

Mothering is easy compared to configuring public education for a child it wasn't intended to serve. It has been a challenge that no formal education could suffice. No amount of tutorials would have prepared me for the transition to public school. Up until that point, Amos had been receiving services at home and participating in a pediatric therapy program at our community hospital. I now found myself talking to professionals at a long table in what felt like a clinical setting. A setting that was not unfamiliar to me as a past professional. However, I had no idea what it was like to be THE parent sitting across from the professional at an IEP meeting. It must be a terrible dream, I thought the first time I took my place at the unfamiliar side of the table. The words *SPECIAL EDUCATION REFERRAL* were typed neatly across the top of the paper tucked in an envelope that had landed in my mailbox. I'd spent so much time studying disabilities in education, and here I was, in a room amongst school officials there to decide what was best for my child and to review this new stage in life—his first entrance to school. Most administrators are blissfully ignorant of the power of the seemingly harmless words *special education referral*. I don't blame them. I was, too, before Amos.

*I don't want to be here.*

*I don't want to sit in a meeting.*

*I don't want to read about the many things listed as part of this unfamiliar referral.*

I was not alone though. Amos's teacher was there, and if not for her, I may have run from the room. *She knows and she understands*, I thought. Not because she was a teacher, but because her own son had special needs. When she told me that my son reminded her of her own, it was the ultimate compliment and balm for my hurting heart.

I had been so eager for my other children to begin preschool. Each of them attended a half-day program at a nearby church after their third birthday. They were fully potty trained, and it was an idyllic entry into the world of school. When Amos was not yet three years old, we met with public school administrators and discussed service plans for Amos and his entry to public school. As outlined in state policy, early intervention is provided birth through age two and therapies and services are provided through the school system once the child turns three years old. On his third birthday, he would begin attending school for three full days a week. Unlike the entry into school I recollected with his older siblings, Amos's first experience with school would involve driving and school buses, rather than quaint walks and lunch at home. I would not have chosen this path of education for my youngest child, but I knew it was important. After all, he needed more than could be provided by our neighborhood preschool.

I planned to take him to school later in the mornings and have him ride the bus home with his brothers and sister two days a week. He would travel not on the bus designated for special needs children, but the regular bus. I wanted Amos to have familiar faces on his bus and for his siblings to be proud of this responsibility. He would go on Monday, Wednesday, and Friday, a different schedule than most, but tailored to meet our family's needs.

I was grateful for how accommodating our local school system was in meeting not only the needs of Amos, but our whole family and particularly me. I met with the school psychologist over lunch so she could learn more about Amos and his strengths. Do you know that no one had ever asked me about his strengths before? Over a casual lunch of chicken salad and sweet tea, we talked about his strengths and his needs. His play-based assessment was scheduled that same week, and when I darted into the principal's office a couple of days later to ask a PTA question, do you know what his teacher was doing? She was watching a video of a play-based assessment so she would know what to expect on this day. My heart was filled with thankfulness. After that assessment, Amos was officially enrolled in the public school system.

I remember being introduced to Amos's classroom, which was created to serve children ages three to five with disabilities. This time, I wasn't the teacher or research assistant or early interventionist. I was just a mom and not one thing was even less than perfect. It was the same school that my two older sons attended and where my daughter was currently a first grader. The teachers were kind and generous and loving and friendly with their charges. They seemed like better, laid-back versions of myself, and the children were animated and smiling, eager to move from one activity to another.

I remember the day that I left Amos behind the heavy wood-and-glass door with the kind teacher. An administrator stood beside me as I peered through the narrow shaft of glass, tears running down my face.

"It's never easy when you leave them at school for the first time—every mother feels like that," she said. Her effort to comfort me was well intended, though I was not to be placated and my voice wavered and rose slightly.

"It's not the same—not the same thing at all. This is the fourth time I've done this and it's NEVER felt like this. NEVER. It's not normal to drop off little boys in diapers at public school. It's not the same thing at all."

Yes, it nearly killed me.

Why?

It was because Amos was taking me on a journey that I had never considered traveling. Despite the amazing classroom, my own expectations made me catch my breath. I now belonged to a club that I never wanted to join. It was the first of many moments at school that left me thinking I was not up to the challenge.

The well-meaning administrator quickly relented and softened as anyone should when a tearful mother divulges her heart. That first week of school felt very long for me. I had so many kind friends and even strangers asking how Amos was liking school. Many made a point to also ask how I was doing. I was floored by their kindness and smiled and forced myself to be positive, but I was wilting on the inside. *I hate it*, I longed to say. I couldn't bring myself to admit that I was so lonely and wanted nothing more than to have my son at home with me. I wanted to shout that I didn't know if he liked school. He couldn't tell me and I wasn't there to read his expressions or subtle glances of joy or worry or longing for some activity or type of food. I was his mind reader and useless at home.

Today I understand what it's like to sit on both sides of that IEP table. I have learned to be an advocate, and though it's not the role I imagined playing, when you're the parent of a child with a disability, you have little choice. Belonging to Amos means I have to advocate, and my first lesson in advocacy came from the very best—Amos's first teacher.

I had known who Amos's teacher was for years. After all, my big three had been at the same elementary school and you couldn't help but notice her kind face. I observed her calm demeanor and loving nature as she walked the halls with her own group of ducklings, three- and four-year-olds with varying needs. I couldn't have known then that my own son would one day be welcomed into her fold. Even though I thought she was a wonderful teacher, it never occurred to me that she would ever look after my own child. But life has a way of surprising us. I found comfort in knowing his teacher was that Mama Duck I had admired, someone I knew would love him.

Our school district is a small one—we have one elementary, one middle, and one high school. There is no such thing as an AU classroom (class for autistic children) or an "out of district" referral. There are no private schools that can meet his needs like the expensive ones in wealthy areas of North Carolina. I am not the homeschooling type, which was confirmed when I had a taste of schooling Amos during COVID. Never again. Quite simply, we had one option, and so, it had to work.

When we received the diagnosis of autism, the geneticist asked about the education system where we lived. I explained the smallness, the quaintness, the poverty, and what seemed like the limitations in light of its size. She went on to tell me that families are generally happier in small school systems BECAUSE of the limited options. There was no plan B or alternative setting, so administrators would have to make our elementary school work. Being in a small school system would mean that Amos would not be just a number.

Even more helpful than that fact has been my openness and commitment to communicating with staff in an amicable way. I have always tried to give twice as much as I ask for, whether it means rounding up books and Legos for classrooms, offering volunteer hours, or leading fundraising efforts. Still, I was taken aback when the geneticist said to me at Amos's autism diagnosis appointment, "The most important thing you can do for him is be PTA president."

"I already am," I said. And it was true, when my first child started kindergarten, I immediately signed up as a volunteer and strove to build relationships with administrators and teachers so that the school would see me as a partner rather than an outsider.

The first school year was not the one I envisioned for my Amos.

It was much brighter and fuller than I knew possible and far more transforming than I expected. I watched my youngest son become the loveliest of butterflies. He was given a place in a classroom with other children that shared similar struggles and he benefited from being with them and specialized teachers—parts of a life I had wanted nothing to do with. I didn't know that my beautiful boy would grow into such a complex and amazing soul and I am thankful for the nurturing which transformed us both. Though it was not an inclusive classroom, it was the very best option for him. He was so easily overwhelmed and had never been far from me. More important than being with typical peers was his need for one-on-one instruction in a quiet, less demanding environment.

In those early days, his schooling had little to do with "education." He began to walk on his own into the building rather than insist on my carrying him. He discovered music and learned to clap his small, pudgy hands in some semblance of rhythm. Most surprisingly, he practiced sitting in a chair and listening rather than darting about the room aimlessly as he did at home. A few years later, his teachers and I successfully tackled potty training and we happily said goodbye to the diapers that I wondered might always be a part of our story. I remember picking him up one afternoon, and when I spied him stopping at the water fountain, I moved to push the button, and he leaned forward and got himself a drink. Who knew that mastering a new water fountain could make a mama's heart so proud?

Fast-forward seven years and Amos splits his time between a traditional classroom and an exceptional children's classroom. We had him do an extra year of prekindergarten so he could be with his typical peers and learn to play from their modeling. After the pandemic, I felt he was ready for an inclusive model and lobbied for him to start his days in a typical second-grade classroom. The tradition had been to have children with disabilities join their typical peers for specials like music, lunch, or PE. While that may work well for some children, I wanted Amos to be a fixture in a typical classroom where he would start his day and have a cubby labeled with his name, a desk, and even a special area for calming or sensory input when things may be hard. He does his science and math predominantly in that classroom and his reading and writing in the traditional classroom. He takes spelling tests, calls his classmates by name, and even practices reading passages and answering multiple-choice questions. In another week, the boy who couldn't sit in a circle in pre-K will take his first state-mandated exam. Success means he could pass or only answer two questions. It may take three days, but success is tackling the unknown.

Each school year requires emails and texts, thinking and planning. As a parent, I try not to micromanage administrators and still be an advocate. I have learned to make a point to be appreciative rather than cantankerous. It is a fine line and takes practice. Amos is readying to begin his third year of inclusion at our local public elementary school, where he will be a fourth grader. He may not be able to do everything his classmates are doing, but that has nothing to do with his legal right to access the default classroom.

He has flourished in so many ways. He enjoys his peers now. Where he used to ignore their presence, he now asks to be chased and is quick to join a group playing with Legos.

This year, he's learning fractions and doing word problems. He can name and build a dozen shapes, and while he's not quite ready for multiplication, that's okay. And when he gets overwhelmed or tired or is having a hard day, he makes his way back to the exceptional children's classroom, where he works on science and math and reading with a little more assistance.

Will Amos stay on a traditional curriculum path to graduation? More than once I've been thankful for a background in education. Belonging to a child with autism is not for the faint of heart and I expect each and every year will be a challenge. The beginning of each school year is definitely a struggle, and so is going back after most breaks, and I still wonder if Amos likes school. What I don't wonder anymore is if school is the right place for him. When his teacher texted me that she had forgotten to tell me something, I held my breath and read:

"Amos was tested and made a passing benchmark score! He will officially be promoted to fourth grade. I was so proud of him!"

And this is why I am most thankful for love.

## CARRIE

I parked my car and stepped out, pulling my jacket tight against the chilly day. It was March in New Hampshire, yet spring felt far away.

For the third time that week, I walked past all the other cars waiting in line—moms and dads sitting in the driver's seat, talking on the phone or scrolling their news feeds while they waited for school to let out. I kept my head down so no one saw my face. I was embarrassed and ashamed.

In the tiny vestibule, I waited for someone to buzz me through the door. Once inside, I picked up a name tag in the office. I noticed the air felt charged somehow. Up and down the hallway, people were in motion. One teacher had a walkie-talkie and she was speaking into it quickly. I caught the words *clear the room* and *unsafe*. My pulse quickened. Was there a fire? Maybe something in the cafeteria?

It was only after I was ushered down the hallway lined with kids sitting cross-legged on the floor that I realized this was about Jack. This was about my son. From what I could gather, he threw a computer.

I walked into the classroom. He was huddled in the corner with his head in his hands. He looked up at me and I saw he was flushed. Tears ran down his face. I walked slowly toward him, the way you would walk toward a bird who might fly away at any given moment.

*Broken.*

The word rose unbidden in my mind. He looked broken. Slowly, he stood up. "Please. Take me home," he said softly.

This was spring of 2016. Jack was twelve years old and in the sixth grade. Up to that point, school had been mostly manageable. Sure, he was crushed by anxiety in first grade, and there were the long afternoons of trying to get him to finish homework before he ripped the worksheets to shreds in a rage. But the onset of puberty and the changing social landscape of middle school eclipsed all of that. It threw him into a panic like we had never seen.

Individualized Education Plan. Integrated preschool. Full-time paraprofessional.

Before Jack started school, I had never heard these terms in my life. One by one, they made their way onto our radar, beginning with integrated preschool, which is a fancy way of saying both diagnosed and typically developing children attend the same program. The idea is that the typical kids offer peer modeling, and the diagnosed children increase awareness by way of inclusion. Jack began attending this kind of preschool as soon as we established his Individualized Education Plan, or IEP.

A child needs to be three years old to qualify for an IEP. The first time I got ours in the mail, I held the sheaf of papers in my hand and tried to make sense of them. The combination of goals and measurements of success were a mystery to me—as though they were written in a foreign language. All these years later, I still struggle to decipher them, to be honest.

When he started kindergarten, Jack's team decided he needed a full-time paraprofessional, or para, as they're often called. I've also heard them referred to as an aide. Essentially, it is another adult who is assigned to accompany your child throughout the day and assist with tasks such as transitioning between therapies, managing breaks for regulation, and staying on task in the classroom. Sometimes a para is assigned to a few kids, but Jack always had what's called a 1:1, which means that person spent the entire day just with him.

Now, as we started to consider how to help him through the rest of sixth grade, a new phrase began to circle our conversations: *out-of-district referral.*

An out-of-district referral is for students whose academic needs aren't being met by their local schools. The district pays for an outside school that offers the type of help and setting your child needs. It could be a public school, a private day school, or a residential school where your child would live full-time.

Joe and I desperately wanted to keep Jack in our district. For starters, most programs were over an hour away, and we didn't want him on a bus for that long every day. But mostly, I had this image of all five of my kids crossing the same stage at the end of senior year and accepting a diploma from our kindly superintendent. Now it seemed like even the diploma was out of reach.

Three months and one disastrous field trip later, we met with his team at the beginning of June. Seated around an oval table, his teachers and therapists took turns talking about the challenges he continued to face in the classroom. They detailed his deregulation, the occasional threat he posed to other kids. Listening to them felt like an out-of-body experience.

By the end of the meeting, we all agreed the out-of-district referral was the logical next step for seventh grade. Public school wasn't working for him anymore. This was an all-time low for me.

My son couldn't make it in public school. Again and again, this reality hit me. I mean, public school is supposed to be for *everyone*. The kids who pick their nose, the kids who bite, the kids who are prodigies, and even child stars. Everyone gets a chance to go to public school.

As parents, we're inclined to tie our own moral compass to our children's behaviors and appearance. If our child is overweight, we feel judged for buying too much junk food. If our daughter gets pregnant in high school, it's because we didn't emphasize good values. And if our son can't make it through a day of sixth grade without swearing at a teacher, well, we question ourselves. Where did we go wrong?

The truth is, by the time Jack came home from school most afternoons, I was armed and ready. Many days, I'd already gotten a call from his teacher or case manager. He threw a book. He bit the recess monitor. He punched a wall.

As soon as he walked in the door—or sat in the car, if I

had to get him—I unleashed. *We don't throw things at school! We don't bite or kick. We know better, don't we?*

We, we, we. It was as though he was acting out on my behalf. After my stern lecture, I'd start threatening everything that was important to him—*Scooby-Doo* after dinner with his siblings, or the movie we had planned for the weekend.

The problem with this method is it doesn't work. You can't punish a child at 4:00 in the afternoon for something they did before lunchtime. You can't create a teaching moment after dinner if your child couldn't sit for circle time in the morning. Oh, we tried it! We took away his beloved television at night. Many afternoons, I admonished him all the way home for his behavior. Thinking about it now makes me sick to my stomach.

Kids like Jack can only match the highest nervous system in the room. Once elevated, he is incapable of regulating on his own. Essentially, he was moving from one stressful place to another—from school to home—without a chance to recalibrate. It wasn't working. He didn't connect the dots. When he got elevated in school, he didn't remember the quiet night before without television and attempt to behave.

After a few months in this cycle of shame and blame, I knew we had to try a different tactic. This was a regulation issue, not behavioral. We had to figure out the *why*—the trigger or reason—behind the *what*. In this instance, the behavior was our *what*—kicking, lashing out, swearing.

The terms *tantrum* and *meltdown* are often used interchangeably. Yet I learned there is a distinct difference between the two. A tantrum has a goal: more cookies, another movie, a later bedtime. A meltdown, on the other hand, is a response to the environment; the lights are too bright, the music is too loud, the socks are too scratchy.

Once you distinguish between them, you can handle them

differently. If you sense your child is attempting to gain something, you renegotiate the goal according to behavior. One cookie, or ten more minutes of television. If it's a meltdown, try removing the stimulus—lower the lights, take the socks off, turn down the music.

This was a critical piece of information for me when it came to Jack's recent behavior at school. How would I categorize his outbursts? Did he have a goal in mind? Did he want to get out of work or come home early? Not really. He wanted to stay with the other kids and finish the day. So, it had to be a reaction to the environment.

As anyone who has ever stepped inside a school during the day knows, it's loud in there. The hallways are buzzing between periods. The cafeteria is noisy. The gym is full of kids bouncing balls off the floor and the backboard. On top of that, you can smell the food being prepared for lunch. I often think of gravy.

Once I considered all the ways in which Jack's five senses were immediately engaged the moment he stepped foot inside the school, I could better understand why he remained so deregulated throughout the day. And while we couldn't exactly remove all the stimuli, it gave us the chance to consider building more sensory breaks into his day—a quiet space in the counselor's office, or a chance to walk down the hallways alone.

Every day after school that terrible year, Jack would walk in the door, throw his red backpack on the floor, and go straight upstairs. Fully clothed, he'd climb into my bathtub and huddle there. He never turned the water on—he simply closed his eyes and cocooned inside the porcelain.

The first few times he did this, I felt uneasy. What was this new routine? After a week or so, I realized he was working on regulating himself. He needed a small space to feel emotionally safe. I decided to take my cues from him.

During the day I bought special treats at the grocery store—avocados, a certain kind of pretzels he liked, Parmesan cheese for spaghetti. In the morning, I smoothed his crumpled sheets and made his bed just the way he liked it, with the pillows stacked neatly and his beloved stuffed bunny nestled amongst them. We started lighting candles at dinnertime to help everyone relax at the table.

Schedule became important. I tried not to surprise him with last-minute appointments or errands. I wanted him to relax into our family's routine as much as possible. I thought after the unpredictability that was school at that time, the least we could do was keep a consistent rhythm at home. Dinner, television, shower, bed. Weekends were for breathing, not rehashing all that went wrong at school.

It seems trivial, to make sure dinner is on the table around the same time, and that we follow a regular bedtime routine. It's hard to imagine a neatly made bed could shore the rising tide of autism's rage and chaos. And yet it did. It provided a framework into which Jack could relax and recharge. Nothing resolved overnight. But after a few weeks, I sensed an ease in him—in all of us.

That fall, Jack started seventh grade at Vista, a much smaller school in a nearby town. Our hearts were broken, but deep down we knew it was the right choice. In this program, he was in a classroom of eight to ten kids, with a high ratio of teachers to students.

Over the next five years, we considered moving him back to public high school, but he was successful at Vista—gaining ground academically and learning to navigate his smaller peer group. His undesirable behaviors lessened, and he began to thrive. When he was in tenth grade, we started to consider the possibility of a high school diploma.

In the state of New Hampshire, there are a set of education rules that state the baseline requirements to graduate high school. Local school boards then have control to add or remove additional requirements. Our district has two diploma tracks: twenty credits or twenty-four credits. They both legally hold the same weight. Students who are unable to complete either track receive a certificate of attendance.

Foreign language and algebra are a state requirement; however, Vista waived the foreign language part for their students. Jack was required to complete algebra and, with the support of Vista's academic team, did so in his senior year.

And so, in the spring of 2022, Jack stood in the kitchen and pulled a red gown over his dress shirt and tie. He proudly placed the matching cap on his head. He turned to me and smiled. We were a long way from the sixth-grade classroom. Finally, what was once broken had healed. In life alongside autism, the moment where you stand will not last forever.

Yet Jack's academic journey didn't stop there.

I've said many times that since the day Jack was born, I longed for a crystal ball to see his future. I tried to figure out what third grade, middle school, even puberty might look like. But I never once imagined what he might do after high school.

The day we dropped my oldest son off at college in Philadelphia, I watched Jack carefully examine the dorm room. Slowly, he began to trace the windowsill and the desk with his fingertips. It's as though I could see the wheels turning in his mind. He was imagining a place like this for himself.

We returned home on a Sunday, and the following morning I sat at my desk and began researching programs for neurodiverse students. Time and time again, I was reminded of the limited spots all over the country. In the end, there were four programs that were a good fit. Four programs between tentative steps toward independence and a life here in his childhood home.

We filled out forms. We submitted paperwork detailing his medication, his diagnosis, and our guardianship arrangement. Then we waited. Every day Jack would check the mailbox. Every day I checked email. Slowly, as the snow began to melt, we had three rejections, explaining Jack wasn't a good fit or it wasn't the right time. I could barely bring myself to tell him.

"When is the right time?" he asked. My heart sank.

Then one day, a letter came in the mail. Jack walked in the door, holding it jubilantly in his hands.

"Mom. It says yes."

In all honesty, this was the program we most hoped would work out for him. Less than three hours away, it is a fully scaffolded residential space. There is staff there from 7:00 in the morning until 11:00 at night. He has a life-skills coach, a social and emotional coach, and an academic team.

There are forty-four students in this program, all neurodiverse. He has a suite with three other kids, and they share a bathroom and a small kitchen. There is also a community dining space with tables and areas for board games and puzzles. Kids are encouraged to connect and build relationships.

The first semester, Jack took three classes at a nearby college. With the help of his academic team, he went to the Office of Disability and asked for accommodations—something we didn't realize you could request at the college level. And although there were some speed bumps socially, overall he adjusted to the demands of his new school setting.

Dropping Jack off for the first time was perhaps the hardest thing I've ever done. Over and over, people asked me if I was ready. The truth is, a mother is never ready to alter the familial landscape upon which she has built her life.

Yet I knew it was time. The right time.

# 10

# What Kind of Autism Is It?

## KATE

We don't blend in, Cooper and I. Not that we ever did, but I'll admit when he was smaller it was easier. We got by with the grace strangers bestow on energetic toddlers and precocious kindergartners. But thirteen. Well, thirteen is a whole different story.

Thirteen is five feet, four inches tall. Thirteen is a men's size ten shoe. Thirteen can be mistaken for a man. Except, cognitively, he's not thirteen because he has autism. The kind that seems to freeze certain points of his development. The kind I didn't know existed before I belonged to him.

The weight of his autism isn't always visible at times. I know that because most days I help him carry it. With armor on, I pave the way, while softening his edges to the world. Our whole family does, really.

Cooper has what's known as an invisible disability. Meaning he has a condition that can't be seen by the naked eye. It can be confusing for people and leaves me wondering if we need to look a certain way in order to get grace in this world.

In simple terms, an invisible disability is a condition that is not visible from the outside, yet can limit or challenge a person. Autism is a perfect example. Unfortunately, the very fact that the symptoms are invisible can lead to misunderstandings, false perceptions, and judgments.

We've all been there. You see someone pull their vehicle into a handicapped spot, get out, and walk into the store. You look and can't find the disability. Your first reaction is most likely to judge. Our family knows this judgment well.

I have a friend with a son very similar to Cooper and she told me that because he gets fatigued easily on walks and can refuse to move, they often use a wheelchair when out in the community, even though he is capable of walking. She said people are much kinder when he appears disabled. It's a bizarre concept to grasp. As a parent, I don't want my son to appear disabled, but if he did, would his disability be more accepted?

Cooper looks like every other thirteen-year-old boy, except he's not. He can't wait patiently in line. He can't sit quietly at a table. He needs constant supervision. He can't cross a street alone and he can't say his name when asked. And social norms, those are not a concept he grasps.

Last summer there was a miscommunication of who was watching Cooper while we were staying at a very crowded campground. I wasn't there at the time, but Jamie said his stomach dropped when he realized Cooper was gone. He knew to check the water first. Drowning is the leading cause of death for children with autism. As he ran, he said he heard a stern voice saying *"What are you doing on my boat?"* before he saw Cooper sitting on a pontoon, oblivious, a man standing over him, confused and frustrated.

It makes sense. I get it. The man saw a teenage boy trespassing on his boat and demanded an answer as to why. Jamie said as he explained autism and Cooper, the man's angry demeanor softened, and he began to see what was in front of him the whole time: a boy, head down, swaying to the music from a cartoon playing on his blue Kindle, his hands dancing in the sunlight, laughter escaping his belly.

Cooper's disability is invisible until it's not.

I don't think about autism on a daily basis. In fact, I may not even say the word for periods of time. This is just our life, and we don't know any different.

The truth is, though, Cooper has the kind of autism that no one talks about. The kind that can't successfully fly on planes or go to restaurants. The kind that needs lifelong care and can make people nervous sometimes. You won't see it on one of the trendy prime-time TV shows like *The Good Doctor* or *Love on the Spectrum*. He isn't the poster child picked for autism awareness month and he isn't a savant who can count cards to bankrupt a casino. His autism is not a superpower either, and while I have focused on sharing the beauty in living a different life, it's important for me to share the realities too. Because if I don't, if we hide or if we pretend, or just look to Hollywood, I am doing a disservice to individuals like him.

Cooper has level 3, severe autism. In 2023, the Centers for Disease Control and Prevention (CDC) reported 26.7 percent of people with autism spectrum disorder have severe or profound autism. That percentage shocked me. I had no idea it was that high.

There are three levels of autism when it's diagnosed. Level 1 describes people considered more independent with lower support needs or high functioning, and level 3 describes autistic people living with intense traits and high support needs with labels like severe, profound, or low functioning. Level 2 is somewhere in between.

If you peel back the many layers of the autism community, the topic of profound autism is polarizing. I've been told countless times online that it doesn't exist. And yet we are here, existing, practically screaming for our place on the spectrum.

The reality is severe autism is challenging, life-changing, and lifelong. I'm often asked what is the hardest part. People assume aggression or lack of sleep. But it's more than that for me. Nothing is easy in our world. Not one hour, one day, or one week. We have learned to manage it, but when asked what I long for, it's ease. A day of ease.

When Cooper was diagnosed, I convinced myself he was high functioning. I told myself he would be quirky, not disabled. I wrapped the term *high-functioning autism* around Cooper and myself like an invisible cloak protecting us from the realities of the other end of the spectrum.

I convinced myself that this would all eventually be fine. It would work itself out. Once we got all the resources, supports, and services in place, it would be easier. We all know beginnings are hard, but kids grow up and they need you less. They learn to help themselves. They develop hobbies, make friends, and learn independence. They eventually move out and start their own lives.

Of course, Cooper would always be autistic, but I assumed even though his trajectory was different, he would eventually catch up. Even if it was slow, he would still get better. Because life can't be hard forever.

In a way we are frozen in time. He and I. Mother and son. Everyone around us seems to move on and we stay in the same place.

When your baby is born, every other baby the same age is their peer. Until they're not because your baby is different. Then your child is diagnosed, and their peer group becomes this smaller subset of kids. Kids with autism. It takes time, but you get comfortable. You find your place once again.

But then the kids with autism seem to get better. They start talking and they are able to integrate into classrooms with their neurotypical peers. They can go into the community and do all the things you wished for your own son. And suddenly, their peer group shrinks again. You are the 26 percent. And you find yourself jealous once again of other kids. Only this time, it's other kids with autism.

And at your lowest point, you'll wonder why some kids get to improve. Why do some get to talk. Why do some seem to get better. And why didn't your son.

I don't know one other individual like Cooper, even in the autism community. I find myself at events created for families like mine and look around and wonder why I have the only child lying on the ground kicking and screaming.

It took me many years to learn that the 26.7 percent are out there—they are just in their homes, too afraid to go into the community for fear of danger or judgment. This is one of the main reasons I share. Because we are here. Hiding in plain sight.

And for every boy or girl with autism who runs on the high school track team or gets to be on the homecoming court, there are boys and girls with autism like my son who hurt themselves or other people. Who pick at their skin or spit or scream. I never want to diminish any person's challenges, wherever they are on the spectrum, and that isn't what this is about. But this is the autism that no one wants to see or even hear about.

At age thirteen, I dropped my cloak and am doing everything I can to embrace the severities of my son's autism while advocating for him and his future.

When I speak to crowds of people today, I describe Cooper as the most flamboyantly autistic person you will ever meet. There is no hiding it, not that we ever would. But I could call him high functioning, quirky, moderate, it doesn't matter. Cooper is Cooper. Diagnosis or not. He has profound autism. And he is happy. I can say that confidently. My son is happy being himself.

*What kind of autism does he have?*

I get that question a lot lately. It typically comes from someone new to my life. A fellow sports parent or a grandparent at the park.

When I tell people I have four kids, ages three to thirteen, people ask questions.

Where do they go to school and what sports do they play. How is sleep going and managing technology.

I tell them about each of my kids, with pride and love and humor. I share stories like all moms. The stories are what connect us.

I share about toddlers who don't sleep and five-year-olds who push the limits. Tips to get grass stains out of white baseball pants. The challenges of raising these tiny humans. And my yellow-haired boy who has autism.

*What kind of autism does he have?*

The question comes from a curious place, typically. A kind one too. And sometimes I will hear hope in a person's question. Hoping it's the "good" kind. I think for so long our society has painted severe nonverbal autism with a dark color. A stain, even.

Describing Cooper's autism has always felt like a contradiction to me. I want people to know his challenges, but I don't want him to be limited. I want the world to know how hard it is at times, but I don't want pity. I want accommodation for his needs, but I also want acceptance for who he is.

But the real challenge is convincing people that he is more than just a diagnosis. He is a boy first.

Today he was so excited to go to school because it was his turn to pick out the afternoon movie. He picked *Cars*.

Next week he has his first school dance, and he is going with his personal care attendant. I ordered him a tuxedo T-shirt. He has two best friends that I thank God for every single day.

He can spell and read some and tell time. He wants to take the Amtrak train to California to see the whales.

He adores birthday parties. He can say twenty-five or so words. He uses sign language and a speech device and has no trouble getting his point across. He tattles nonverbally on his siblings daily. He has the best laugh you will ever hear. His progress knows no limits to his dad and me.

Yes, we have hard times. We've had even more sad times. But we also have joy, humor, and happiness.

He is just a boy. A typical, average, everyday boy who happens to have severe autism. He is a brother and a son and a grandson and someday maybe a brother-in-law and an uncle.

His name is Cooper. He is unapologetically himself.

He has the kind of autism that not a lot of people talk about. But we do. Because he is so much more. He is the sum of his parts. Good and hard. And no one should be reduced to just their hard parts. No one.

And I remind myself, if we fixed all the parts of Cooper that the world thought were broken, there would be no more Cooper. He is exactly who he is supposed to be, in a world that doesn't understand him.

Often, I say autism isn't the problem. The problem is the world's reaction to autism.

The other day, Cooper and I were walking along a sidewalk. We were waiting for Sawyer to be done with baseball practice and Cooper was getting antsy in the car. So, we walked as we often do.

He was anxious, half running, half pacing. He wanted to leave but we couldn't. Not without Sawyer. He wasn't directly bothering anybody, but we were being noticed.

I was focused on Cooper, not really paying too close attention to the people around me, when I heard, "Autism, right?" I turned to the woman who said it and nodded my head yes.

She said, "I'm here waiting for my son, and I heard and saw you two, and you are so patient. You are doing a really good job."

I felt the tears stinging in the corners of my eyes when she said her last sentence, "It gets better. Maybe not today, maybe not tomorrow, but it does get better. I promise."

She walked away before I could even say a word. After I got Cooper buckled in the car, and Sawyer was entranced by his phone, my tears started to flow.

I needed her words on that day more than ever.

It gets better. Maybe not today, maybe not tomorrow, but it does get better.

I don't know if she meant he will get better, or I will get better, or maybe even the world will get better. I didn't have a chance to ask.

I just know on my lowest days now, I tell myself it gets better.

## ADRIAN

*What kind of autism does he have?*

I've never been sure of what to say.

When Amos received his official diagnosis of autism at age three, we were not told the severity and I didn't know to ask.

*Severity.*

Who knew there was such a thing?

I've since learned that severity refers to an individual's symptoms in two primary areas: social-communication and patterns of behaviors or interests that are restricted or repetitious. The American Psychiatric Association (APA) defines severity levels in their Statistical Manual of Mental Disorders, also called the DSM-5. As Kate shared earlier in this chapter, there are three levels of severity—level 1 requires support, level 2 requires substantial support, and level 3 requires very substantial support.

Testing for autism is not a simple thing like a blood test or MRI. Accessing a qualified professional who can diagnose is also difficult. Not only do families have to gather information, secure a referral, and find a provider within driving distance, waits can be years in North Carolina. Amos was diagnosed at a specialized autism center in the state of Georgia. The assessment lasted several days and he was observed playing with toys as well as interacting with me. Prior to the appointment, his therapists filled out lengthy questionnaires and several of his teachers were interviewed. We gathered records from early intervention and had his pediatrician share his developmental history with the center, as well.

The autism diagnosis was not a surprise then because our neurologist had shared a few months earlier that she believed it was his diagnosis. I recently pulled out his original assessment and gleaned little from the many boxes that were each marked with a perfect *x*. Though no level was ascribed to Amos, I would say he falls in the low to middle of severity.

He can speak, but can't tell you a story about his day.

He is a good reader, but struggles to answer questions.

He loves to play chase with his peers, but lacks the ability for complex games.

I will say that though he will never not have autism, he has made such progress in so many areas and continues to do so.

He is able to complete schoolwork in a not-so-timely way.

In the last few months, he has proved himself able to sit and wait in a store or a restaurant.

He is still learning to handle disappointment by not throwing objects and struggles with following a schedule with too many transitions.

A few years after the autism diagnosis, we added other pieces to the puzzle, like anxiety, ADHD, and even a genetic disorder. It wasn't until Amos's behavior became too much to handle that we sought the help of a pediatric psychiatrist. It was at that appointment that we learned about common co-occurring conditions like anxiety and ADHD. According to the National Institutes of Health (NIH), additional challenges that often travel with autism include limited expressive and/or receptive language, and developmental delay and/or intellectual disability.

Genetics also became part of Amos's autism story.

Researchers believe that 20 percent of children with autism also have a diagnosable genetic condition. The American College of Genetics recommends that those with an autism diagnosis also be evaluated by a geneticist. All states in this country require newborn testing for twenty-nine health conditions, which include genetic disorders amongst other conditions like congenital diseases.

When Amos was born after an emergency C-section, his newborn screen came back normal. Our doctor did share that he had hypospadias and a sacral dimple and I noticed that one eye seemed unable to focus. His development seemed behind and I noticed his inability to hold his head up and his lateness in smiling.

I took him to a developmental pediatrician who noted the anomalies we learned at birth. He also noticed his low-set ears and widely spaced nipples. He ordered a microarray—the simplest of genetic tests. Six or so weeks later, the results came back and, again, were normal.

I was still worried.

We made an appointment with a geneticist, and six months later, our extended family underwent whole exome sequencing (WES). Initially, Amos, my husband and I, and my parents were tested. When a variance of concern was identified, my mother's brothers were also tested. Because her typical brother was found to have the same variance, it was taken off the list as a possible genetic anomaly.

Three years later, we received a call from our geneticist that another variance had been identified. We were asked to submit more blood work, and at the end of this past summer, we received a call solidifying his genetic diagnosis.

It's called MSL2.

It's only been a month since my conversation with the geneticist and it doesn't change much about Amos's trajectory other than solidifying the foreverness of autism. I thought that a genetic diagnosis would offer me some peace.

It hasn't.

Instead, we were handed a report and officially told that the person we ordered would never exist. You will find that this new person is the same one you have loved since you saw the line on that pregnancy test. There is no ascribed set of directions for parenting this child. Few speak the language that is required by the families who live alongside a disability. Regrettably, there is no crash course on navigating the unplanned life.

Autism is a dance, I would tell you.

In those early days, I was filled with fear of the unknown and what I deemed to be a scary future. Today I would tell you that I focus on today and the near future. Autism is so different for everyone and that includes both struggles and successes no matter the severity.

*What kind of autism does he have?*

I don't know.

I didn't know when he was diagnosed and I don't know today.

It doesn't matter so much anymore.

## CARRIE

*What kind of autism does he have?*

I hear this question a lot about Jack. People seem eager to classify the autism spectrum in some way—to organize it into neat boxes with a subtitle. They want to know if he is a savant, or if he has the kind you see on television. And the short answer to both is no.

"Is he, you know, *high functioning*?"

This is usually the follow-up question. For some reason, people drop their voice a little on the last two words, as though they feel guilty for asking.

High-functioning autism essentially means a diagnosed person can speak, read, write, and handle basic life skills. It is not a medical diagnosis, but rather an informal term used to describe those whose daily life is not as disrupted by the spectrum disorder.

There are two important things to keep in mind when talking about autism. First, it truly is a spectrum with a wide range of symptoms, characteristics, and behaviors. Although the diagnosis typed onto the bottom of forms and education plans have the exact same letters and words, I have yet to meet two people with autism who are exactly alike.

Just as autism varies from person to person, it varies within an individual over time. As Jack gets older, his autism changes year by year. I'm often reminded of a snowflake inside of him, drifting, melting, and then crystallizing. Every so often his autism seems to lie dormant for a few minutes, hours, or even a day. Then, without warning, the snowstorm will begin again.

Jack was diagnosed at eighteen months old, but we noticed some red flags when he was an infant. He was born a little over a year after our first son, so I had an easy way to benchmark milestones. Although doctors and family reassured me over and over that every child develops at his or her own pace, I still couldn't ignore the nagging feeling that something was amiss.

It started with signs that are difficult to capture or explain. He never really engaged with us at all. He seemed disinterested in his surroundings. He didn't appear to be attached to either Joe or me.

There was a vacancy to his eyes that I couldn't quite describe.

On top of that, he was very difficult to soothe. He cried for hours, and although he slept through the night at six weeks, he abruptly stopped when he was four months old. He's struggled with sleep ever since.

What eventually landed us a referral for what's called *early intervention*—or services available to babies and young children who are demonstrating developmental delays—was his inability to manage solid food. Around a year, he still lacked the motor skills to move food effectively around his mouth, resulting in incredible frustration during mealtimes. It took nearly six months of testing before we received the official autism diagnosis.

Throughout elementary and middle school, many of Jack's issues were related to sensory integration and his own internal regulation. If he was feeling overwhelmed or unsure of himself, he became excited and deregulated. He started to stim and jump around, and he sucks on his middle two fingers to soothe himself. He might also start whining at a high pitch. It's as if a little snow squall begins inside of him, and eventually builds up into a full-blown storm.

When Jack was in first grade, he was assaulted by anxiety. Much like a blizzard, it came on quickly and quietly. Only instead of delicate silvery snowflakes, he was pelted by violent mood swings, deep phobias, and long sleepless nights. It was an incredibly trying time for our entire family, watching him struggle and fight against his invisible demons. He was disappearing before our very eyes.

Jack's development never seems to be a steady climb—instead it's like the steps on a staircase. He'll make a great leap in one area, and then stand motionless for a while before bounding up another riser. New behaviors always emerge right before he takes that next step. When he was five, his toileting regressed and he wet the bed at night. Halfway through first grade he became very explosive at school, screaming and lashing out at other kids.

In sixth grade we had him tested by a neuropsychologist so we could figure out his latest bout of anxiety and behaviors. Over the course of four weeks, I brought him to the office where a young doctor met with him one-on-one. Gently, she coaxed answers from him on standardized tests meant to measure how he processes information, as well as his social and emotional skills. The results took our breath away.

I remember sitting in her office with Joe next to me, listening to a whole new set of deficits. I was wearing a dress that I'd gotten from Stitch Fix and it felt too tight in the overheated room. From the sound of a car starting in the parking lot below us, to the panic spreading through my rib cage, I remember it all.

"Well," she began, "he has some issues with working memory." I looked at Joe and back at her. I nodded my head. I'd heard of working memory.

"Picture our working memory to be this entire table," she continued. She spread her hands over the wood surface. "We have all this space to arrange our ideas." She fanned some of her papers out to demonstrate.

"We can organize the things we're thinking about. We can put some things here," she said, gesturing to the right. "And other things here." She moved a folder to the left.

"But Jack, well, his working memory is more like this." She made a small circle with her hands in the empty corner of the table. "He doesn't really have as much."

Looking at her hands, I carefully considered her words. He doesn't really have much working memory. His table is empty. Like a gust of wind on a rainy day, autism swept all his cerebral papers and folders and Post-it notes to the floor.

"It's as if we all have a filing cabinet in our minds," she continued, stepping inside of my reverie. "It's where we store all the information we absorb throughout the day. Jack has his own kind of filing system, but it's hard to know what that's like. His information is, well, it seems complicated."

I uncrossed my legs and then crossed them again. I glanced at Joe in the chair next to me. He seemed to be squinting at something on the wall.

"His cognitive thinking is quite impaired. He's probably less than 2 percent of his peers at this point, but it's difficult to tell because his anxiety gets in the way." She cleared her throat. "Based on his scores, his reading comprehension is close to that of a first grader. While I was testing him, he often said things like he feels like a loser—that he feels alone.

"When I showed him a math problem, he would tell me he's dumb at math, he can't do it."

I struggled to stay focused. I pictured Jack in first grade. He was so cute. I had bought him a red backpack for the first day of school. His name was stitched across the front in white letters.

"You see, he doesn't process language the same way we do. For Jack, listening to people talk all day is like you or me sitting in a French class, except we don't speak French. He only understands bits and pieces here and there." I remember feeling a powerful wave of regret and fear, like nausea.

"I do think he's depressed."

Now, at nineteen, Jack still doesn't have the television kind of autism. He doesn't know how to count cards in Vegas or solve medical mysteries in a busy hospital. He doesn't paint masterpieces or write concertos. He has the regular old kind of autism with delayed communication, limited eye contact, rigidity, and anxiety. He also continues to struggle with working memory and depression.

The term *high functioning* is one I grapple with, to be honest. Yes, Jack is obviously high functioning. It's hard to dispute that. Yet high-functioning autism doesn't translate to easy autism. I feel guilty just admitting this. Here I have a son who is in a college program, attempting to make his way in the world. In the face of so many challenging autism profiles and behaviors, how can I complain? There are people who would long for my problems.

The truth is, there is a price to pay for having one foot in each world, and that price is knowing you are different. People often ask me when we told Jack he had autism. It was a conversation we'd been putting off, to be honest, but when he was ten he came to us—to me, specifically, as I was trying to make a cup of coffee the day after my fortieth birthday—and made his announcement.

"I have autism."

I set my mug down, the one ironically emblazoned with the phrase *Best Mother Ever!*, and turned toward him. I tried to ask him how he knew, and what it felt like, but he turned abruptly and walked upstairs.

Ever since then, he has been aware of all the ways he doesn't fit in with his neurotypical peers—and often points out how he doesn't fit in with kids with autism either. He knows when a sibling leapfrogs over him, especially when it comes to things like driving or dating. It's very painful to watch him try to find his footing.

What does high functioning look like in everyday life?

Jack can bake a cake, but he needs to check and recheck the recipe continuously because he doesn't store information in his mind while he's working.

He can sign his name at the bottom of a paycheck, but he cannot grasp the concept of a mortgage or a lease. Once he turned eighteen Joe and I obtained guardianship to safeguard his finances and remain a part of his medical appointments.

He can open and read the mail, but he is easily persuaded by advertising and political campaigns.

He can have a conversation, but he often scripts—reciting passages he's heard or read somewhere else.

He can cross the street on his own, but he has very little understanding of personal space. He'll cut in line, bump into strollers, and, no matter how many times we've practiced, doesn't understand how to hold the door for someone else.

Jack struggles with a concept called *social inferencing.* He talks to everyone exactly the same way: his grandfather, his bus driver, the guy in Chipotle. Family, teachers, strangers—they have the same level of context to him. He uses the same tone of voice and asks the same kind of questions.

He also has limited *theory of mind*, or the understanding that other people might have a different belief, opinion, or emotion than his. He thinks in very concrete terms.

And he is honest. Unflinchingly, fearlessly honest. Let's just say the phrase *lack of filter* was created with Jack in mind. There is a kind of levity that comes with his candor. We affectionately refer to his observations and running commentary as *Jack-isms.*

Like the time he told his bus driver Doug I was in the NBA. Doug smirked at me one afternoon when I stepped outside to say hello and suggested I work on my three-pointers. As he pulled away, I asked Jack why on earth he would tell him I played in the NBA.

"Because. You say it every time you sweep the floor. Or clean up the mess. You say NBA. NBA. NBA."

"No, Jack. I say I have an MBA. MBA! It's a master of business administration."

"Oh. Same thing."

Then there was the time I had a hysterectomy to remove a large fibroid. Thankfully it was benign, but it gave Jack enough material to last for years. Actual conversation between actual people at our local Dairy Queen:

Teenage employee: "Yes, can I take your order?"

Jack: "My MOTHER. Has no UTERUS."

Employee:

Jack: "I'll have a large chocolate cone. Extra sprinkles."

*What kind of autism does he have?*

It's the kind that is difficult to capture in a chapter, in a book, in a conversation. It changes almost day by day. It is him, and yet it is not him.

# 11
# The Autism Family

## KATE

*Describe how your child's challenges affect your family.*

I was filling out yet another questionnaire for Cooper, and this was question number thirty-two. In parentheses after the question, it said…*in four sentences or less.* The paperwork is never-ending when you have a child with a disability and often leaves me wondering why this process hasn't been simplified yet.

The questions are mostly about Cooper, his development, and his challenges. He's thirteen now, and I'm still describing his birth and digging into my memory vault to remember when he first rolled over and sat up and crawled.

Over the years, though, I've started to see an expansion

in the questions. Sprinkled in are questions about our family, marriage, and siblings. The needle is moving. An autism diagnosis doesn't affect just the diagnosed child. It affects the entire family. And in every single presentation I give, whether it's to moms and dads, educators, medical providers, or therapists, I say the following sentences, loudly and without a waver in my voice.

*"We are failing families of children with disabilities. I am not placing blame or even defining the 'we.' I am simply saying 'we' as a society are failing these families. And the reality is, Cooper is fine. Because he has me and his dad and his siblings to advocate for him. He is exactly who he is supposed to be. It's the rest of us that need help."*

I often see nods in the audience. Maybe even hear some gasps. I've seen social workers puff out their chests and sit up straighter as if I'm blaming them directly. I'm not. I just know the stress this has put on my own family, my marriage, and my other children is exponential, and that we can't be alone in this.

We are told countless times to just ask for help. And it's implied that if we ask, the help will come. It doesn't. There are families out there screaming for help and given another form to complete.

"We" are failing families of children with disabilities. And it must stop.

The answer to the question, describe how your child's challenges affect your family, isn't black-and-white. And it most certainly can't be summed up in four sentences.

There is nothing in our family's life that autism doesn't impact. There are no decisions made without factoring in autism either. I've been told in the past that we shouldn't let Cooper's diagnosis control us. And I will bravely say here, for all of the parents who are too afraid to say this themselves...I don't know how not to. Because everything has to be looked at through the lens of autism. We may not all carry the label, but we all are impacted in different ways.

Take my marriage, for instance. We knew our life would change after our first son was born, but we also assumed that after a period, our life would resume as normal. We assumed this because that was how it was for our friends who had children before us. But our life never went back to the life we had pictured. A stark line separating before and after.

Jamie and I have been married in total for sixteen years. On paper we have moved seven times, been pregnant six times, experienced two miscarriages, had four babies, loved four dogs, and even divorced each other and remarried again. When I share that last part people often gasp.

People love to hear about our unconventional love story. I think because they look at us now, smiling and laughing, and wonder how we could have gotten to the point of divorce. Or maybe they are experiencing their own marriage struggles and love to see a happy ending. The divorce rate is high in families like mine.

I may not be an expert in much of anything, but I can say with certainty, marriage is hard. Harder than I ever expected it to be. Add in autism, and it's even harder.

*You were so young to go through what you did together.*

My mother-in-law said that to me once, and while such a simple sentiment, it felt profound to me. She was looking at our wedding photo on the wall in our living room. Jamie and I were kissing under an umbrella in the rain next to Lake Superior. My dress was white. His tux was black. We stood out amongst the blues of the water. There is no question we were madly in love. We could never have anticipated what was coming our way. Or the way it would strip us both bare and leave our raw, vulnerable, ugly parts exposed.

When faced with our greatest challenges, we turn into different people. Grief. Struggle. Fear. Anger. Worry. All elements that change us. The stress on our marriage felt insurmountable at times.

The truth is, the day "Cooper has autism" was said out loud, we were expected to be experts. We were expected to know exactly what to do in an unbelievably hard situation. We were expected to know how to grieve. And we didn't. To put it bluntly, autism humbled us. Everything we thought we were and would be was no more.

I wish I could go back and tell myself that it was scary because it was unfamiliar, not because we were incapable. We were capable. And how very brave it is to continue to show up in a story that looks so different from what you thought it would be, because for so many years I felt like a failure.

In the beginning, I chased hope for our son all over the state. It felt like we were living our lives in doctors' offices. We moved three times, all for more services for Cooper. We started to feel the strains of the isolation. We missed the friends that were lost. We missed the people that we used to be. The sleep deprivation became unbearable. And the pressure on Jamie and me to keep living the lives we imagined started to build.

We started to disagree on everything. My husband thought we should keep living our pre-autism life. He saw all our friends with young children doing all the things that families do. He wanted that to be us. He thought our son was fine. I knew he wasn't. Jamie accused me of seeking out a diagnosis, as if I was searching for something to be wrong. I wasn't doing that, but at times I doubted myself, wondering if I was looking for something that wasn't there.

Then the financial strains really kicked in. One of us had to quit our job to meet the demands of autism. And boy, did that interfere with the high price tag on all the private therapy. I could feel the perfect life I had pictured slipping away.

I took the lead on coordinating our son's care. A role that

completely consumed me. I was researching, finding therapies, fighting insurance companies, battling the county and the school district. I felt like I was on the roller coaster alone and no matter what I did I couldn't get my husband to sit with me on the ride.

Our conversations soon became about our son's care and solely his care. I'd talk about new therapies with a renewed spirit almost weekly. I'd find a new diet or tactic that was going to help our son. My hope would be restored. I would be on top of the world. Until it failed.

And with each failure the resentment built between us. He resented my willingness to try new things and I resented his ability to not worry. It became easier to carry the weight of autism alone. I made the decisions. I dealt with the consequences.

I know he wondered what had happened to the woman he married. The woman who was vivacious, fearless, and adventurous. What he didn't know was I barely recognized myself.

During our hardest years, and divorce, we were at an impasse. I needed him, or so I thought I did, to help me carry the weight of autism. He needed me to be the woman he married. I didn't understand yet that she was gone, and I spent way too many years trying to get back to myself. For him. For me. It took us those years apart to realize that we would never be ourselves again. Because that version of us before autism was no more.

Time has a way of healing and softening our edges.

Thankfully, having a child with a disability hasn't broken us yet. We are still here, trying and often failing, but keeping love at the center of everything we do. Love for each other and love for our children.

It's taken me a lot of self-growth and healing to say that my husband is not my autism person. But also, the more important part is that it's okay that he's not. Jamie loves and adores Cooper. He bathes and dresses him with tenderness, he tickles and wrestles him with endless energy, he goes to every single appointment, and pushes Cooper in a way that I cannot. But he doesn't carry the emotional weight like I do. He doesn't agonize about the future and life after we are gone. But what he does do is carry the rest. He fills in the gaps in our family when I cannot.

The other day I was driving Sawyer home from hockey practice, and I told him how I was writing a chapter about our autism family. I explained a bit about the context of the chapter and then I asked him how he thinks autism affects our family.

I didn't know what he would say, and I thought possibly nothing. Sawyer is knocking on the door of teenagerhood and isn't sharing as much with me as he did when he was younger. But I can say with certainty that I didn't realize that Sawyer would carry so much, that he would worry so much about his brother.

I am learning that this next season of my life will entail seeing autism through my other children's eyes and walking alongside them on their own journeys as siblings. At times, I feel prepared, anticipating and knowing what they are feeling. Other times, I feel completely lost, not knowing if I am saying and doing the right things.

I have worked so hard to acknowledge the complicated feelings that come with special needs parenting. And also, to not let them harden me. I truly believed that once I did that my work would be done. What I didn't know was that each of my other three children would go on their own grief journey in their own space and time. The pressure I feel walking alongside them is immense at times.

*"You always leave, Mom. Remember last Halloween when we had that party at the neighbor's house? And we all went? But then you had to leave after just a few minutes."*

I was a bit stunned, and I felt an initial feeling of defensiveness because I remembered it differently than that.

*"Yes, buddy, I did leave. But you got to stay. Remember, you played pool in their basement and had a dance party. Mom and Cooper left but you stayed with Daddy, Harbor, and Wynnie."*

We had made our way as a family of six to the Halloween party, and Cooper lasted fifteen minutes. Which in my book was a success. I thought I did the right thing by taking Cooper to the comfort of our home and leaving the rest of my family to enjoy the party.

This is the balance I always talk about. I often say as a mom I'm straddling two very different worlds. Autism and neurotypical. Arms outstretched with a foot in each. Trying to bridge the gap between the two.

It's taken us a lot of years to figure out what works for our family. Almost like a complicated algorithm. One stays home. One goes. We switch off. We have help from grandparents and personal care attendants when we can. We make plans knowing we may have to cancel. We host when we can. We educate about autism and the path less traveled.

I think the point is, we can't force our Cooper to enjoy the "norms" of the world and it's not fair for our other children to miss out, so we do our best to figure out a balance. And know that it will look a whole lot different from every other family.

It's no secret that my biggest guilt moments in this life surround Sawyer. I worry constantly that I have failed him. That I've overcompensated. That I've spoiled him. That I haven't done enough. I thought I had been sacrificing my needs to accommodate my family and Cooper, but I was sacrificing a lot more than just my needs.

*He fidgeted with the buttons on the radio as he said, "I guess, Mom. Yeah, it was fun to stay. You just leave a lot."*

I let the shot he fired hit me squarely in the chest and let myself absorb his words. Because it was the truth. He wasn't wrong. His feelings are never wrong. He looked little sitting next to me. Much younger than eleven years old. I forget sometimes that he is younger than Cooper and I'll find myself expecting more from him. Or for him to act older than he is because he is the younger "older" brother.

Resentment. It bubbled up right there on our drive home, just the two of us. Not resentment toward Cooper. Resentment at this hand we've been dealt. Resentment that it's not easier. Resentment that it's unfair sometimes. Resentment that we must make choices.

I thought about the high price of having to make these impossible choices. Was I missing more than I was gaining?

I knew the autism family would be complicated—I just didn't realize the stakes would be so high. But we do our best. We keep living. And we keep trying to merge these two worlds.

A lot of families hide the realities of autism. They don't talk about it. I have a friend who whispers the word *autism* in front of her other children like it's a dirty word. We don't hide it here. We have talked about it since day one. We do that to normalize it. We do it to help Sawyer, Harbor, and Wynnie understand and because we don't want it to be a secret. Or shameful. Cooper is Cooper, and his beautiful parts by far outweigh his hard parts. That's what we need to remember. So, we talk as a family about autism. We share. We live out loud.

One of the best things we have done is immerse ourselves in the world of disability. We joined Miracle League Adaptive Sports and bring our whole family. We host events for families like ours too. We rent out pools and trampoline parks and movie theaters. And after every single event, I hear from fellow parents that it is so good to feel normal even for just an hour.

We have also found something that works for our family. The list of places we can go successfully is tiny, so years ago, Jamie and I made it our mission to find one family activity we could all do together. For us, that is boating. It is our escape from reality. Once we found something that worked for our family, I watched the relationships between my kids grow. It took time, but there was no leaving early or not being able to go. There was no resentment.

As I look to the future, watching our family age, I am focusing on prioritizing my husband and my other children individually. They each need time, to have their own autonomy separate from autism, and to know they are special. While we will never be empty nesters, we will be down to just three of us. Cooper will have siblings at home for fifteen more years. It seems like a long time, but it will go fast.

I am learning to ask for help and to take it when offered. It sounds so simple, but asking for help is hard, especially when it feels burdensome. It's not. Ask for help. If Sawyer or Harbor can ride with teammates to a game or get dropped off, we take it.

I am also focused on embracing our reality. Not fighting it either. This is our world. Cooper has become the nucleus of our home, the rest of us orbiting around him. We don't fight the differences; instead we embrace them and do what works. We come and go, to baseball games, to work, to playdates, and he happily waits in the window for whomever has gone to return. And we wait and hope for the day that he can join us.

You can't tell Cooper's story without telling the story of us, the autism family.

One day, I believe that Jamie and I will sit down together, many years from now, and say, "It was hard, but we made it. Together."

## ADRIAN

The story of a marriage and family is a complicated one.

Mine is no different.

My husband, Thomas, and I have been married for almost twenty-two years and had been married three years before we became parents. Innocent and naive, we planned for strollers and cribs and tiny day gowns. We had not concerned ourselves with actual parenthood. Our once-naive selves adjusted and life settled into a comfortable groove.

For the first seven years of parenthood, ours was a typical family.

Unlike Kate and Carrie, who were introduced to autism early in their parenting journey, our transition to parenthood was fairly uncomplicated. Three children arrived in rapid succession and our early years as parents were free from the stickiness of autism. We traveled as much as we could afford, went camping, saw plays, attended outdoor concerts, and trekked through the woods.

We moved through the world as a family of five. Our troubles in public spaces centered around squabbles amongst children or the occasional spilled drink. Yes, the ease of those early days disappeared with the gift of Amos.

How has it changed us?

As the mother of three teenagers and the wife of a somewhat reserved husband, I hesitate to answer. I prefer to let them answer for themselves, but I CAN share MY perspective of the impact Amos has had on our family life.

I'll begin with my husband.

Thomas has always been the quiet one behind the scenes. I met him my first year in college and knew him several years before we dated. While I was outgoing, talkative, and never missed a party, he was calm, cool, and collected. He also was the one planning the party. While the other college boys would lavish me with exuberant greetings and invitations, he was much quieter and stood on the sidelines, hardly a nod and just a hint of a smile.

Of course, I was intrigued.

Our friendship grew, and in our early twenties, fate brought us together again. I was having a party at my parents' beach condo, and I was surprised to see Thomas. Tan and handsome, he said hello and flashed a smile before heading up the stairs, and I was a goner.

The moment he was out of sight, I fell back on the old once-white couch and said aloud, "I'm going to marry him." Funny how you choose a spouse and really have no idea how they will react to the most important things in life.

Prior to our wedding, we participated in mandatory premarital counseling as required by our priest. We talked about all sorts of things that may go wrong in our marriage and what potential stumbling blocks may lie ahead.

Infidelity.

Establishing boundaries with in-laws.

Financial decisions.

Even the possibility of fertility issues.

We did NOT talk about having a child with a disability or about being a family with a disabled member. Unlike the above issues, this future scenario was not a choice.

There would be no claiming a mistake or even walking away. Having an Amos never crossed our minds. I guess not the rector's either.

What would he have said?

How could he have known what to say?

I imagine something along the line of "What if you get a baby or a child you didn't order? How will you manage? Will you be able to handle it?"

He didn't ask and we sailed into the sunset of what we thought would be the perfect marriage.

For the last ten years, autism has dictated the direction of our family.

We received the diagnosis when Amos turned three. It was about this time when we could no longer venture into the world and explain away his differences with toddlerhood. As he grew older, we stood out more and people were quick to assume that he was simply an unruly child. He became more unmanageable and our movement as a family was less cute and more of an imposition. We were no longer privy to the once-frequent wry smiles cast our way. Those admonishments to enjoy the chaos dwindled while I outwardly struggled to attend to my three older children and their autistic sibling.

Amidst the unplanned life, my husband was the rock that I never dreamed I needed. Though I run the household, he is willing to do anything I ask.

Before Amos, he took the children out to play while I got dinner on the table. Because we had three under three, it was all hands on deck for baths and bedtime. As they grew older, he began coaching teams and attending school events. Most every evening, we would have an early dinner and go outside as a family. Shoot baskets.

Ride bikes.

Meander the neighborhood and climb favorite trees.

Amos's arrival meant that duties were split. Thomas handled sports practices, making breakfast, and school transportation. I did the grocery shopping, signing up for sports and summer camps, and picking them up in the afternoons.

It hasn't been easy—life with four kids never is, but add special needs and you get an accelerated kind of chaos.

In those early years, we were getting acquainted with what it meant to live a life out loud. Hauling a three-year-old with autism everywhere was a grand adventure and we tried to shrug off the rolling on the floor, the hiding beneath the table at dinner, and the wet pants. But sometimes, it was too much for all of us, and I worried, too, about what would happen when Amos got bigger and wasn't so "cute" anymore. What would I do when I couldn't pick him up in my arms anymore? But still, I knew that dwelling on my fears for the future would mean we would miss out on the wonderfulness of today.

Over the years, Amos has become more able to care for himself. He can change clothes, use the bathroom independently, and get himself a prepared snack from the pantry. I think what is hardest is not being able to leave him at home alone. Running a simple errand in our small town meant that I left his siblings for ten or fifteen minutes at a time. I can't do that with Amos and that lack of freedom weighs heavily on me. This year, his three older siblings will all be away at school, and I wonder what life will be like.

Will we enjoy giving him our time and attention?

Will he be lonely?

Will we be lonely?

My husband, Thomas, has continued to be the voice of reassurance. In the early days of autism, I was struggling. Life felt so hard. I felt like I was losing friends because we could no longer join casual family gatherings or leave children home alone. I wondered aloud if life would ever be what it once was. I spewed a load of worries, and rather than console me or agree with me or correct me, he paused before saying, "Well, autism will smoke 'em out."

I guess that's how our marriage is too.

We are in this together.

Through thick and thin and ups and downs.

Not just in parenting Amos, but all our children. No one loves them or cares about them like we do, and that responsibility looms extra large when one of them will never truly fly the nest. Maybe that's too simplified, but it's the truth.

We've learned to talk about the hard moments and encourage one another to voice their feelings and concerns.

We have tried and failed activities a zillion times. When my family fusses about taking Amos, I listen while pointing out that there is no shame in being different, or at least there shouldn't be.

In that same breath, I've committed to having a family life where the squeaky wheel doesn't always get the grease. I have learned to juggle and prioritize the siblings who have a tendency to get lost in the shuffle of autism. After all, we have four children and none is more important than the other. Each needs different things at different times (sometimes at the same time) and my husband and I do our best.

We are learning as a family that life is not as much about charting our own paths as it is following the trajectory that fate lobs each of us. It has not been an easy thing to learn as an adult, much less a child. Amos's siblings have learned about the reality of life far earlier than we ever did. So many feelings exist when you belong to children like Amos, diamonds in the rough. I have to continually reassure the feelings of his siblings. Looking back, we have had to leave many a party early or one of us has had to stay home rather than watch a sporting event.

"Amos ruins everything," the small girl said after we abandoned a Halloween party because Amos was overstimulated with the noise of fun.

"No, he doesn't," I said.

*But he does*, I thought to myself. *Maybe not everything, but an awful lot.*

Life with Amos has been a lot of things. Awesome, certainly, but easy? Nope, no way, nada, no sirree, Bobby.

Later that evening, I talked to my daughter and told her that I could understand how she felt. It did feel like we had to live according to what was best for him a lot of the time. It's hard on all of us, and no matter how much we plan and try, sometimes it's going to happen, I told her. Autism, being three, having extra special needs, or just being a little brother, all those things make life tough. I conveyed that I was still thankful for OUR life and I wouldn't trade it for any other in the world.

Talking through our reality has helped us make big decisions regarding the trajectory of our family. Years ago, we decided to hire a nanny/caregiver for Amos, even though we weren't sure we could afford it. I had gone back to work and it was a crucial part of our effort to prioritize living a typical life alongside autism. What that means is that sometimes Amos is left at home. Maybe for a family wedding or graduation or a sporting event or even certain family vacations.

No one has four children so that they can leave one at home though.

I long to have Amos with us, a part of our family. It wasn't until recently that I learned that my children did too. This year, we had made plans for my husband to take the three teenagers on a ski trip in Wyoming. As the time grew closer, I felt uneasy about this plan. I was sad to miss it but was unwilling to leave Amos, as I had just been gone on a special trip with my senior. I struggled and came to the decision that we would all go. I would be Amos's person and they would ski and do dinners and all the things that had been planned. The last time Amos had been to Wyoming was in my belly and he was thrilled. Of course, the travel experience fills Amos with delight and he spoke of nothing else but how many sleeps until the airport, the flight to Chicago, and skiing in Jackson Hole.

The morning we left, my daughter said, *"This is the first family vacation we have taken."* I was quick to point out that we had been to Florida to see grandparents and gone to the beach in the summer, but she stood firm and clarified this trip was a family adventure and we had never moved as a unit on one of those.

She was right.

I found a letter that I had written when Amos was four where I wished autism would scamper off and leave our family of six to seek out grand adventures without worrying about noise or too many people.

And still, he is not ready to be a part of everything we do as a family.

My oldest son is graduating from high school this year. I wish Amos could go.

One of the hardest parts of being an autism family is not knowing what's on the horizon.

When Amos was diagnosed, I assumed—or maybe just hoped—that autism's edges would be smoothed out over time. I believed the need to explain his disability would fade away much like the sharp pink of a morning sky in the path of a hurricane.

That day has never come.

Rather than an impending storm, the boy named Amos has exuded love and light and rained manna on our family.

Each and every day, we have to make choices.

How are you supposed to know if you are choosing wisely?

We guess and try and do our best. I'd like to think that is enough.

I've had to accept that I can't do everything.

I can't be everywhere.

Maybe being everywhere is not as important as being THERE.

# CARRIE

This chapter was one of my toughest to write. Not because I don't have a lot to say about an autism family, but because I don't know where to begin. I don't know how to squeeze seven lives into a few pages. You might say I don't know how to capture the parts of us that are not shiny.

I guess the best place to start is with my marriage.

Joe and I met in college when I was nineteen years old. We both worked at Uno Pizzeria in the Crossgates Mall in Albany, New York. He was a short-order cook and I was a server. I remember he leaned up against the cash register and told me his plans to become a dentist, because it seemed like a good career for a family. *A family.* Hearing the words roll so easily out of his mouth took my breath away.

As summer leaves turned golden, we meandered together through a sunlit campus made of stone archways and concrete stairwells. It was dominated by a large fountain at its center. He carried my books. Empty-handed and awkward, I turned to see his eyes in the yellow light.

The next ten years passed by like a slideshow.

Peanut butter and fluff sandwiches eaten picnic-style near the parking lot.

Saturday afternoons at the movies, late-night pizza downtown, followed by brunch on Sunday mornings.

Graduations, with diplomas held aloft. New jobs—him in scrubs, me in pencil skirts and blazers.

Eventually, a sapphire ring with little white diamonds, followed by a white dress and a black tuxedo in a small-town church.

A brick house on a tree-lined street, both of us armed with paintbrushes and color swatches. Then kids, one right after the other.

By all accounts, marriage is hard. Tying up your life with someone else—familial baggage, traditions, religious values, Netflix preferences—it's almost unnatural. The idea of sharing the same bed and the same meal as another person for the rest of your life would daunt even the happiest couple.

Then you add kids. Kids are at once the worst and best thing for a marriage. Sure, you can argue it solidifies your union even more and brings you closer together. But kids also expose every weakness, every crack in your marital foundation. Our dynamic was established immediately—loud, explosive arguments followed by quiet and, eventually, grace. Twenty-five years later, this is the marital music to which we still dance.

I've been asked how we made the decision to have more kids after Jack was diagnosed. I like to joke that we didn't *decide*—that happenstance and poor planning led us to five children in less than six years. Basically, we were careless.

Autism is often called a family diagnosis. When Jack was little, autism factored into every single decision we made. What time we ate dinner, if we could go to the park, whether or not we accepted invitations to holiday parties or barbecues.

Yet at the same time, it was so tightly woven into our family's landscape, it was nearly invisible. We hardly noticed it on a day-to-day basis. Now, as our kids get older, it's become nearly a separate entity all its own. One by one, they tentatively ask about their role in his future. They wonder if they should stay close to be near him geographically. It hurts to think of them restricting their own flight to aid him with his. Yet this is our reality.

We assure them he will be cared for financially. He will have a place to live and supports in place.

When I think of our family, I think of couches. Though the style and fabric has changed over the course of twenty-five years, this piece of furniture remains our command center, our battleground, our comfort zone.

The first one was white with an embroidered design. We'd only been married a few months and couldn't afford new furniture. Joe stood over the sewing machine in our apartment, piecing together long strips of fabric. He finished the cushions and sewed the rest by hand, using a running stitch taken from his book on oral surgery. Once it was done, we had a Couch Party to celebrate. He made coconut shrimp.

We were gorgeous back then, the kind of gorgeous you can't even appreciate yourself. We were tan and lean. Our youthfulness glowed.

From there, a light brown microfiber sectional. We rocked infants and read to toddlers. After Jack was born, it's where some of our worst arguments happened, as autism took a foothold within our family. We exchanged uneasy glances late at night while we took turns soothing and walking our angry, mysterious baby.

Once he was officially diagnosed, however, we didn't sit together as much. We didn't exchange the glances, and we didn't take turns soothing. I think this was because, overnight, I became The Person. I was the only person who could feed Jack his mashed bananas that he spit right back out, or rock him to sleep so he would wake up twenty minutes later screaming.

I threw myself headfirst into specialists. I read articles. I researched therapy. I was frantic, and I thought I was the only one who understood him. There I sat on my island of invented expertise, like a carping queen in her ivory castle.

And of course, I took Jack right along with me—the two of us on our own little island. This was not good; for me, for Jack, or for my marriage.

When you think you are the only one who can do everything, who can do it perfectly, and you sneer and roll your eyes when someone else tries to help, then you will wind up doing every single thing yourself. And this will make you mad. A little sad, too, but mostly mad.

If you are anything like me, you will blame your husband since, clearly, he is very lazy. He is perhaps a little bit stupid because he doesn't understand that the special diaper cream *must* go on every time you change a diaper, and if the bananas have any lumps, then it won't work. Also, the green bowl is best because the bottom is flatter.

So, you blame and blame and maybe you feel resentful. Resentment is like a tiny seed that plants itself in your heart and your mind. Except instead of blossoming into a beautiful, silky flower, it grows into an ugly weed, when all you really need are colorful petals.

Back then, I thought it all mattered so much. I thought that if I didn't do everything exactly right, then Jack wouldn't outgrow his autism and our life would be miserable. That's what the voices in my head told me, anyway.

Well, we were pretty miserable, but it wasn't because of autism. It was because I was trying to control my life's unfamiliar landscape through ridiculous details like diaper cream and baby food. It was because Joe's opinion ceased to matter. It was because I was alone and angry and sad on my island, and I didn't even know how I got there.

People like me use smugness and bananas to protect a small inner light. This light flickers like a tiny candle on a windy day. The wind is trying to control our vulnerability and stamp it out because it is scary. It makes us feel defenseless. We build a wobbly fortress around our candle out of sticks and stones and green plastic bowls. We must hide it from the wind, and the world, and maybe even ourselves.

Don't stand in the way—that's what I want to tell you. Don't block the light from him, or her, or the world. Come out from beneath your pile of sticks and take a deep breath.

Trust your partner, and remember, there is no "perfect" way. The wind will stop blowing, I promise. You will stand straight and tall and honest in the still, tranquil air and nothing bad will happen to any of you. It is in the quiet space of light where life is lived best.

As the mom, I often say I am the Manager of Moods. It's the aspect of motherhood I least expected—the way I constantly try to manage the nervous systems of six other people, plus my own. It doesn't help that Jack is wired to match the highest nervous system in the room, or that Joe is naturally calibrated around a twelve (out of ten). For as long as I can remember, they have a unique tendency to elevate each other. One gets loud and agitated, and the other follows—a nervous-system game of cat and mouse.

It makes me anxious. I hate it. In the beginning, I tried to manage them both. Their moods, interactions, arguments, and opinions. When you have a diagnosed child, there is a triangle of sorts: mother, father, child. Firmly we sit in our angled corners, convinced we know the best way. Then one day I simply let go. I stopped trying to be the safety net upon which they fell, breathless and irritated and divided.

I remember the exact moment when this happened. Jack was fourteen. It was early March, and we were at a middle school concert with plans to go out for dinner afterward. The metal sky spit a cold rain. He didn't want to be there. He fidgeted while the singers performed. At one point, he looked straight at his father and shouted the worst swear word he could. Joe stood up angrily and steered him toward the door. A folding chair clattered to the floor as they moved. My inclination was to follow—to soothe and mediate.

But I didn't. I stayed and watched the next song, then the next. I was tired of being in the middle. That was five years ago. Since then, like a painting under the artist's brush, they emerged vibrant with color. They found each other. The sharp angles didn't disappear altogether, but they became smoother. Softer. Something closer to circle than triangle.

At times, watching them is like watching a most chaotic dance. They seem out of sync, out of rhythm. But I can only play observer to their most intense moments. As much as I hate it, it is this downshifted role that helped them establish and reestablish who they are to one another.

When we moved to New Hampshire, we donated the tan sectional. I was glad to see it go, to be honest. In its place, we bought a red pull-out sofa with cushions that were sewed onto the back. For years, we snuggled toddlers and babies on it. When the kids were in elementary school, we watched movies on snow days and ate toast on sick days. It sits in the basement now—teenagers lounge on it while they play video games.

Our current couch is blue. We bought it just before COVID. Another sectional with a chaise on one end, and what we call "the nest" at the other. The day my mother died, we sat down on it and watched one of her favorite movies. *Beaches*, with Bette Midler.

It was a mistake. I thought I was ready. A mere six hours after I learned she'd passed, I thought I was ready to watch the movie we watched together during a rare moment of goodness between us when I was in high school. Joe held me while I sobbed during the credits, tears slipping down his own face.

Night after night, we sat on that couch debating whether or not Jack was ready to go to a program after high school. Then we rehashed it all again the following night. Carefully, we listed everything we were afraid of. For Joe, someone taking advantage of Jack was his biggest fear. I, on the other hand, worried that giving up on this opportunity would be a mistake—that he would wind up missing the chance to gain some independence in a supported space. Often, I went to bed before Joe, feeling as though we had nothing left to say. All of the ground had been covered.

A mother's grief demands oxygen. It fills the room with color and sound. A father's grief is quiet. It is an after-hours affair, when everyone else has gone to bed and the lights are dim. Watching his silhouette in the darkness, I knew Joe was grieving something, even if he couldn't quite name it. He was desperate to protect his son.

A young mother once asked me how I made sure I paid enough attention to all our kids. Her face was so earnest, so open and honest, I wanted to give her a hug. And for a split second I considered listing strategies for emotional child management in a larger family, when another thought popped into my head entirely. Without hesitating, I suggested she worry less about the attention her kids get and more about the attention their marriage gets.

From there, our conversation took a wildly different turn. Marriage counseling. Date nights carved out in the busy weekly schedule. How to be okay with going to bed angry so you may wake prepared to forgive in the morning.

These are things Joe and I did, without shame or regret. We arranged for a sitter every Saturday night so we could go out as husband and wife. And about ten years ago, when we felt stuck within our cycle of rupture and repair, we met with a counselor. Once a week in a somewhat small room, we perched on the edge of our armchairs and confessed our rage, our petty slights, our bewilderment, while a kindly gentleman in glasses nodded and soothed.

We untangled our familial baggage and made plans for better communication. We healed. Perhaps the greatest gift from our time in this room were the therapist's gentle words at the end of each session, spoken softly as he opened the door and released us into the evening air.

"Remember, you love each other."

It brought us to a place where we are married on purpose. After all, we do most other things in life on purpose. We raise our kids, go to the gym, download books, order pizza—all on purpose. Yet marriage often slides into the shadows, untended and ignored. Ours did, anyway.

Now I notice the small things. The way he offers me the first bite of every meal, or how he reaches for my hand in a crowd. Coffee in the morning, silly texts throughout the day—these are all the little love letters between us.

Still, there are parts of us that are not shiny. Just the other night we argued. Joe accused me of being already elevated—in a bad mood before he even walked through the door. He wasn't wrong. We had dinner plans with friends. I wanted to get there on time, but his class at the gym ran late. I stood in the kitchen watching the clock until I heard his car in the driveway.

I followed him when he left the room to go take a shower. On the way up the stairs, our voices took on a jagged edge. Whenever we argue, I feel like the worst parts of me are exposed: my pettiness, my righteousness, my shame. At the same time, I see the worst of him. I forget all about the good parts.

Can we love the unshiny version of ourselves? I guess that's the question. I guess you might say that's what we're still learning to do.

He slammed the shower door. I huffed out of the room. I went back downstairs and sat at my desk, seething. I thought once more of my mother and the tears on Joe's face. I walked back upstairs to find him. Unshiny me. He was standing in front of the mirror, combing his hair. He turned, palms outstretched. Forgiveness has always been his superpower.

We still sit on the couch at night after dinner. Me on the chaise, Joe in the nest. We wait for the lights to sweep up the driveway—teenagers home from work, from the movies, from their secret lives. When our oldest calls from college, we swap the phone back and forth between us. We catch each other's eye and smile at a funny text Jack sends. We marvel at his progress in his college program.

Here, we're briefly young again. We're briefly gorgeous.

We are the culmination of our battle scars, our jagged voices, our stolen moments.

Unshiny.

Yet good.

# 12
# A Different Kind of Success

## KATE

At one of my lowest points on this autism parenting journey, I found myself chatting with a man at an event for parents of kids with disabilities. I was standing in a room of my supposed peers, yet feeling like an outsider. I had just completed a yearlong competency-based leadership training program for adults with disabilities and parents of young children with developmental disabilities, and while I had learned so many things, I felt a sadness deep inside of me.

The other kids with disabilities weren't like mine. Cooper didn't speak or participate in any activities. I felt funny, not knowing how to describe him beyond "autism."

The man I was chatting with had no problem describing his four children.

"My oldest is a doctor. The next is a lawyer. One works in finance. And my youngest works eight hours a week at our local grocery store."

It was apparent he was proud of all of his children, but I noticed a change in his voice as he spoke of his youngest daughter.

"She has limited communication and a diagnosis of autism, although, when she was diagnosed years ago, they didn't call it that. She was just Maggie. No one could tell us what the future would hold for her, but my wife, she refused to give up."

He went on to tell me that she is adored at her job. She stocks shelves and collects the carts. She even takes public transportation all by herself to and from. I stood in awe, listening to him brag about his daughter.

"People assume that I am the proudest of my son who is a doctor or my daughter who is a lawyer. And they are wrong. While I'm proud of all four of my children, I am the proudest of my youngest daughter because I know how hard she had to work to do the things she is doing."

Before our conversation ended, he said one more thing to me.

"My daughter is the definition of success. Or at least she should be."

That conversation has stayed with me for years. Today, I call it a Godwink, or a sign of hope given at the most opportune moment. That man helped me redefine what success looks like for not only Cooper, but myself. And he showed me that we can be happy and proud even while living this different life.

When Cooper was diagnosed with severe nonverbal autism, I didn't know if he would ever be a success story. And

I only say that because before I knew Cooper, and others like him, success looked one way to me.

Success was graduating high school, an acceptance letter to college, a happy marriage, a good-paying job, a beautiful home, children in the backyard playing. Those were the things I wanted for myself and my own children. So, upon hearing the words *severe nonverbal autism* in relation to my firstborn, the word that came to mind was *overcome*. For him to be successful, and ultimately for our family to be happy, I would need to help him overcome.

I foolishly assumed if we did everything all at once, all the therapies, early intervention, even diet modifications, we would help him, and he would eventually catch up and get back on track for the success I imagined.

I knew he'd always have autism. I was never one who thought it would go away. But I did think we would help him, bit by bit, and eventually he'd be where he needed to be. Which at the time I thought was alongside his peers. I share this truth vulnerably. I can't rewrite the way I felt in those early days, and if I did, I wouldn't be helping anyone. Before autism, there was just my baby. After, it felt like there was just autism. I had to find the boy again.

I assumed he'd go to kindergarten and learn to sit in a circle and walk in a line and even read and write. He'd develop friendships and get invited to birthday parties and find an extracurricular activity that excited him. And buried way deep down, I thought for sure he'd start talking. Eventually, someday, because everybody talks.

I'd hear stories about kids saying their first word at eight, ten, and fifteen, and I'd think, *We still have time*. I'd mentally count how many years we had to reach the goal like those other kids did, ticking the years off on my fingers. I would obsess on the stories of hope and their ages and the relief I would feel when we made it there. I'd find out what those parents did to help their kids and I'd be rejuvenated. And I'd picture how this would end.

Cooper would be the success story that parents of newly diagnosed kids hear about today.

He'd be talking. He'd be living on his own or with a buddy, or with support, but in theory on his own. He'd have a job. Take the bus or maybe even drive. And I wouldn't be worrying anymore about how this all ends. Because he'd be fine.

I would even go as far as picturing myself laughing with his dad while we reminisced about how worried we used to be. We'd giggle about those nonverbal days that were long gone and how we made it.

I'd imagine people saying:

*"You know that Cooper boy from* Finding Cooper's Voice? *He didn't say his first word until he was ten. And now he doesn't stop talking."*

As he aged, I watched him fall further behind. Slowly at first, then faster, until there was no comparison to his neurotypical peers. No matter what I did, I couldn't help him. But I still held on to hope that this would get better. If I just tried one more thing.

But that didn't happen. Cooper didn't get better, nor did he seem to make improvements. I found myself at my lowest point, not only as a mom, but as a person, in a battle with hope. I felt like I had failed my son as I watched all my friends' kids move on with their lives and grow up and we were frozen in time.

I had to stop running from autism and searching for a different boy buried inside. Cooper was Cooper, unapologetically, and exactly who he was supposed to be. I was not. I needed to become the mom he needed me to be. Because the truth is, his success starts with my acceptance. And inviting autism in to stay.

When this book arrives on the shelves of bookstores, Cooper will be fourteen years old. We will be living the days I was most afraid of in the beginning. But I can also say I know we will be okay because we have survived every hard day so far. Better than okay, even. We will be successful. And I credit the transformation both Cooper and I made over the years.

Cooper will most likely never do any of the things I once considered vital for success. And at the same time, he is doing things I never dreamed possible. Every single day he does something that amazes me, and I am reminded that Cooper has given me the gift of sight. He has shown me what things really matter.

For years, I felt a little uncomfortable saying all of Cooper's giant wins. Not because I wasn't ecstatic but because I didn't know if others would understand.

How goals scored, tests aced, and driver's licenses can also equal a new sound, a new food, and a new life skill.

There are no small things in autism, and while they may not be on a developmental checklist, they are huge to us.

Cooper eats popcorn now. Which is supercool because we have family movie night every Friday and he wants to participate.

Last year he managed the countdown calendar to Christmas. And every morning, he would show that he changed the counter. Then he would point to the fireplace. I rave about how huge that really is. Counting, Santa, delayed gratification, patience, communication, joint attention. I can barely list all the reasons.

He can make his own toast now. And fill his cup with water from the fridge. Two skills we have worked on for years.

He can use the remote. When he learned to use it, I swear it felt like he climbed Mount Everest. He can type words into YouTube. And he loves *The Loud House* now, which is a nice change.

He held the door for me the other day when my hands were full. He's learning about wearing deodorant. He puts his shoes and coat in the closet every day.

He asks, even begs, his little brother to play downstairs with him. He's learned to tattle. Which is a riot. And a huge skill.

He tells us when the bus gets here. He watches for it and communicates that it's arrived. SO HUGE.

He can plug his iPad in to charge. And he does so every night before he falls asleep.

He has learned to dress himself, although not always accurately. He can put on his own shoes and find his backpack and jacket. He uses the toilet independently and willingly hops into the shower.

He rides a bike now. It has three wheels, and he chooses it at choice time at school. His para sends me videos sometimes.

He brings the groceries in from the car after each of my trips to the store. He grunts over the weight of each bag he carries and meticulously puts away each item, mostly in the wrong spots. Dry noodles in the fridge, dog treats in the freezer. We don't mind, though, and often laugh as we search for certain items.

He plays Miracle League baseball once a week all summer. He doesn't own a glove. And his favorite bat is blue. He hits off a tee. And he doesn't need any help to grip the bat anymore. He runs the bases with such spirit and joy you can't help but smile. Oh, and he rarely runs alone because he has two best friends who play on his team. They met at school. And two brothers as well and a grandpa and a mom and a dad. And we all typically take turns running with him.

It's pretty special if he chooses you. Because he gives these high fives that start up high and then go low and end in a chest bump. There is nothing better.

He texts me daily on his very own cell phone. When we got it for him, we had no idea what it would look like for him. It's better than I ever imagined. He texts me his hopes and dreams daily with sentences and GIFs and memes. The other day, before I was about to give a keynote speech, he called me, "Cooper Swenson" popping up on the screen. I sobbed when I heard, "Hiii, Mawwwm."

Last week Cooper had his first playdate. When I told him after school about the playdate he gasped and clapped and jumped. I was so nervous, but I knew he was in good hands. I had prayed for so long that this would happen, and as the moment stood before me, I felt overwhelmed with love for him. We are connected, me and this boy. I don't know a life without him attached to me. But I am learning that, one day, there will have to be. He waved to me when I left and blew me a kiss.

He is still considered nonverbal, but has learned to communicate in the most beautiful ways. On the morning of my most recent birthday, I sat next to him on the couch and said, "Cooper, it's Mom's birthday today!"

I don't know what I expected. Not words, of course. But a cheer. A smile. A gasp. But nothing. He looked back down. It stung. Like a tiny bee sting or a poke in the side. But the pain is duller these days. It doesn't take my breath anymore. It's just enough to take notice.

That's how it's changed over the years for me. What used to drop me to my knees now stings. We've gotten stronger, he and I.

As I made my coffee, steps away from him, I thought back to being twenty-eight, and when I first became a mom. I was such a different woman then. Untouched by autism. Oblivious to the beauty and possibilities in being different. I knew nothing of adversity.

Not really.

And then I heard it.

Sid the Science Kid on PBS singing "Happy Birthday" on my son's iPad. I looked back to see the biggest smile on my sunshine boy's face as he pointed to his ear and then to his iPad, nonverbally telling me to listen.

"It's my birthday! And we will have cake and balloons and presents…" said Sid.

Every single day he amazes me. And I get the gift of being present for each achievement because I know how hard he worked for each of them.

Some days I feel the pressure to teach him everything. But I try to remind myself that we have time. Our kids are lifelong learners.

He may learn to write a sentence or wash his own hair at twenty-five. He may learn to truly speak at age thirty. And how incredible would that be? It won't mean any less because he achieved it late.

In fact, I have a feeling it may be even more remarkable. And this mama will celebrate twice as much. These kids, these unique, beautiful, in-their-own-time kids, have a lifetime to learn this stuff.

Figuring out autism and all the complicated parts takes time. And in the most beautiful way, we are happy. Sometimes it feels like we don't get to be, but we do. We get to laugh and experience joy and celebrate Cooper's success too.

I have no idea what the future holds for Cooper or me or our family. I know it will be filled with messy, complicated, sometimes even painful moments. But I also know it will be filled with joyful and beautiful moments too. And all we can do is live each moment fully and into the next.

Because what's next is going to be amazing.

# ADRIAN

My whole life, I measured success in a very specific way. It was the way that had been handed down through generations of my family. Work hard, get a good education, and success will be yours. I bought into the program, and by the time Amos came along, I was well on my way.

Success was a well-executed plan that had resulted in a happy marriage, a PhD, a parcel of children, buying a home, and even scheduling the many appointments needed for a life filled with sports and camps. It was easy to be proud in those days of parenting typical children and my self-adulation lurked beneath the surface of a naive woman.

My whole existence before Amos had been about checking off large square boxes, and now I saw tiny blips of wonderment. Small achievements that I had been too busy to notice in my efforts to reach a contrived view of success.

This child was slow to smile, laugh, and after saying "Mama" at ten months, no words came for well over another year. There was no pointing or babbling or waving bye-bye. He paid no attention to a stranger at church or family friend who stopped by to visit. Though his love for me has always been apparent and broadcast with outstretched arms, he hardly acknowledged the rest of our family. I wasn't even sure if he knew the names of his siblings or could hear someone when they called his name. While his peers were playing T-ball and having playdates, Amos was learning to hold a cup or eat from a spoon.

The success I witnessed with Amos was so novel I didn't recognize it at first.

It was a cold winter night, and like many a Friday evening, our family popped popcorn and agreed upon a movie. The big three lay in front of the crackling fireplace snuggled like puppies amidst blankets and pillows. Amos the toddler wandered from room to room, not one to sit still, much less watch a movie. In an effort to entice him to join us, I called out the names of each person in the room. Amos paused and glanced and turned his blond head in the direction of each one. Surprised, I directed him to hug them, and one by one, he did as he was told. Daddy, then Russell, then Blair, then Thomas. Again and again, I called out their names, and in his signature lopsided gait, he toddled across the rug and hurled his small body into each of their arms. He grinned with his eyes as much as his perfect mouth and crowed with delight.

"Yay, Amos!"

He cheered for himself and we echoed his words, jubilant for the four-year-old boy who had not only learned to give a hug, but even better? "He's finally figured us all out," my oldest son said, tears shining in the blue eyes that matched his youngest brother. He had. He knew them. He had known me from the very beginning, but that's how it is with the mamas of extra-special little people. Each of them had given their whole hearts to Amos, and finally, he had offered a token of reciprocity. It was the gift of love, the gift of acknowledgment, the gift of a name, and the gift of a family. We sat on the edge of our seats and shouted and cheered for the boy who ran into welcoming arms. It was an introduction to the real definition of success.

I was learning to marvel at the paths of *all* my children.

The life I had planned and expected never happened, but an even better one did. *This is joy*, I tell myself, as I navigate a messy life, usually in exercise clothes, cursing as I step on Legos. Having Amos in our family has been the brightest light I've ever known. He's the one who has taught us to catch the beauty and joy in the tiniest successes.

*He can zip his pajamas*, I remember my daughter yelling from the kitchen.

*Mom, he's holding his cup with one hand*, my oldest son said.

*He found where I hid my popcorn*, another son laughed.

*He brought me his plate when I asked him to,* I proudly told my husband.

We have learned to delight in all the small successes and choose joy. At ten years old, Amos continues to develop. He can sit patiently for a few minutes in a store if we have to wait; he can say hello and tell people how old he is; he can even swim across the pool and play a simple game of chase with his peers.

Those successes have made life smoother for the rest of our family and gave us the courage to take Amos on that family ski trip this past winter. He even went skiing, though it was not smooth sailing. He rolled and kicked and I dripped with sweat before we even got on the snow. Just stuffing his stocking feet into those hard boots felt like a win. On the final day, his ski instructor and I juggled him between us and rode up the chairlift. Because what goes up must come down, we held our breath and began the descent.

Damn if he didn't do it.

Made it the whole way down upright with lots of assistance and what looked like reins attached to his skis and steered by the instructor. I skied backward and enticed him to chase me and keep moving. As we neared the end, I heard his siblings cheering from the ski lift. I wiped away tears as we gathered for a family photo to capture a scenario that I never dreamed possible.

Success doesn't have to be something as grand as a ski trip.

A simple trip to Walmart can be progress and a huge win. I remember one quick trip to a nearby town to do some shopping. I hadn't realized until we were halfway there that Amos had not put on shoes. Life with Amos meant this was not something to stress about and we continued on our way to go shopping. He was allowed to choose one Lego set and success was having this choice happen without a meltdown.

He wavered but ultimately chose the space shuttle and began planning the building process immediately.

*When you get home, you will build ALL the Legos. Just Mommy and Amos. Isn't that right? ALL the Legos.*

At the checkout, we held up the line as he insisted on scanning everything in our cart all by himself. I accepted my role as observer, and as I watched him flipping items to look for the barcodes, I wondered if someday this skill could be turned into a job. It's what mothers like myself do.

With his diagnosis, my perspective on accomplishment changed dramatically. I giggle now with the thought of that girl who believed that she could beat fate. Life doesn't abide by our wishes and that realization can come with the gift of the most wonderful freedom. If not for Amos, I would have passed down the biggest lie on which my foundation had been built.

Success isn't wrapped up in checking those many boxes.

It's moving in a direction that betters the world.

It's more about counting raindrops than measuring a heavy downpour.

Amos is the epitome of success and I would be lost without him—he is my weather gauge, my barometer, my why, and the axis on which our family swivels. He steers our family to all that is good and hopeful and amazing.

## CARRIE

If you had told me five years ago that Jack would one day live in a college program, I would have stared at you blankly and shaken my head in disbelief.

For as often as I wished for a crystal ball to see into the future, I never looked much further than adolescence. I never considered what life would be like for him as a young adult.

I never thought about programs or residential places for kids with his kind of autism profile.

For nineteen years, autism connected Jack and me in complicated ways. As long as I can remember, I fought for him. I spoke for him. I hoped for him. I often joked that the umbilical cord never quite severed between us. At times it stretched, sure, but he remained attached to me in ways my other kids began to outgrow. He orbited me in the house—calling my name up to a dozen times an hour. If I was out alone, he would listen for my car in the driveway and greet me at the door as soon as I pulled into the garage.

Dropping Jack off at his college program was perhaps the hardest moment of my life. Nothing prepared me for the way we all stood in the parking lot after we moved in his belongings and set up his room, and after we said our goodbyes, he turned one way, and we turned the other.

It's been said again and again that in this life alongside autism, there is no manual. There are no instructions for how to manage meltdowns, get through puberty, or navigate your new expected role of advocate. Watching Jack turn and walk into the building that day, I realized there are no instructions for how to untie yourself from a tender child who needed you for so long. You forget what life was like before he disrupted your world in an exquisitely magical way.

I read somewhere that it's easy to trap bees in a jar because they focus on the bottom and the walls. They never look up and understand there is freedom above them. I didn't want to let Jack go. At the same time, I didn't want him to wait for me another moment. I didn't want him to watch the world through glass. I wanted him to reach out and know his own sky.

You could say the separation from him began months—maybe years—before that day in the parking lot. It's a process I call *untethering.* To me, it's a triangle of sorts. There are three corners: physical, emotional, and interpretive.

Physically, I knew Jack could sleep somewhere other than our house. When he was around five, he would sleep at Joe's parents' house for a night or two. Sometimes he would go with his brothers, and sometimes he went on his own.

Once all the kids were old enough, we started to look into summer camps—informal programs run by the YMCA with a little structure but mostly centered around play and having fun. Although we didn't realize it at the time, this was a great way to prepare Jack for his program after high school.

All of us, including Jack, were pretty nervous the first time we dropped him off at the campground. But he was with his brothers and the staff was very informed about his diagnosis and his needs. It turned out to be a great way to introduce him to the idea of community living—this was especially important for eating in a large group. Many kids on the spectrum have trouble sharing meals with a lot of people because the sounds and smells can add up to a difficult sensory experience.

When Jack was about twelve, we stopped managing his medication. Since Jack is a steadfast rule-follower, we were confident he could take the dosage safely and as instructed before bed. Carefully, he'd fill the small Dixie cup we kept in the kids' bathroom with water. We showed him how to handle the childproof cap and shake one into the palm of his hand. Eventually, when he needed a refill, he'd leave the bottle on a little wooden table we have in the hallway upstairs.

Once he was accepted into his college program, we decided to familiarize him with the doctor portal. One afternoon after school we sat at my laptop, and I showed him how to log in to the website and message his doctor. After that, we used Google Maps to find a pharmacy within walking distance to his residential space and set up an account.

Next came emotional untethering. This was much, much harder. Emotional untethering meant moving beyond the physical, concrete aspects of medication and sleeping away from home. For so long, Jack's frontal lobe was connected to mine. Even as a teenager, he rarely made a decision without checking with me first. What to wear, when to eat, if he should bake cookies. Slowly, I began to disentangle us. Like the sun making a long, unhurried arc across the sky, so too is the disentanglement of mother and son.

As I've mentioned, there is a duality in kids like Jack: his physical age and his emotional spirit. When it comes to raising a special needs child, there can be a tendency to parent only the younger versions—infantilizing our kids long into adulthood. At the same time, codependency can be easily created. As the mother, I thought I was the only one who could understand him, or advocate for his needs.

It forced me to consider my relationship more carefully and come to terms with a few things. Jack isn't my friend. He's not my companion. He is my son. In some ways, *untethering* is a word wrapped around a stop sign—it is a process of stopping all I did for him, in hopes he can start doing it himself. Because if untethering is wrapped around a stop sign, then codependency is the sly lean into the red-and-white yield. I was determined to keep us both upright.

The truth is, Jack was becoming a young man. At six feet, five inches tall, he has facial hair. His voice is deeper than his father's. I wanted to make sure he was respected in the outside world, and not always considered childlike.

Practically speaking, untethering meant I told him to stop waiting for me whenever I left the house.

I stopped calling him Big Guy.

I stopped suggesting what clothes he should wear.

I stopped ordering for him in restaurants.

I stopped monitoring how much soda he drinks or cheeseburgers he eats at a barbecue.

The first time I pulled into the garage and noticed he wasn't waiting for me, I put my head down on the steering wheel and cried. What was I doing? What was this all for? Still, I persevered.

His first few months at the college program were not as successful as we'd hoped. He was in constant contact with us—sometimes up to thirty texts a day. He checked in with us every few hours, explaining what he was having for lunch, what his roommate was having for lunch, what the lunch lady was having for lunch.

I remember one afternoon in particular. I was trying to get some work done at my desk when my phone kept going off with text after text from him, even though I'd asked him to wait until later that afternoon to connect with me. I felt a surge of rage and frustration so strong, it was all I could do not to hurl the phone against the wall.

Even from afar, we were a *we*. Our frontal lobes were still connected.

I forced myself to sit back in my chair. I spread my hands out in front of me with my thumbs touching and my forefingers extended, making the shape of a *W*. Slowly, I moved my hands apart and tucked my thumbs in, creating two *I*s. This was my visual—I need to move him from a *We* to an *I*.

We started telling him we would check for texts once a day. Then we suggested he call in the evening to tell us news from the day. In his own wily way, Jack would figure out ways to keep engaging us. What time would we check? Was everything okay? Could we check in earlier?

It took a full year. And every time I was tempted to give in and answer his text, or I felt myself lured in by some good old-fashioned manipulation, I stopped and forced myself to make these shapes with my hands. *We* to *I*.

It is easy to feel guilty when we set boundaries with our kids, like it's bad parenting or we're being unsupportive. Yet the concept of boundaries reaches back to eighteenth-century crop holders, who set boundaries in the soil in order to allow each harvest to flourish and grow. They exist for a very good reason. Desperately, I wanted my boy to blossom into this new life.

Slowly—so slowly it often felt like we were standing still—the texts became less frequent. He started to skip a nightly call here and there. I started to breathe a little easier. The umbilical cord was stretching at last.

He came home for a short time over the summer, and that's when I realized how much I continued to speak and mediate for him. For so long, I interpreted Jack to world and world to Jack. It occurred to me that it was time to slide out between the two and let them begin to figure one another out themselves.

This happened in a restaurant. We'd taken him, my oldest son, Joseph, and Joseph's girlfriend out for dinner. This was a rare combination of kids for us, but the younger three were busy.

When the server came to the table, Jack ordered pepperoni pizza. But when the food came, she brought something different. I think it was mushroom truffle—something I knew he wouldn't want. Once he realized the mistake, he abruptly announced that it wasn't what he'd ordered.

I could feel my nervous system rise. I leaned forward in my chair, ready to intervene. But then, much like my moment at the middle school concert with Joe, I decided not to get involved. I forced myself to sit back and fold my hands in my lap. I tried to ignore the pit in my stomach while I waited to see what would happen next. Would he be rude? Or start to twitch nervously?

In moments like this, I wonder how this story will turn out. How long will I look over my shoulder? How long will I wait for the chaos to descend? How badly I want to know the ending.

Across the table, Joseph shifted in his seat and looped his arm around his girlfriend's shoulders. He knows this dance all too well. I held my breath. For a long, awkward moment, no one spoke. Then, out of nowhere, Jack made an announcement.

"I will try this pizza. If I don't like it, I will be ordering dessert."

We all smiled and agreed that, yes, this sounded like a great plan.

He tried a bite and ate three slices.

In the fall Jack went back to his college program. He was thrilled to return—ready to head back to the space he now calls *home*. And although my heart squeezes when I hear him call it that, I know this is good.

The other night, I asked Joe if he'd heard from Jack during the day. He shook his head no. "Me neither," I said. We both smiled at this small triumph. In life alongside autism, success is often in the details.

How will this story turn out? I have no idea. I can only tell you what is, as opposed to what will be. It is the story of brotherhood, motherhood, changed minds, and beating hearts. It is the story of the wind at our backs and the sun on our faces. The ordinary, dazzling story of metamorphosis of boy to man.

It's easy to assume the story begins and ends here. I don't know where it began. I don't know where it ends. But I believe the middle of it happened in a garage, with my tall boy's silhouette making shadows on the wall.

"Mom. I always come to the door to see if you have groceries to carry inside."

People ask me how I let him go. All I can say is, when I notice it's raining, I look to the sky. And I hope he remembers his own umbrella.

# 13
# What Does the Future Look Like?

## KATE

This chapter almost didn't make it in the book. We had it in the original outline, but when it came to writing it, Adrian and I both said we didn't want to predict the future. I think we were both scared to even make a guess of what forever could look like for Amos and Cooper. Neither of us wanted to limit our kids, nor did we want to have unrealistic dreams. We also didn't feel comfortable diving into topics like guardianship, group homes, or day programs because neither of us are there yet. So, we scrapped it. But then, upon review, in the eleventh hour, it was obvious that it was missing.

People want to know what forever looks like for Cooper, Amos, and Jack. Each of them uniquely made with their own strengths and challenges. Our followers see their own children in our boys, and they wonder how this will all end up.

Will they be able to live independently? Or will they live in a group home? Drive? Work a job? Get married? Will siblings be involved? What will happen after we die? All valid questions.

The truth is, for Cooper, I can't definitively say. For so long the future felt unknown, a black hole, even. I couldn't picture Cooper as a man. There were just too many uncertainties and unknowns.

No one ever talks about autistic children growing up. Never.

As parents, we are told to take it day by day, even hour by hour. Focus on the present. Don't worry about the future. And for so many years, Jamie and I did just that. We were reactive, not proactive. We managed every curveball autism threw at us. Simply put, we survived.

In the most beautiful way, age became just a number with Cooper. It stopped mattering. For many years, Cooper's kindergarten photo stayed on the wall, freezing him at that age. There were no grade levels in therapy, no school pictures either. Even the seasons cease to matter when you have a child who doesn't like to play in the snow or go to the beach. The markers in time that most take for granted disappeared.

In a way it's like we became solo members of our own club. And we get to make the rules. We get to focus our goals and hopes and wishes around what's best for him. What he truly needs and what makes him happy, not what's age appropriate.

He loves Thomas and Barney and Dora. He loves visiting train depots and scouring gift shops for old-man train documentaries in VHS format and magazines no longer in print.

He loves lining up brightly colored pieces of paper throughout our home and bringing me black-and-white magazine clippings from the 1960s with details about trips to Canada or the Ozarks. Trips that cost $50 and no longer are happening.

He is uniquely made. Parts old. Parts young. Not one part his actual age. He will grow and age at his own pace. On his own time. Some parts leaping. Some parts frozen in time.

To survive, we focused on finding joy in standing still. That is until recently—I opened Cooper's backpack to find a form mixed in with his speech device, a change of clothes, and an art project I know he didn't make.

The form said "transition planning." Three pages of questions, none of which I had the answers to. Heck, I hadn't even been brave enough to think of the questions yet.

Where would Cooper live after he finished high school? Would he work? Was college a goal? If not, what kind of job would he be able to do? If he couldn't work, who would care for him during the day? Where will he live as we age? Are we financially prepared?

I stared for way too long at that form, my tears soaking my face. Because in my hand were all the questions I had been avoiding for thirteen years.

Of course, Jamie and I had discussed the future. In the beginning, many of our conversations ended with me crying or us fighting. The reality of our future felt terrifying. But as the grainy picture came into focus, it showed us three rocking chairs on a patio and cross-country trips on Amtrak. We agreed that Cooper would live with us forever. That was the plan.

But lately, as parts of Cooper's autism are getting harder, cracks have begun to emerge in my plan. How can we do this forever? And without resentment.

Jamie wants to travel. He wants to retire in Arizona and live his final years on the golf course. He wants to be done caring for kids at some point. His feelings aren't wrong. And I get it. But there is no carefree living when you are a caregiver. I can't imagine doing any of this when I'm seventy years old. Bathing my adult son. Laying my body gently over his during a meltdown. Living in a world of Wi-Fi and trains and Elmo. Those are the things I will be doing when I'm seventy.

When I share our story, I often feel the pressure to put a bow on everything I say about autism. When I bring up my worries about the future, I hear that I am being negative. But truthfully, I am not. I am being realistic, and I am terrified.

*"I don't want my son to lose his home and us (his parents) in the same accident."*

A fellow mother said that to me on a podcast a while back. Her son was sixteen at the time and they were already starting long-term care transition planning. I felt a little bit uncomfortable with the conversation. Maybe even a little bit of judgment toward her, because I want to keep Cooper with me forever. But she wasn't wrong. In fact, she was right. If something was to happen to her and her husband, her son would lose his home and his parents in an instant. She wanted to make the decisions for her son's future. She wanted to be in control of it. And she feared if she waited too long, she wouldn't be able to.

After the podcast was finished, I immediately called Adrian. I shared the woman's plans and how I hoped to keep Cooper with me forever.

"You can't keep Cooper forever, Kate. Because you won't be here forever."

Her words stung. She was right though. I won't be able to care for Cooper forever. He will have to live without me someday.

As parents, we are faced with impossible, heartbreaking decisions. And I will say for everyone that needs to hear it… it's not fair.

I recently turned forty-one. Surpassing forty forced me to think about turning fifty and sixty and seventy. But more importantly, that means Cooper will one day be twenty-two, thirty-two, and forty-two. What will that look like? The other day, I was helping him shower, which is a huge accomplishment. For years, he was terrified of the shower, and I worried about bathing a teen in the bathtub. But, of course, like he always does, he surprised me one day and hopped right into the shower as if he'd been doing it for years. He still needs my help to wash his body and hair, so I reach an arm in and get the job done.

It is in those most vulnerable moments when I feel our ages the most. Sometimes the tears fall from my eyes as I think about who will gently wash his body and make sure the soap is out of his eyes before he opens them. This is a gift, not a job. An honor, not a burden. If I let it, the fear will consume me. But no matter what, I make sure the tears are gone before he opens his eyes and smiles at me. Me growing older means that he is too. And one day, I will be gone. I don't have all the answers yet. I don't know if I know all the questions yet. *One day at a time*, I always say.

Now, I am a realist. And I've always known that we live our lives, hopefully long ones, and then die. But I've never been afraid of it. Because I always imagined myself old, my children grown, their children grown, as well. I didn't imagine any loose ends. I didn't imagine leaving a boy who will never understand why I left him. One who will wait in the window for me to return. A boy who is so incredibly vulnerable to all types of abuse. One who needs love, patience, and a mother to care for him.

I can plan for the logistics. But I can't plan for the love. Who will hug him after I am gone? Who will wipe his mouth, and make sure his waistband isn't cutting into his sides, and write endless words on his whiteboard?

Who will be me after I am gone?

The panic started a few months back. It comes in the middle of the night, at 2:00 a.m., when I can't fall back to sleep. Or more recently, I found myself frozen in the driver's seat at a stoplight on my drive home. It was like a movie scene. The light was green, yet I didn't move. My foot was placed firmly on the brake. Cars honked. I could hear them. They drove around me, some gesturing at me. But I was paralyzed.

We had just spent the week at a cabin rental in northern Minnesota for spring break. We can't fly but we can drive and stay in a cabin. Three kids fished and rode ATVs and played outside. And Cooper, he snuggled up in a big comfy chair and watched it all through the picture window. It was perfect until it wasn't. Which sums up our life honestly. Cooper had a very challenging meltdown. I could try and explain what caused it. A television that didn't work right. A fear of getting burnt in a fireplace that wasn't even in use. Loud siblings. Me leaving for a few hours. The list goes on and on. But really, I could sum it up by saying autism happened. It was more intense than any he'd had in a long time. It lasted hours. When it was over, I felt the weight of autism more than I had ever remembered. Thoughts running through my head...

*No one else can do this. No one will ever be able to care for him but me. No one else could ever love him enough to do this.*

I grieved for two weeks after that spring-break trip.

As I sat at the light, I had a flash of the future. I was gone. So was Jamie. Cooper was living in a group home. He was a man. And he was being abused and no one was there to help him. I heard his screams in the silence of my car. I'm not sure how much time passed before I snapped out of it.

Instead of hiding, I shared my fears and worries out loud every single day. With my husband, my family, my friends, and my followers.

I grabbed grief's hand and walked with her, exploring and feeling the feelings. I created scenarios of the future in my head and planned the best I could for each of them. And then I created one more scene in my head. I imagined it working out. Beautifully. I pictured him safe and warm. I pictured his siblings gathered around him, hugging him, and holding his hand, gasping at the train on the screen of his cell phone. I pictured him laughing his deep belly laugh while thrusting two fingers up in the air and demanding two more cookies, the ones with the thick frosting. I imagined him happy.

A while back, Jamie and I found ourselves driving around a picturesque town for twenty minutes or so alone. We had no kids with us. There was no loud noise or fighting, endless questions, or music from an iPad. It was just us, driving around looking at holiday lights, Christmas music playing softly.

Eventually we found ourselves in the parking lot of what looked like a brand-new apartment complex located right on the river. It was breathtaking. After looking at the sign, we saw it was for folks over fifty-five years old.

Our conversation became about the ease of living in a place like that. No grass to mow. No sidewalks to shovel. We even spoke of walking outside and taking our boat for an evening cruise. There were restaurants and bars and places to get coffee all around.

A silence filled the car. My thoughts turned to Cooper. I am sure Jamie's did too. The proverbial elephant in the room is always with us. We will never have an empty nest. Never.

We sat for a while taking in the white lights framing the windows. Tears began to fall from my eyes. Then from his. His hand reached for mine.

*"Cooper would love this,"* I said.

Without skipping a beat, Jamie responded, *"He absolutely would. He would love this."*

## ADRIAN

Considering Amos's forever has never been fun.

When he was ten days old, I knew his forever would be different from that of my other children. I didn't know that TALKING about forever would be so heavy though. How often the world emphasizes its importance—not even a simple meeting about his education can occur without an interrogation about his future. I think the powers that be mean it to be inspiring.

A chance to dream big and put magical wishes to paper, yet it never fails to spring tears from my eyes.

The question of his future propels a whirling torrent of fearful thoughts, and I struggle with the guessing about, the worrying about, and the planning of my boy's forever. So often you hear parents voice their sentiments about their special child's future. "He will always live with us," say many a mother, but that sentiment defies logic. As much as I'd like to keep my son tucked beneath my wings, someday I will fly, and so, he must fly first.

After I'm gone, what will become of him?

Despite my commitment to acknowledging the truth, that question is still my boogeyman—the black hole that pulls me to confront my greatest fears. I can't imagine anything worse than uprooting him after my death, and so I have to consider the hard stuff.

Questions like where he will live, what he will do on holidays, and who will see to it that he sees the dentist twice a year or gets a regular haircut. These are scenarios that every mother of a special needs child must think about.

What does our empty nest look like?

After all, it will never truly be empty, because even if

Amos is not in my physical space, he will always hold court in my mind and own my heart.

I long for Amos to be independent, not in the traditional sense, but to have his own life.

He deserves his *own* life—one filled with laughter and plans—a life where he is the main act, not the tagalong.

I imagine him living with a few friends and surrounded by kind caretakers—maybe near the ocean or the mountains. Maybe near a big airport so he can travel to all the countries on his bucket list. I want his siblings to love him as their precious youngest brother, not act as replacement parents.

I don't want them to be up at night worrying about his needs being met, medications being filled, or making sure he is scrubbed and shaved. I hope they envelop him in the regular parts of their lives, and with that, I mean holidays with his siblings and summer vacations. I imagine him living close enough to at least one of them for convenient weekend overnights or special trips to his favorite places or on his favorite airline. I long for his place to be one of importance amongst their future families.

Though he will be their responsibility, I don't want him to be a burden. Maybe they wouldn't feel like that, but our goal is to simplify his future by preparing now.

We go on trips and to the grocery store and even sporting events, just so Amos builds up the ability to participate in activities and interact with the world. Simple outings can be made complicated by a long line or an unmet expectation, but we go because we have to build up his endurance for the world.

Eventually he won't have me to help him through, and so, to ensure his best future, we practice.

This past spring, I took Amos to several of his big sister's track meets. For years, we could not take Amos to any school event. Even the activities crawling with loud toddlers and preschoolers were not structured for families like ours. Amos doesn't easily wait in lines or follow three-step directions. Athletic events are particularly tricky for us.

We try each year, and this year, we finally had success. The track is a wonderful place to practice, largely because the area has only one exit. This year, Amos did not attempt to zigzag between runners on the track or slip under the chain-link fence. Instead, he navigated the bleachers and happily read the signs of business sponsors. I stood along the fence with all the other parents—parents who don't belong to children who require constant surveillance and intervention. It's been a goal to stand there, to experience what it means to be a regular family socializing with friends and allow Amos some freedom to navigate the world without my looming presence.

Eventually, he made his way back to me and set up shop at the concession stand.

I overheard him request a hot dog from the middle school student at the counter. When he produced no money, they produced no hot dog. He walked back to my position along the fence and I asked him if he would like to buy something. With his yes, I pulled out a few crumpled bills and gave him simple instructions to hand over the bills in exchange for a hot dog. He did as instructed and then returned to the bleachers and the comforting familiarity of those signs.

Later that afternoon, I handed him a ten-dollar bill and told him to bring me the change. I knew he didn't know what that meant, but he came back with his popcorn tucked in the crook of one arm and my bills clutched in the other hand.

"Here's your change!" he said proudly.

The baby whose future filled me with fear now speaks in sentences and I marvel at how far he's come. Yet he will depend on the care by others to live his best life. Though ours is an amazing family, it's not enough. I will not be here forever and his siblings will have families and lives of their own. Because I want Amos to have his own life, too, we will depend on help. But luckily there are resources for families who have children with special needs.

Rather than place children in sterile buildings with minimal care and no education, the federal government decided that children could be better cared for by their own families, whether in their homes or long-term living situations chosen by their families. In order to make this happen, the Waiver program is a federal program created to support those families. The Waiver program is run by the states and implemented in a variety of ways. The common thread is that when a child is granted the waiver, he or she will be provided health care (through Medicaid) and care services for the length of his or her lifetime.

Unfortunately, the majority of states have lengthy wait lists, and families can easily wait for a dozen years or more for services. Like so many, our family sits on the wait list for the Waiver of Unmet Needs. But our family receives services like developmental therapy and respite while we wait for the waiver. We receive developmental therapy hours where a caregiver works with Amos on self-care goals like teeth brushing and community goals like going to the movies.

Amos has been on the Waiver wait list since he was three years old and we were told the wait would be about seven to nine years. We are hopeful that he will receive the waiver by the time he finishes high school, which will be when he is twenty-two years old. Having a plan for Amos's health insurance and care offered through the waiver makes the fears of the future sting a bit less.

I can't tell you what life will look like in five or ten years or even twenty years, but I am thankful for the now, the daily successes and progress as Amos learns to navigate the world. I'm thankful for our amazing caregiver, excellent teachers, kindhearted friends, and an inclusive community. Maybe the best part of forever is right now.

## CARRIE

I have a scar on my left index finger. I got it in high school, in a class called Technology. In retrospect the name is ironic, as we didn't use anything that resembled technology.

I was carving something out of clay. We were using a metal tool shaped like a spoon with sharp edges. I turned to talk to my friend Ruth, and it slipped and caught my finger. Forty-plus years later, you can hardly see the scar. But every now and again I find myself rubbing it absentmindedly.

Tonight, I sit at my desk. The evening sunlight dances across the floor. I am in a mood I can't describe—equal parts pensive and happy. I am attempting to finish this chapter, because although we're not sure yet where it will land in the book, this is the one I've chosen to write last.

What does the future look like? It's a great question, if only I knew how to answer it.

At this point, Jack is finishing up his second year in his residential program. In the next few months, he will move to an apartment of his own. Using a floor plan he got from the landlord, he has been busy taking new measurements of the rooms and making lists of what to buy on Amazon. New towels, a bath mat, pots and pans. This is his wheelhouse, if you will. Organization is his superpower.

*Splinter skills.* This is a term I recently learned in connection to autism. You would think I'd have heard of them all by this point, but it seems like we keep coming up with new ways to deconstruct this tricky disorder.

*Splinter skills* refers to abilities that are disconnected from their usual context or purpose. Because they are just a "splinter," or fraction, of a meaningful set of skills, splinter skills aren't always useful in real-life situations. They are commonly found in people diagnosed with autism.

For example, a child with autism may memorize all the statistics around baseball, but not understand the game itself. In Jack's case, the concept of a lease or a mortgage is meaningless to him, but he excels in setting up his apartment.

I often say there is a duality within kids like Jack—his physical age versus his emotional age. At nearly twenty, his body is rounding the corner into adulthood, while his spirit and heart remain somewhat stuck at perhaps twelve or thirteen. And when it comes to launching him into the world and making room for some independence, the stakes feel very high.

In my lowest moments, when I am mostly likely to catastrophize, or imagine every bad-case scenario, I often go right to the worst. He could bump into the wrong person at the wrong time and get assaulted. He could get arrested. He could be taken advantage of by people with less-than-good intentions.

Sexuality. Online dating. Social media. These are a few of the things we are trying to figure out as we raise a young adult diagnosed with autism.

As Joe and I work to balance keeping him safe while also preparing him for a semblance of his own life, I keep one eye trained on the proverbial crystal ball. What will Jack's autism look like in the future?

The other day I realized I have never seen an old man with autism—a man well past his seventies. A little hunched, maybe using a cane, his white hair in tufts around his head.

Once, at a party, I saw a man in his thirties. His resemblance to Jack took my breath away. I heard him before I saw him. His voice was several octaves too loud. He leaned in close to whomever he spoke to—a breach of personal space. He walked the length of the bar, asking other patrons their name, their reason for being there. I tried to guess his exact age. Thirty, perhaps? He was desperate to tell his story about autism.

My mind wandered to Jack, tucked away in his program thousands of miles away. I thought about all the times we asked him to lower his voice, to keep his hands still. The times we practiced how close to stand when you talk to someone.

So often, I wondered if I was shaping and reshaping him too much for the world's liking. I worried I was trying to erase who he was—changing his own story to make it palatable. But can we hear the story through the fog of symptoms? The loud voice, the twitching, the breach of personal space.

Does he need to change for the world? Or the world change for him? What is the answer? This is what I ask myself.

At the party, the young man eventually made his way toward me. He offered to show me a video of him and his mom on his phone. I nodded my head and smiled. People around us smirked. They rolled their eyes. With each reaction, my heart sank.

When Jack was diagnosed with autism, I felt like I had a clock strapped to my back. Now, nearly twenty years later, I am still racing against time. I am racing to explain him to the world and the world to him. The fact of the matter is, autism is no longer cute or quirky.

Whenever I thought about Jack's future, my mind hovered on the practical.

Will he get a driver's license? Will he manage money? Will he have a family?

Maybe. Once upon a time, that was what I would have said to each of these. Now I am less sure.

Is there a point where the progress stops? When *maybe*

becomes *never*? Lately, I think of all that will likely never happen.

He will likely never drive a car, winding through back roads as autumn's sun streams through the trees.

He will likely never run for office, or own a business, or plan a vacation.

He will likely never hold his own child.

Likely.

Never.

I know you want to stop me here. You want to remind me of hope. I know all about the hope. I subsist on hope. I breathe it in like barbed silk. Smooth at first, yet deceptively thorny. Sometimes, hope is not enough. This is the heartache with which I am familiar.

I read a lot of posts and memes that declare autism is a gift.

Autism is not a gift. No one hopes their baby is born with it. No one hopes their son or daughter will struggle with communication, social cues, or isolation. No one hopes they will one day stand in a courtroom and appeal for guardianship.

To say autism is a gift is a disservice to the mothers and fathers who advocate tirelessly for their child—who wake up in the middle of the night panicking about what will happen when they die. It is an injustice to the siblings who grow up alongside this diagnosis, who know that, one day, they will assist in caregiving.

It is especially unfair to the individuals themselves who work their hardest for what comes easily to most. Who sit on life's sidelines as our culture celebrates trophies, awards, promotions, and status.

Inside the bell curve are tiny steps forward, the unexpected smile, the good day at school, the first bite of a new food, the tiny triumphs that propel us to another day. These are the gifts.

The gift is the surrender. The surrender to a life we didn't ask for, yet love all the same.

Financial independence. A driver's license. Fatherhood. Autism keeps all these things out of his reach. He is vulnerable, and often misunderstood.

What is his future? Our future?

Will autism repeat itself again, a duplicate strand of DNA showing up once more?

Will someone hurt him? Take advantage of him? Break his heart?

Will he live alone forever?

What will happen when I die?

I don't know what the future holds.

Sometimes, I make my own version. I imagine a day where everything is clear. This is the day I think of when I hunger for more—a made-up day.

Or is it?

Early June.

Joe and I sit on the front porch. The grass is green, the leaves on the trees vibrant.

Through the window you can see a calendar hanging in the kitchen. The year reads Sunday, June 21st, 2054. Father's Day.

His favorite dessert sits in the refrigerator—the lemon tart I've been making since we were in college from a recipe I clipped out of a magazine.

I look over at this man. I smile.

He takes my hand.

"They're here," he says.

One by one, cars pull into the driveway.

A mismatched jumble of people spills out onto the grass. Sullen teenagers, chubby toddlers, son- and daughters-in-law.

Kids.

Grandkids.

Another car approaches. Self-driving, it shuts off on its

own. He steps out into the sunlight. At nearly fifty, silver threads his once-dark hair.

They circle him, like petals around the heart of a flower.

This is family.

Sharp edges, scars that heal, made-up stories to get through the day.

Timeworn recipes of lemon, of heartache, of worry, and hope.

A small boy walks over to the car.

In his young face, I see the smile of my children. I see their youth. I think of Star Wars pajamas, of childhood, of birds gone free in the sky.

He reaches out a hand.

What you don't know can tell you everything.

"Uncle Jack! We have the same name."

Jack.

Jack.

He is the gift.

My son.

My sun.

# EPILOGUE

It's late summer now. Warm, sunny days give way to cooler evenings. Fall, all colorful leaves and back-to-school shopping, is well on its way.

After nearly ten months of meeting, writing, editing, and revising, this book is finished. It is the collaborative effort of many late-night texts, Zoom calls, and Google documents. Messy conversations, and a lot of soul-searching.

What to add? What to leave out? What do people need to know as they navigate their own journey alongside autism? These are the questions we asked each other, and ourselves.

The cover took the longest to decide. The three of us desperately wanted to capture our three boys in a single image—which is harder to do than one might think.

Cooper is fourteen now. He's learning to ride a trike and

has an Amtrak trip planned to Chicago with Kate, which he reminds her of a dozen times a day.

Amos is eleven, and still loves all things travel. He is hoping to take a cruise around the world one day.

Jack recently turned twenty. He has a new apartment and a job washing dishes in a pizza place. He continues to take classes in broadcasting and social media.

Our boys are growing up.

We take the fiercest pride in every triumph, no matter how small. Yet beneath our rib cage, worry continues to beat its drum.

Autism. Over time, this diagnosis became the lens through which we view life's details.

*We can't die.*

This is the mantra of every special needs mother. *We can't die.*

Yet immortality belongs to no one. This is why we tell our story.

This is why we share about the medication, the behaviors, the marital discord, and the grief.

We told it even when people warned us not to share.

We told it when we didn't think it would mean anything to anyone.

We told it as an insurance of sorts, hoping against all hope someone will pick up the baton and carry it when we no longer can.

We hope reading our words inspired you to share your own. It doesn't have to be a book. It can be a blog post, or a short essay, or even a conversation. Autism shouldn't have to be a secret any longer.

Collectively, we have to share our moments of light, our gentle intentions, our radical grace, our reckless mercy, our tender, tender resilience.

Because if compassion is a house we build, then storytelling is the key to the front door.

It is the entrance to our messy kitchens and our lopsided picture frames and our wildly unguarded hearts.

It is the only way to open the windows and bring in the sun.

* * * * *

# POSTSCRIPT
## Autism Is Not a Tragedy

### KATE

Nine days after *Autism Out Loud* became a reality, the autism community was turned upside down and inside out. On April 10, 2025, Robert F. Kenndy Jr. announced a "massive testing and research effort" to determine the causes of what he called an "autism epidemic." As if that wasn't a bold enough statement, he also claimed that the US Health and Humans Services Department would find the cause of autism by September.

This bold declaration wasn't made quietly either. Instead, it was announced on the national news, interrupting regular television programming for all of the United States, and leaving me staring at the television with my hand over my mouth.

My immediate reaction was dread. I knew in my heart this wasn't going to go well. What is that old Proverbs saying? "A house divided against itself cannot stand." It refers to the ruin that occurs when members of a group fight each other. The autism community is a divisive one. The Neurodiversity Movement is at war with the parents of autistic children. There is an ongoing debate over ABA and treatments for autism, and even the use of language like high functioning versus low functioning, special needs versus disability, and so on. I've often thought how much further we could be as a community if we could come together.

And yet at the same time, other feelings quietly bubbled up inside me. Feelings from an exhausted mom who has been navigating this often isolating life for close to sixteen years. Shock that severe autism finally entered the conversation. Intrigue, hope, gratitude even.

Could they really find out the cause of autism? Was it possible? Right or wrong, I would give anything to know why my son has autism. Why is he so severely affected? Why him and not his siblings? Is it my fault? Should I have done something differently?

And then, just six days later, on April 16, at another press conference, Kennedy referred to autism as a "tragedy" and an "epidemic" that "destroys families." He also made claims that people with autism "will never pay taxes, they'll never hold a job, they'll never play baseball, they'll never write a poem."

That's the moment everything went sideways.

The ding of text messages received on my phone in the days following his announcements sounded like a chorus as friends and acquaintances wanted to know my thoughts. It didn't end there. A guy I went to high school with and haven't seen in twenty-five years, my mailman, even the cashier at my local grocery store, all wanted to know my opinions. Was autism a tragedy? Did it destroy our family?

Now if you know me in real life, or through my smaller subscriber groups on social media, you know that there are two topics I never, ever talk about.

Politics, and vaccines in relation to autism.

I've been sharing in the public eye long enough to know that rarely, if ever, does good come from debating those two topics. Opinions are never changed. Views are never swayed.

And yet, both topics were front and center. Now, one could argue that autism isn't political and I would agree with you. It's not. But it was.

If you are anything like me, polar extremism makes me want to hide.

Seeing and hearing about autism in the news felt surreal to me. I often say that my son has the kind of autism that no one wants to talk about. It's not shiny or pretty, and he needs an unbelievable amount of support. For some reason, that makes people uncomfortable.

But up until this point in time, I longed for people to peel back the lens and see us and him. I thought it was what I wanted. To be seen. To be understood. To finally have people take notice of this complicated, mysterious, hard, sometimes sad, yet often magical life alongside autism.

I was wrong.

Reading and hearing about my son's disability, mostly being shared by people who don't live it, was a bit unsettling.

So much fighting. A lot of us versus them. Finger pointing. Blame. Name calling. I struggled to know whose side I was on.

When I drilled down into the real controversy, it seemed that some felt like finding a cause for autism would equal eugenics. Or a cure. That terrified those who felt their autism or their child's autism was a gift. And yet, the parents whose children have never spoken or hurt themselves and others felt hopeful.

Another controversy seemed to lie in the claims that people with autism "will never pay taxes, they'll never hold a job, they'll never play baseball, they'll never write a poem."

Some felt these statements meant that individuals with autism couldn't live meaningful lives. While on the other hand, parents of children with severe and profound autism were thankful to finally be seen. When I spoke to them, they felt optimistic that help would come from this.

What I noticed though is the loudest voices seem to forget that we are talking about real people and real families.

I always say autism is a family diagnosis. And I don't mean that in a genetic way. I mean that autism affects every person in our family. And differently.

Autism is a person.

A family.

A mom and dad.

Brothers and sisters.

A whole life.

Here are my thoughts. And they are my thoughts only.

Autism is not a gift. Nor is it a tragedy.

Autism is not an identity. It's a disability.

Autism is heartbreaking at times. And magical at other times.

Autism has brought so many wonderful people into my life. The best people really.

My greatest fear is dying and leaving my son.

We need more help. Where is it and when is it coming?

My son is amazing, and I thank God for him every single day.

I would take away his autism in a heartbeat. And until you've watched your child injure their own body or lay awake at night wondering who will care for them after you die . . . you don't get a say in that one.

I am so proud of my son and, honestly, he works harder than anyone I've ever met.

Having a sibling with a disability is hard and feels unfair at times. I don't know how anyone can deny that. But it sure does bring kindness, empathy, bravery and love, too.

Autism did not destroy our family. This is hard and even sad sometimes. But it's also made us strong and loyal. We take nothing for granted and we are thankful for what we have.

I want to know why my son has autism and why my other children don't. It's okay to ask why. And I believe it's from asking why that we will get more services and support. That's what I am hoping. I pray that from conversation comes help.

See, my thoughts are in between gift and tragedy. It's in our reality. It's in our every day. That's where we reside. It's "and," not "or." It's the grey area.

We live autism out loud. Whether it's in the news or not. And when this news cycle passes, we will still be here.

Living alongside autism. Praying to be seen and hoping to blend in.

This life, it's not what I pictured and it's hard at times. But boy, do I love my son.

And while my boy will never pay taxes or write a poem, or possibly even hold a job, he does play baseball. Our whole family helps him run the bases. There is nothing better than watching an adaptive baseball game. Trust me on that one. If you haven't seen one, you're missing out.

## ADRIAN

*Why do so many kids have autism?*

It is the question families get asked the most. In September of 2025, a White House press conference was held where Donald Trump, Robert F. Kennedy, Jr., and Dr. Mehmet Oz shared potential autism causes as well as treatment. There were broad warnings from the Department of Health and Human Services about vaccinations and taking Tylenol when pregnant. President Trump warned women against Tylenol use in pregnancy; his exact words were "fight like Hell not to take it." The FDA started a label change for acetaminophen saying the potential link between the medicine and neurological disorders in children, and they issued letters to physicians sharing the same information. The agency also started approval of Leucovorin calcium tablets as a treatment possibility for autism.

Mothers like myself were filled with self-reflection. Did I take Tylenol? I tried to remember being pregnant with number four. I even scoured my own medical records to look for evidence, though none was there. I remembered that I'd had a beer and I had been on another medication before I knew I was pregnant. Was that it? At the end of the day, we blame ourselves. But it's quite a contradiction to blame oneself for a beautiful human. Now what? Do we rush out and beg for a prescription? Like so many families like ours, I was left feeling more unsure than before the big announcement.

There is always going to be selling an idea and autism is no different, but what does the research say? Research shows that autism is genetic. The most recent study estimates that 80 percent of autism can be linked to genetic mutations. When Amos was four months old, we begged our pediatrician for genetic testing. We spent the next ten years looking for a genetic diagnosis, and three years after two rounds of Whole Exome Sequencing (WES), we received a call from a researcher in Canada. Further bloodwork solidified that Amos was one of fifty people in the world with a newly discovered variance called MSL2. I was filled with relief. Relief because families like ours want to know, but we need correct information, *not* vague potential causes not rooted in research.

Science does not lie. A study of 2.5 million children born between 1995 and 2019 looked at the use of acetaminophen during pregnancy. About 185,000 children were exposed prenatally to Tylenol and yet, they were no more likely to be autistic than the children *not* exposed. Tylenol is the current scapegoat in the world of autism, and while knowing "what" causes autism is not terrible, pointing to the wrong reason will not help families. It will not only spread misinformation but undermine the continued need for research. Families like mine deserve better, and so does my Amos.

My Amos is a spectacular being, perfectly imperfect, and I struggle with saying aloud that he is anything that needs to be prevented. How can you separate the autism from the boy? He adores traveling and can recite a zillion different airlines and tell you to which countries they embark. He knows almost every flag for every country in the world—quite literally hundreds of them. He can even hum their national anthems. His brain is a myriad of secrets and treasures, yet he struggles to tell me what he did at school. I do not expect details but would love to know if he went to art or PE, or what they are studying in history. Instead, when I pick him up in the afternoon, he greets his service dog in the back seat and then makes me repeat, "Good girl, she's a good girl!" Every day I perform the script and then we go to McDonald's, where he orders from the back seat window. Two plain cheeseburgers and a sweet tea, he says, and because his articulation is poor, I repeat it. Every day it is the same and that is just the way he likes it. While other boys his age are shooting baskets on the neighborhood goal or playing sports, autism keeps us on the fringes of society. Our cocoon is simple, joyful, and sometimes lonely.

He has made so much progress this year. He can go

upstairs and put on his own pajamas. He routinely asks when his older siblings will be home again and remembers the date. He is thriving in a traditional fifth-grade classroom with a tremendous amount of support. He is still on the "standard course of study" and I long for that to continue. We know through his genetic diagnosis—there are several adults within the fifty people discovered in the study—that he will never live a fully independent life. The more we know, the more we can support Amos to be the best version of himself.

There is an umbrella that explains the many parts that make up my special child—autism, ADHD, anxiety, and a genetic diagnosis of MSL2. Some would say that autism is not a problem—I'm not one of them. Some would say that autism should be extinguished—I'm not one of them, either. My son has autism and he will always need some level of care. No matter what we do, his disability influences his future and requires extensive plans. My son is amazingly imperfect. Different, not less. Sometimes I try to imagine him as a typical child and I never can. He is who he is meant to be and I am his mother. Would I choose autism? Probably not. Would I choose Amos? Absolutely. But still, I long to know the why behind the wholeness of him.

## CARRIE

*"Did you take Tylenol when you were pregnant with me?"*

The house is quiet. Joe went up to bed an hour ago. I am enjoying some time to myself, watching a show Joe doesn't like, when my phone buzzes next to me on the couch.

Jack. Jack-a-boo. Jack-attack.

Reading his text, my stomach sank. Just twelve hours earlier, Robert Kennedy, Jr. stood at a podium and made remarks regarding people diagnosed with autism, one of which asserted that mothers who used Tylenol, or acetaminophen, while they were pregnant have an increased risk of a child with autism.

Jack was diagnosed with autism almost twenty years ago, and two decades later, not a single day goes by when I don't wonder why. Why him? Why us? Again and again, I go through my pregnancy and the first days of infancy. What did I do wrong?

This is the burden special-needs moms carry. We are never absolved of the mistakes we don't even know we made. Time and time again, the finger seems pointed at us. Time and time again, we are called upon to defend ourselves.

At twenty-one, Jack is old enough to drink alcohol, rent a hotel room and vote in the election. Although he doesn't possess the language to explain it, I can tell he is trying to figure out where he stands, as a human being, as a student, as a young man, in the larger backdrop of headlines and current events surrounding his own diagnosis.

I cannot die.

I have repeated this mantra to myself until it alone became a living, breathing truth.

But I am starting to realize, much like the idea Joe and I once had that little-boy Jack might one day outgrow autism, this is a form of denial. Denial of the future, and of what it takes to plan financially. Of what we'll need Jack's siblings to know in order to keep their beloved brother moving forward in his life.

So now we are delving headlong into things like Social Security Income (SSI), Social Security Disability Income (SSDI) and Disabled Adult Child (DAC). We're a long way from the initial vocabulary autism bestowed upon on us—phrases like *working memory*, *joint attention* and, my very favorite, *theory of mind*—but I still feel like I'm playing catch-up with a language I will never fully understand.

Yet Jack's triumphs continue to show up in small, unexpected ways that many wouldn't even notice. A few weeks ago, he texted me and asked if I could send his suit. I wrote back and asked why, and he said there was a dance he was thinking of attending.

A dance. For the boy-turned-young-man. The one who, for as long as I can remember, hated crowds, loud noise, and music other people choose.

For as long as I can remember, I built cocoons for this boy. For twenty-one years, I have raced from place to place, creating what I refer to as safe landings. I call ahead of time. I fill out the endless paperwork. Via the phone and email messages, I explain his triggers, his behaviors, his quirks, his appetite. First, preschool. Then kindergarten, and summer camp, and karate class. Finally, a college program designed for the neurodiverse.

I explain all that I have explained before, that yes, he handles his refills. Yes, he administers the pills himself. Yes, he is what they call medication compliant.

But he may not answer you right away if you ask him a question. I describe his words like so many bees in a hive: First he must search through the buzzing before he can figure out what to say.

His autism isn't going anywhere. There is no cure. Anxiety will be a lifelong battle, as will his obsessive-compulsive disorder. Still, I can't help but hope a wild hope that maybe one day he will overcome all he continues to face. One day, the perpetual barrier between him and I will be gone. At long last, we will talk. Instead of exchanging information about the weather and celebrities like two court reporters, we will have a meaningful conversation.

I want to talk to my son.

What is it like to have the kid who doesn't fit anywhere?

Let me tell you.

It will break your heart into a million pieces every single day.

Cocoon-building. This is what I do. I thought I would do it forever. I thought I would explain him forever.

This week, he sent me a text about his job. He spent most of the summer searching local job sites. He ironed his dress shirt and checked—and, if I know Jack, rechecked—the bus schedule. Time and time again, he went on interviews. Finally, an offer came through for part-time work.

And I realized that for perhaps the first time, I have not built this cocoon. He did it all himself. Now, he communicates with his manager. He schedules his shifts and asks for time off. In fact, I have never even been to the grocery store where, week after week, my son cuts fruit and packages it to sell for people searching for shortcuts.

Cocoons.

Where this most tentative caterpillar eventually emerged, radiant and colorful

Whether it's TV shows like *Love on the Spectrum*, words spoken at a podium, or headlines in the news, I am glad whenever autism is part of the discussion. It doesn't matter how messy, or ill-informed, or tough it is. It's here. We are here. Autism is no longer the secret it once was.

These conversations light a fire. This incredible autism community—full of warriors, of caregivers, of mothers and fathers and brothers and sisters—will do the only thing we know how to do. We will use the flame to bring our loved ones out of the shadows and into the light. Together, we will carry one another's weight.

Growth is disruptive.

For some things, there are no shortcuts.

In the darkened living room, I reach for my phone.

"No, buddy," I type back. "I don't think I did."

# ACKNOWLEDGMENTS

## KATE

Thank you to my husband, Jamie, and four wonderful children. As cliché as it sounds, there is no story without you. Each of you have made me who I am today. A huge thanks to Jennifer Weis, Erika Imranyi, our team at Park Row, and HarperCollins for believing in me again. Writing a book is hard. If you know me, you have heard me say this. The experience is both internally challenging and rewarding. Adrian and Carrie, Amos and Jack, you bring me joy. It is a gift to share my story alongside yours.

To the friends who have sat with me in the dark on this journey, thank you. Thank you for not rushing me through. And to my very own yahoos, thank you for showing me the bright side of all of this. It's you and your kids. I didn't know this much laughter was possible. I could never do this life without you.

Lastly, to my followers. Thank you for loving my boy,

Cooper, our family, and our story. There was a time when I thought no one would know my son's name. I feared we would disappear into the secret world of autism. But you, you believed in our story. You encouraged me to keep sharing. Thank you.

## ADRIAN

To my family, your support and cheering me along has made this book possible and I am forever grateful for the opportunity to be a daughter, sister, wife, and mother.

To my cowriters Kate Swenson and Carrie Cariello, your wisdom and mentorship made this possible and I thank you.

Thank you, Jennifer Weis, amazing agent and brilliance behind the trifecta book. Thank you to the amazing team at Park Row, HarperCollins, especially Erika Imranyi, whose expertise made this process seamless.

Lastly, to my followers who have cried tears and shared my laughter. I am so appreciative that they showed me our story was worth telling.

## CARRIE

My deepest gratitude to those who held my words in the palms of their hands and saw the book before it was whole.

To each and every follower who found a piece of themselves inside our story, and rooted for us on the days we couldn't even root for ourselves.

For Kate and Adrian, who continue to take me under their virtual wing, make me laugh, and always push me to reach new heights.

For Jennifer Weis, who helped transform a phone call into a project.

For Erika, who steered our wayward ideas and patiently coaxed edits in the final hour.

Joseph, my oldest son. Our fearless leader.

Charlie, the middle child, the boy with the chocolate eyes. May the stars always shine.

My daughter, Rose. You are perfect as you are.

My youngest, Henry. The boy I nearly lost. And then I found.

My husband, Joe. It is your voice I hear as I type.

And Jack, Jack-attack, Jack-a-boo. Watching you take flight is breathtaking.

Mostly, for my mother, who always told me to never put anything in writing I didn't want the whole world to read.

May you finally know peace at last.

# NOTES